Making Their Own Way

MAKING
THEIR OWN WAY

Southern Blacks' Migration
to Pittsburgh, 1916–30

PETER GOTTLIEB

University of Illinois Press
Urbana and Chicago

Publication of this work was supported in part by
a grant from the Andrew W. Mellon Foundation.

This book is printed on acid-free paper.

Library of Congress Cataloging-in-Publication Data

Gottlieb, Peter, 1949–
  Making their own way.

  (Blacks in the New World)
  Bibliography: p.
  Includes index.
    1. Afro-Americans—Pennsylvania—Pittsburgh—Social
conditions.   2. Afro-Americans—Pennsylvania—Pittsburgh
—Economic conditions.   3. Pittsburgh (Pa.)—Social
conditions.   4. Pittsburgh (Pa.)—Economic conditions.
5. Rural-urban migration—United States.   I. Title.
II. Series.
F159.P69N44 1987   305.8'96073'074886   86-7041
ISBN 0-252-01354-9 (alk. paper)

To my parents,
Sidney and Margaret Gottlieb

Contents

Acknowledgments

I have been inspired and assisted by many people in the long process of writing this book. My interest in the general subject of the transformation of rural people under industrialization was first stimulated by the British historian E. P. Thompson and other lecturers at the University of Warwick, Coventry, England, during my junior year. I found encouragement in my desire to study an American case of this social process at the University of Pittsburgh, where I received my graduate degrees. David Montgomery, my adviser, went through the writing of the thesis with me chapter by chapter and helped me make the connections between what I discovered about black migrants and the larger changes taking place in the American work force. I also benefited greatly from the seminars in rural development and economic growth given by Julius Rubin, whose interest in southern agriculture was hardly incidental to my decision to investigate southern rural blacks. Larry Glasco provided helpful criticisms of my thesis chapters, and Reg Baker coached me in the use of the computer to process a mass of quantifiable data.

I was fortunate at Pittsburgh to have a number of friends and fellow graduate students in American social history who were willing to put aside their own work to help mine. More than any of these friends, I owe much to Ron Schatz, an outstanding historian and close friend since our days together at the University of Warwick. Though undertaking a very different kind of study for his doctoral degree at Pittsburgh, he improved my research with his recommendations for the thesis. I am also indebted to a number of other friends at Pittsburgh for their contributions and assistance: James Barrett, Peter Rachleff, Nora Faires, Mark McColloch, Steve Sapolsky. Without these friends, my first explorations of American social history and of black migration would have been much less exciting and productive.

August Meier has done more than anyone else to press the material of my graduate study into the mold of a scholarly monograph. His forceful and imaginative editing has been faithful to the original direction in which I had started but never lax in improving the clarity of my arguments. Susan L. Patterson at the University of Illinois Press made many additional corrections and editorial changes that brought the manuscript closer to her high standards. I wish to thank several other people whose suggestions and insights on different drafts of this book were very helpful: Elizabeth Pleck, John Bodnar, Kenneth Kusmer, Maurine Greenwald, Keith Dix, and Peter Shergold. Emory Kemp of West Virginia University gave me a crucial boost with his enthusiasm for this study.

The sound advice and encouragement from these teachers and friends have been matched by help of many kinds from my own family. The entire project of research, writing, and rewriting has been inseparable since its inception from Laura Moss Gottlieb's companionship. She not only gave numerous drafts the benefit of her editorial skills, but also offered unfailing moral support. Rita Lovell Moss, Lil Harrington, and Marsh Harrington all were wonderfully generous in giving me the space and time I badly needed to complete portions of the work on the book. I am deeply grateful for having such supportive companions and family members.

Much of what I most wanted to write about when I began this study depended on the cooperation of former migrants to Pittsburgh. Several dozen men and women in Pittsburgh and its suburbs allowed me, a stranger, to enter their homes and ask them many questions about their life experiences. Their help was unique and of the highest importance to my conception of this study. I would not have been able to write this book the way I have without their information. Librarians and archivists provided access to other extremely valuable sources. Frank

Zabrosky and Jeff Flannery at the Archives of Industrial Society gave me generous latitude in using the rich materials in the collections of Hillman Library. Staff members at the National Archives, Library of Congress, Carnegie Library of Pittsburgh, and the Pennsylvania Historical and Museum Commission also were helpful in responding to questions and locating important documents and photographs. The interlibrary loan staffs at Hillman Library, West Virginia University Library, and Pennsylvania State University Libraries all provided indispensable services. Abby Curtis of the Cartography Lab at Pennsylvania State University helped prepare the maps that accompany the text.

Irmi Keiderling and Beverly Hendrickson have done excellent typing of drafts under the pressure of short deadlines and have also helped to proofread parts of the manuscript.

This book is dedicated to my parents, my first teachers, both for encouraging my writing and for their love.

Introduction

FROM THE EMERGENCE of slavery until the Civil War, the black population of the United States shifted slowly to the Southwest, driven in the direction of the plantation economy's geographic expansion. After Emancipation ex-slaves and their children continued moving southwestward, seeking the fertile agricultural land in the east Texas, Mississippi Delta, and Red River regions. Occasionally, the freedmen pushed out of the South to escape harsh treatment or extreme deprivation. The "exodusters" who moved from the lower Mississippi Valley to Kansas in the 1870s represented one case of this kind. Western lands proved difficult for impoverished blacks to settle, however. Northern cities in the late nineteenth century, the portals of industrial America for millions of European immigrants, were not attractive to the mass of southern blacks. The foreign-born influx met the labor requirements of rapidly growing urban areas, leaving few opportunities for Afro-Americans.

A perceptible northward shift in southern blacks' movement began in the 1890s, as some members of the first generation born in freedom began leaving their native region for the cities of the Northeast. But the mass migration of southern blacks is usually dated from 1916, when the stream from the South became a surging tide that ran deep and strong through World War I and into the 1920s. Many people realized at once the significance of this increasing northward movement. Newspaper editorials and magazine articles commented frequently on the decisive break with the past heralded by this rapid population shift. By the mid-1920s experts on black community and

1

social institutions were appraising the effects of migration to northern cities. Since then, southern blacks' movement to the North has become a fixture in general treatments of blacks in U.S. society as well as in numerous studies on a diversity of topics from race riots to black nationalism.[1] Retrospective views from many vantage points have confirmed the belief of those who witnessed the migration: southern blacks movement presaged lasting changes for the migrants, and for racial practices and habits of mind at every level of American society.

Given the importance bestowed on blacks' northward migration, it is surprising how little we know about it. Detailed descriptions of the migrants themselves are rare. Though we have an abundance of generalizations regarding the dynamics of their geographic movement and absorption into northern urban social structures, seldom can we find systematic investigations of variations in black migration patterns or insights into the nuances in the migrants' experiences. Despite the important studies of the 1916–30 population movement that have been written, the main problem confronting the student of black migration today is the scant treatment previous writers have given to critical facets of the transition from southern to northern life.

Six studies, published between 1919 and 1932, furnish our basic knowledge of the migrants and their migration. The works by the U.S. Department of Labor, Emmett J. Scott, T. J. Woofter, Jr., Clyde V. Kiser, Edward E. Lewis, and Louise V. Kennedy treat the northward movement in similar terms.[2] The authors' main concerns lie in the causes and effects of northward movement. The questions raised in these studies deal primarily with the material factors that set southern blacks in motion and those that confronted them in the cities to which they came. The authors argue that southern blacks began northward journeys under the force of circumstances between 1914 and 1916. As a sudden response to northern labor demand and poor southern agricultural conditions, the migration swept to the North great numbers of blacks unprepared for urban life. Though the migrants earned more money in urban occupations than they had in the South, they were forced to adjust their customary way of life to the rigors of modern industrial society under severe handicaps. The crowded and unsanitary housing they occupied, the inadequate recreational and health facilities available to them, and the poverty of black urban communities in general claimed a high toll among the newcomers in ways familiar to these students of urban problems: disease, high mortality, and crime.

Both the strengths and weaknesses of these studies sprang from the fact that they were researched and published while the migration was still in process. Their value lay in the wealth of detail they provided on many aspects of southern blacks' status in their areas of origin and destination, accumulated painstakingly by observation of the migrants at different times and places. Viewing the migration at such close quarters, however, produced distortion in the authors' perspective. They frequently highlighted the most dramatic episodes in the northward movement, omitting less conspicuous long-term developments that preceded and followed the journeys. The consequence for their analyses was that the causes and effects of migration seemed to overwhelm the migrants themselves. The general impression conveyed to the reader was of a routine agricultural life shattered by forces beyond the understanding of rural blacks, of frantic departures from country homes and groping entrances to northern cities, and of a backward people thrust quaking into the industrial heartland of the world's most technically advanced society.

Recent studies of black migration by Florette Henri, Robert Grant, and Hollis Lynch bring a different perspective to the northward movement.[3] Instead of stressing the causes and effects of the migration, these authors emphasize the theme of the migrants' struggle against racial proscriptions in the South and the North. From a vantage point provided by the civil rights and black power movements of the last two decades, they argue that migration from 1916 to 1930 is significant mainly for the heightened race consciousness and aspirations for social justice it stimulated among millions of Afro-Americans. Though these authors rely on the earlier investigations of the northward movement for their evidence, and though their concern with social issues deflects attention from the dynamics of migration, they have begun the task of enlarging the migrants' role in their own journey to northern cities. Henri writes: "The getting there [to the North] was a tremendous feat of initiative, planning, courage, and perseverance . . . not by one or two 'exceptional individuals' . . . but by at least five hundred thousand perfectly average southern Negroes."[4]

Most of the recent literature on black migration approaches the northward movement in terms of its significance mainly for Afro-American history. Yet the shift of black population from southern rural to northern urban environments clearly resembles in some ways the worldwide country-to-city migration that has paralleled the rise of commercial and industrial economies. Keeping in mind the specific historical context of black migration in industrializing America, we can draw on studies of the same basic process in other places and at different times to further our knowledge of blacks' experience in the United States. This is in a sense what recent investigations of black "proletarianization" in Detroit and Milwaukee have accomplished.[5] By viewing blacks' urbanization as a change in the occupational composition of black city populations from service to industrial jobs, these studies provide a basis for understanding twentieth-century Afro-American history in the framework of broad social changes that have influenced cityward migrants in other developing economies.

Social scientists from many disciplines have provided models of geographic movement that enrich our understanding of southern blacks' journeys to the North. Demographers, economists, psychologists, and geographers have all contributed in the last thirty years to a more sophisticated appreciation of rural-urban migration.[6] Recent studies in the United States, European, and undeveloped countries have demonstrated that migration can best be seen as a social process involving both the areas of origin and destination. The investigations have shown that in many instances, including the movement of white Appalachians to northern manufacturing centers, migrants initially remain in close communication with their rural homes and only gradually shift their primary involvement to the urban communities to which they moved. Kinship and communal bonds do not break when individuals migrate. On the contrary, sociologists and anthropologists have indicated that these relationships are influential in many aspects of the migration and settlement in new, urban homes.[7] These insights suggest important questions about southern rural blacks' stages of out-migration, about their relationship with family members, other migrants, and northern blacks, and about their adjustment to urban, industrial communities.

Our understanding of southern blacks' migration between 1916 and 1930 can be extended in another direction mapped out by European and American social historians. E. P. Thompson, David Montgomery, Herbert Gutman, and others have surveyed the experiences of preindustrial urban and rural workers in their encounters with factories on both sides of the Atlantic.[8] Among the pervasive changes that industrialization brought about for artisans and peasants, the transformation of work itself has been emphasized by these scholars. The concentration of production in workshops and factories undermined hand manufacturing and drew into the sphere of industrial labor men and women unschooled in the demands of task work, minute divisions of labor, and factory discipline. The clash between the customary work practices of these new employees and the routines of industrial labor welded motley groups of preindustrial workers into a new working class.

Industrialization, rural-urban migration, and the transformation of work have been closely related changes in modern world history. Since the late eighteenth century, the emerging factory system and its attendant urban growth have afforded avenues of escape from stagnating agricultural regions. In search of wage earnings with which to improve rural standards of living, men and women from every corner of the world's agricultural hinterlands have moved to industrial towns and cities, bringing with them traditional work habits. In the mines, mills, and factories these recruits to industrialism have been initiated to the requirements of mechanized production.

Southern blacks' migration to northern cities from 1916 to 1930 represents one chapter in this story. And we can hardly hope to comprehend the changes in the lives of the black migrants who came to Pittsburgh without examining their labor in both rural and urban settings. To the questions suggested by anthropological and sociological studies, we must add others that relate work experiences to the movement from south to north. Three general questions are investigated in this connection: what kind of work did black migrants perform in the South? What occupations did they enter in Pittsburgh? And how did their previous work experience and their migration affect their status as northern industrial laborers?

Synthesizing the insights of historians and other social scientists, I portray in this study black migration and the black working class in formation in Pittsburgh, Pennsylvania. I have viewed these processes through two lenses: one directed at the migration from the rural South to the urban North, and one turned toward blacks' work experiences in agriculture and industry. But my study presents geographic movement and various types of labor as interwoven elements in the migrants' experience. Northward migration is not seen merely as an episode in Afro-American history but as an unfolding social development closely linked to economic, cultural, and social growth in both the South and the North. The general organization of the study derives from a view of migration and industrialization as historical processes with definite outlines in time and space.

My focus here is on the southern black migrants alone, and not on Pittsburgh's black workers as a whole, nor on the black community of that city. These newcomers from 1916 to 1930 did not comprise all of Pittsburgh's expanding black proletariat, although the southern-born men and women I am considering became the largest percentage of its black workers. Their family life, work, households, neighborhoods, and leisure pursuits are the heart of this history. The wider black community in Pittsburgh and the conditions confronting all blacks in the city naturally became part of the setting for the migrants' transformation, but I discuss them only as they directly concerned the process of migration and the formation of the black working class.

I make three major arguments. First, I contend that the kind of urban laborers blacks became in the early twentieth century was determined as much by what kind of work, culture, and society they engaged in before moving north as by the nature of the occupations they entered when they reached their destinations. This is to say that for Afro-Americans, as for most twentieth-century unskilled workers, their preindustrial coloration was not shed like a snake's skin, but blended with the new attitudes, values, and patterns of behavior they developed in the industrial environment. And what was often attributed by northern observers to racial temperament or peculiarities was in many cases actually the manifestation of a southern black culture, which played a large part in the migrants' adjustment to industrial life.

Second, I elaborate the point made by Henri and other recent writers that the overarching change in southern blacks' lives came about through a process of *self*-transformation. This study confirms that the uprooting, northward movement and adjustment to urban life were not solely the work of impersonal social and economic forces. Black migrants often consciously entered the migration process, eagerly sought some of the changes flowing from it, and pursued in specific instances their own definition of advancement through geographic movement, even when it opposed the designs of more powerful groups. I argue, however, that the ways in which blacks shaped their own experience reflected their southern rural way of life as well as their historic aspiration for freedom, justice, and opportunity. This analysis of southern blacks' values, customs, and goals also reveals that the migrants' preindustrial attitudes and behavior sometimes undercut their ability to contend with hostile groups in Pittsburgh and helped to force them into a subordinate status, despite their resistance.

Finally, I indicate that the reciprocal influences of the southern migrants and the established black community strengthened the emerging class divisions among Pittsburgh blacks. The nature of the demand for southern black labor brought to Pittsburgh industrial recruits seldom seen in earlier years: black farmers from the Deep South who were able quickly to master unskilled industrial tasks. Employed by the thousands in work places in Pittsburgh and the surrounding mill towns, they soon made their presence felt on the shop floors, in the black community, and in the labor movement. Pittsburgh's resident black population reacted with deep ambivalence to the new black workers' impact on their way of life, and black profes- ·

sionals began a campaign to make the migrants over in the image of the urban middle class. The hostility implicit in this effort encouraged the newcomers to build their new northern homes around their own kinship and friendship associations and to maintain whenever possible the ties they had with former southern homes. The migration forced an encounter between upper and lower levels in Pittsburgh's black community, and through this encounter the identities of both groups grew more separate and more sharply defined.

While population transfers from rural to urban areas have been relatively rapid in recent history, the transformation of traditional agricultural peoples into urban working-class groups has been a more drawn-out change. An analysis of all the ramifications stemming from black migration obviously cannot be undertaken in an investigation of the years from 1916 to 1930 alone. The half generation that this study covers nonetheless affords an intensive examination of the most important social changes that attend migration and class formation: uprooting, patterns of geographic movement, adaptation to city dwellings and jobs, the relations between the migrants and the organized working-class movement, and the beginnings of the migrants' settlement in cities.

The years from 1916 to 1930, moreover, cover a unified era in the history of black urbanization in the United States. On either side of this span lie periods during which the wellsprings of Afro-American migration and the dynamics of class formation were quite different. Though there were indeed fluctuations in the demand for black labor and in general economic conditions from 1916 to 1930, these fifteen years form a coherent whole so far as the fundamental conditions surrounding black migration are concerned. In southern agriculture there was an unevenly paced but gradual deterioration in blacks' status, though no fundamental change in farming practices took place. In northern industries these years represented one of the longest periods in U.S. history during which blacks could relatively easily find jobs working in the basic industries. Urban conditions in general were inimical to the migrants' well-being, but migrants could, if they chose, establish homes and raise families without the threat of severe economic disruption.

Pittsburgh provides a suitable locale for studying the development of an industrial population from the raw social material of rural migrants. Not only was this heavy manufacturing center regarded by contemporaries as "capitalism's first city," but it was also reputed by southern blacks to be one of the best places to look for industrial jobs, if not necessarily to settle down. Hundreds of thousands of foreign-born and American families preceded southern blacks to Pittsburgh. Just a few years before 1916, the Pittsburgh Survey had been completed. One of the most extensive studies of an American city's social life, the Pittsburgh Survey showed that the city was above all a place where rural peoples staked their energies and powers of endurance in the hope of economic security.

My study approaches black migration through time, place, and social process, but the key to understanding the fundamental historical changes in question is the migrants themselves. For this reason, I have attempted to flesh out the shadowy figures of southern blacks who came to the North between 1916 and 1930. What has been said about them so often lacks detail and substance that we can hardly say we know who they were. One of my chief objectives has been to focus this analysis wherever possible and appropriate on the migrants themselves, both individually and in their own family and community groups. This effort has led to extensive collecting and interpretation of sources that reveal the migrants' actions, speech, attitudes, values, and customs with the least possible interpretive or editorial mediation. Such sources have problems of accuracy, authenticity, and consistency that are sometimes more difficult to detect and correct than the traditional sources on which migration students have relied. But if we want the early generations of black migrants and industrial workers to lend their views to our understanding of their lives, there is little choice but to use these sources judiciously.

NOTES

1. Studies of urban black communities conducted in the 1920s gave prominent place to migration from the South. See, for example, Chicago Commission on Race Relations, *The Negro in Chicago* (Chicago: University of Chicago Press, 1922); E. Franklin Frazier, *The Negro Family in Chicago* (Chicago: University of Chicago Press, 1932); T. J. Woofter, Jr., ed., *Negro Problems in Cities* (Garden City: Doubleday, Doran, 1928).

2. U.S. Department of Labor, Division of Negro Economics, *Negro Migration in 1916-17* (Washington: Government Printing Office, 1919); Emmett J. Scott, *Negro Migration during the War* (New York: Oxford University Press, 1920); T. J. Woofter, Jr., *Negro Migration* (New York: W. D. Gray, 1920); Clyde V. Kiser, *Sea Island to City* (New York: Columbia University Press, 1932); Edward E. Lewis, *The Mobility of the Negro* (New York: Columbia University Press, 1931); Louise V. Kennedy, *The Negro Peasant Turns Cityward* (New York: Columbia University Press, 1930). Kiser's monograph is an exceptional study of black migration that does not fit the mold of the other works cited here.

3. Florette Henri, *Black Migration: Movement North, 1900-1920* (Garden City: Anchor/Doubleday, 1975); Robert B. Grant, *The Black Man Comes to the City* (Chicago: Nelson-Hall, 1972); Hollis R. Lynch, comp., *The Black Urban Condition: A Documentary History, 1866-1971* (New York: Thomas Y. Crowell, 1973).

4. Henri, *Black Migration*, 80.

5. Richard W. Thomas, "From Peasant to Proletarian: The Formation and Organization of the Black Industrial Working Class in Detroit, 1915-1945" (Ph.D. thesis, University of Michigan, 1976); Joe W. Trotter, Jr., *Black Milwaukee: The Making of an Industrial Proletariat, 1915-45* (Urbana: University of Illinois Press, 1984).

6. Carter Goodrich et al., *Migration and Economic Opportunity* (Philadelphia: University of Pennsylvania Press, 1936); Larry Sjaastad, "The Relationship between Migration and Income in the United States," Regional Science Association, *Papers* 6 (1960), 37-64; Everett S. Lee, "A Theory of Migration," *Demography* 3 (1966), 47-58; Lawrence Brown, *Diffusion Processes and Location* (Philadelphia: Regional Science Research Institute, 1968); Curtis C. Roseman, "Channelization of Migration Flows from the Rural South to the Industrial Midwest," American Association of Geographers, *Proceedings* 3 (1971), 140-46; Robert Coles, *The South Goes North* (Boston: Little, Brown, 1971).

7. Sune Ackerman, *From Stockholm to San Francisco* (Uppsala: Annales Academiae Regiae Scientiarum, 1975); Frank Thistlethwaite, "Migration from Europe Overseas in the Nineteenth and Twentieth Centuries," in *Population Movements in Modern European History,*

ed. Herbert Moller (New York: Macmillan, 1964), 73-92; Nancy B. Graves and Theodore D. Graves, "Adaptive Strategies in Urban Migration," *Annual Review of Anthropology* 3 (1974), 117-51; James S. Brown, Harry K. Schwarzweller, and J. J. Mangalam, "Kentucky Mountain Migration and the Stem Family," *Rural Sociology* 28 (Mar. 1963), 48-69.

8. E. P. Thompson, *The Making of the English Working Class* (New York: Vintage Books, 1963); Thompson, "Time, Work Discipline, and Industrial Capitalism," *Past and Present* 38 (1967), 56-97; David Montgomery, *Workers' Control in America* (Cambridge: Cambridge University Press, 1979), 32-47, 113-38; Herbert G. Gutman, *Work, Culture, and Society in Industrializing America: Essays in American Working Class and Social History* (New York: Knopf, 1976), 3-78.

1

The Origins of Black Migration

THE MASS MIGRATION of southern blacks to northern cities that began during World War I had deep roots in the New South. Ever since Emancipation freedmen and their descendants had moved frequently in search of a better living. This geographic shifting that preceded the wartime movement to the North was not random, however. It stood in a particular relationship to the patterns of landholding and labor and to the organization of family and community life. Specifically, black migration in the pre–World War I South was strongly related to the seasonal character of work and leisure in cotton cultivation and to the life cycle of rural blacks. We can discover in these facets of black life the beginnings of the trails that thousands eventually followed to Pittsburgh and other northern cities.

It was the combination of a traditional agriculture with emerging industries of the New South that created a matrix from which black migration emerged. The light and heavy industries spreading across the South were places from which rural blacks could garner cash wages to add to their farm incomes and raise their standard of living. Like preindustrial peoples everywhere from the eighteenth century to the present, southern blacks learned how to adjust their customary styles of work, their household organization, and their family responsibilities in order to derive the benefits of wage employment and still maintain their rural homes. Through a pattern of seasonal migration and temporary industrial work within the South, they prepared themselves for geographic movements further afield.

The deprivation of share tenancy farming and racial oppression stimulated this pattern of movement. Tenant farming became the most common form of agricultural labor in the South after the demise of chattel slavery and provided the framework of economic relations between landless blacks and landowning whites. In its many varieties farm tenancy replaced the slave gang system of fieldwork on plantations with the labor of black families on smaller plots of land rented from whites. Freed by this arrangement from many of the abuses they had suffered under slavery, southern rural blacks after the Civil War quickly became tangled in a new net of oppressive conditions, in which a rigid racial subordination and the ills of the cotton economy itself were interwoven.[1]

In many parts of the Deep South sharecropping soon became the most common type of farm tenancy among black cotton growers. Unlike other tenants who paid cash or a small part of their harvest for rent, sharecroppers possessed none of the things required to cultivate a crop or support a family. The landowners or local merchant provided acreage, mules, implements, seed, housing, and sometimes fertilizer to these poorest tenants. In return, the croppers surrendered one-half of the crops they raised. In addition, they had to obtain on credit everything their families needed from the landlord's commissary, the merchant's store, or a store agreed on between a landowner and a local shopkeeper.[2] The landowner or merchant in some southern states enjoyed the legal right to a first lien on his tenant's crops. The lien represented security for the food, clothing, and farming supplies that the landlord or local store-owner gave the tenant between the beginning of the growing season and the sale of the harvested crops. Most of the landless, propertyless rural blacks in the postwar South had nothing else to offer as security for such "loans." But in the context of increasingly strict race relations and racial subordination in the late nineteenth century, the crop lien became the tool to extract the greatest possible amount of wealth from the tenant and his family.[3] The landlord frequently told the tenant that the crops had not made enough money to pay the costs of the supplies advanced during the growing season and that the tenant would have to work off the debt by contracting with the same landlord during the next year.[4]

Two factors in cotton agriculture made the black tenants relatively impotent to contest the landlords' settlements. One was the general scarcity of commercial banks and similar lending institutions that could offer competition for the landowners who provided credit to black farmers. The plantation owners, storeowners, or credit merchants had a local monopoly on short-term loans. They made good use of this advantage in charging high interest rates on their tenants' accounts and in setting high prices for all the merchandise that was bought on credit. The other factor was whites' sensitivity to any hint of dealing with blacks on equal terms. The landowners kept the only records of tenants' debts, number of bales of cotton picked, and proceeds from the sale of the harvest. Aside from moving to another landowner's farm (an option itself laden with potential hazards), there was little the black tenant could do. The judicial system did not recognize his rights, and he took his life in his hands even to question the landlord's accounts.[5]

The cropper's creditors kept close watch over the work performed in the fields during the growing season. From Lowndes County, Alabama, Carl Kelsey reported: "The size of a man's family is known and the riders see to it that he keeps all the working hands in the field." Either physical punishment or cutting off the cropper's credit brought the landowner's authority to bear on his black labor. Only black field hands, hired on plantations to work by the day, week, or month, had less autonomy in their labor than sharecroppers.[6]

The legal system of the New South supported landowners' and merchants' efforts to discipline rural blacks. The vagrancy laws that originally put teeth in the Black Codes of 1865 and 1866 were perpetuated after Reconstruction, making poor blacks liable to arbitrary arrest and detention. If convicted of a petty offense, blacks could be put on a chain gang repairing roads, cleaning ditches, or performing some other menial "public" work. Other convicts could find themselves hired out to a white employer of mine labor or railroad construction gangs. While such practices made it risky for rural blacks even to loiter in town, other laws made it a crime for them to leave an employer's land before the crop had been harvested. And throughout the South black tenants and field hands who moved away from a plantation before paying off their debts to a landowner could be forced to return to work until the debt was paid. Landlords hunted them down with dogs, guns, and the help of sympathetic law officers. At its worst this practice led to debt peonage for thousands of sharecroppers and field hands. Indebted blacks who escaped the shackles of peonage sometimes had to rely on the willingness of their landlords to allow another white owner to assume their debts. The real slavery of buying and selling blacks before the Civil War gave way to the semislavery of peonage, convict lease labor, and the exchanging of black tenants' debts among white landowners.[7]

Farm owners and renters represented the higher end of the rural economic scale. Beginning from practically nothing at Emancipation, landownership among southern blacks peaked in 1910, when nearly a quarter of all black farms were operated by owners.[8] The percentage of owners among all black farmers varied widely from one southern state to another, but was generally higher in the regions where mixed farming was prevalent and lower in the staple crop areas. Nonetheless, 21 percent of all South Carolina's black farmers were owners in 1910; and in Georgia, Alabama, and Mississippi at the same date the figure was about 15 percent.[9] In the Deep South black-owned farms were also less common in the Black Belt, the region where soil and climate were best suited to cotton monoculture and the plantation system.[10] Partly for this reason, black proprietors devoted a much smaller share of their land to cotton than did tenants.

Black landowners and tenants who rented land for cash instead of crop shares often lived better than croppers and laborers. Owners and cash renters worked less under the scrutiny of creditors than their poorer neighbors.[11] Their ability to manage their affairs more or less independently gave them stature among their black neighbors and made them natural choices for community leadership positions. Their annual incomes, though by no means princely, were greater than the earnings of share tenants. In the Yazoo–Mississippi Delta region in 1913, cash renters made $478 from their harvested cotton, while sharecroppers made $333. A study of farm incomes in Chatham County, North Carolina, in 1921 found black owners with an average income of $597, black cash renters with $289, and black sharecroppers with $197.[12]

As a measure of improving fortunes among rural blacks, however, proprietorship or cash renting was not always reliable. Fluctuations in the yearly incomes of farm owners and cash renters were greater than those of sharecroppers, since white landlords sometimes supported croppers when harvests failed, while black proprietors faced adverse economic circumstances without such protection. "The sharecropping system is safest for the tenant," concluded a study of thirteen Mississippi counties in 1916. "The sharecropper is practically assured of average wages for his work."[13] And precisely because black owners were relatively independent from whites, they were in some ways more exposed to racial hostility than were poorer blacks. Whites could make sure that the few black owners and flourishing tenant farmers in their neighborhoods behaved according to the southern code of race relations by means of threats, intimidation, or economic pressure. Such reactions by suspicious or jealous whites jeopardized the security of even the most successful rural blacks.[14]

Black cotton farmers, whatever the land tenure or income differences among them, shared many of the same burdens. In addition to the common denominator of racial oppression, all cotton farmers felt the stagnation that spread over the cotton region in the late nineteenth and early twentieth centuries. World overproduction of the crop forced the price per pound down to new lows in the 1890s, and there was little improvement until World War I. Low cotton prices compounded the problems that grew from low investment in farm machinery, soil conservation, and education of the rural population. A heavy reliance on commercial fertilizers in particular increased the rate at which the soil lost its natural fertility and at the same time drained resources from efforts to diversify crops, slow down soil erosion, and improve farm practices.[15] Cotton's increasing backwardness compared to other types of agriculture was most evident in the failure to mechanize any of the important phases of its cultivation. Human and animal labor continued to produce crops in the two decades before World War I with routines little changed from antebellum days.

The work of planting, hoeing, and harvesting remained the strongest link among all ranks of cotton farmers. Cotton-growing imposed a routine of labor and leisure wherever cotton was raised as the primary cash crop. The southern climate and soil favored crops with a long growing season. Before the adoption of the mechanical harvester and other machine improvements in the 1940s, cotton's 245-day season demanded periods of very intensive hand labor. All over the cotton South, the rural population for eight months of the year bent to its work in time to the crop's phases of growth. Different tasks coincided naturally with the different seasons of the year, and so did, with somewhat less precise timing, all of the important occasions of group, family, and individual lives.

The annual calendar of cotton-farming tasks began with preparation of the land for planting, which lasted from January until mid-March. During this first phase of the growing season, old cotton stalks and corn stubble were beaten down and plowed under, water holes, ditches, and bayous were cleaned out, and fences were repaired. Planting began in mid-March and lasted through April and into May. When cotton plants had broken through the soil and were strong enough to permit cultivation, the first period of intensive labor began, lasting roughly from May until early July. The necessity of keeping the cotton crop free of weeds and grass required daily stints of long hours. The cotton plants first were thinned out by pulling up those too small to promise good yields, allowing the bigger plants more room for growth. After thinning, the field was made up of rows of "stands," three or four plants to each one. To ensure a good crop, the rows of cotton stands had to be chopped, a process of cutting down grass and weeds to ground level with hoes. The ground between the rows was also repeatedly plowed to form ridges of soil against the cotton plants, protecting them from heavy rain and wind.[16]

The next period of intensive labor began in September and continued through October. At this time of year cotton bolls were picked from the stalks. The quicker the fields could be picked, the better, because sudden rains could damage the crop. The harvest required dawn-to-dusk workdays. Thus the demand for labor exerted by cotton peaked in June and in October. On an index of 100 for the average seasonal labor demand, June's peak reached 127 and October's 130.[17]

During the periods of intensive fieldwork, cotton required the labor of every member of rural black households. Work roles were usually differentiated according to status within the family, age, and gender. Parents had general responsibility for seeing the crop through to a successful harvest and took over specific tasks as well. The most important of these was the coordination and direction of their children's labor. Children's work changed as they grew up, but was crucial to the family welfare even in the preschool years. As soon as he could walk from the family dwelling to the fields, the black farmer's son joined the family work group. At the age of five or six, he could contribute his labor during the cotton harvest. The dexterity and speed demanded of a good cotton picker favored training small children to do the work. Light chores around the family's vegetable garden and animal pens could also be done by young boys. When he could handle a hoe with sufficient skill to chop the cotton rows without cutting down the plants themselves, the boy also participated in the March–June fieldwork. But the indication that he was on the threshold of becoming a full-fledged farmhand was his ability to plow. Plowing was learned roughly between the ages of nine and twelve. By the age of fifteen or so, when he had attained the necessary physical stamina and experience, the farmer's son could be expected to do most of the work of making a cotton crop in both of the seasons of heavy labor.[18]

The black farm girl's work was not necessarily very different from that of her brothers. How similar male and female children's work roles were depended both on the size of the family (and thus the number of people contributing to the family's support) and the parents' attitude toward their daughters' proper work role. In a relatively small family, where the girl's work in the fields was vital to making a crop sufficiently large to sustain the family, her responsibilities during the intensive work periods were practically the same as the boy's: chopping, hoeing, and picking.[19] The main difference in male and female children's work roles was that in addition to fieldwork, girls also had to do household chores of cooking, cleaning, and washing. If parents objected to female family members performing fieldwork, their daughter's labor might be devoted wholly to household work, caring for younger siblings, and tending kitchen gardens and animals. This was more likely to be a girl's work role in a prosperous rural black family. Even modest incomes made many families sensitive to the stigma of poverty that clung to women working in fields.[20]

Farm families enjoyed two lengthy reprieves from intensive field labor, during which either light work or no work at all was done. The first break came during July and August, when the cotton had been "laid by" and no longer needed plowing or hoeing. The second rest period followed the completion of the harvest. When the cotton had been picked, ginned, baled, and sold, the farming community enjoyed a respite from fieldwork until after New Year's Day. Comparing these interludes of light work with the periods of intensive labor on the index of seasonal labor demand, the July–August period declined to 90 and the November–January period to 70. Alternating periods of light and intensive work defined life in all rural regions of the United States and all types of agriculture. The seasonality of life in the cotton South differed from that of other regions in the sharpness of the fluctuation in labor demand.[21]

Alternating periods of intensive and slack work tended to regulate many other aspects of the lives of the black rural population, including market relations, consumption patterns, forms of socializing, education, and temporary migration. Significantly, the mutual obligations of tenant and landlord changed over the twelve-month cycle roughly in step with the phases of the work calendar. Agreements between sharecroppers or tenants and landowners were initiated after Christmas and just before the beginning of the next growing season. In the experience of Ed Brown, a Georgia sharecropper in the 1920s, the time for making the new contracts was well defined. "Unless it's Sunday everyone hired on shares meet the overseer at the barn by sunup January 1." Food, clothing, and medicine, provided on credit by landlords or merchants, could be cut off with the coming of the July–August break. Tenant families during these months were expected to support themselves from home-grown vegetables and meat or wild game. In November or early

December, after all of the cotton had been harvested and sold, landlords, storekeepers, and tenants settled accounts. With wry humor, Ed Brown recalled how the progress of the cotton crop shaped his landlord's attitudes: "Along about April the bossman would say, 'Ed, is *your* cotton gettin ready to chop? . . .' [Around July] I plow my cotton for the last time. It's laid by till time to pick. Furnish money ends. Now the boss ask, 'Is *our* cotton doin pretty good? . . .' By the latter part of September it's all picked. . . . Now Mr. Addison can handle it and just as sure as you're livin he'll call it his'n. '*My* cotton, *my* corn, *my* crop.' "22

The timing of market transactions between white creditors and black debtors produced a marked ebb and flow of cash and material goods in the southern rural community. Between January and July tenants and laborers relied on cash advances or provisions either from their landlords or from furnishing merchants. During the late summer those who had planted vegetable gardens and fattened hogs enjoyed a modest bounty from the land. The only time when most farm families had cash to spend, however, was during November and December, after the cotton had been marketed and accounts had been settled. But even for those who had made money on the year's crops, the amount of cash in hand at the end of the growing season was usually so small that soon after buying Christmas gifts and necessities for the family, they found themselves relying on credit again in January.23

The relative abundance of cash or farm-grown food during the two break periods of the work calendar enlivened the festivities that took place at those times of year. The weeks of July and August were those of church revivals, July Fourth barbecues, homecomings, or visits to friends and relatives. The church activities of this time of year became a focus for community socializing. Each church in some districts would serve as a meeting place for a week, dur ng which the congregations from all neighboring churches would gather for daily services. Pastors from surrounding churches would address the crowds, imploring sinners to join the church. Preachers from outside the district, well known for their oratorical gifts, would also circulate around the country churches, attracting large audiences. After the day's services, the members of the host church would provide a meal for all of the visitors. Tables set up outside the church were piled with freshly slaughtered and roasted meat and garden produce, just ripe for the gathering at that time of year.[24]

The July–August rest and celebration period was also a time for visiting relatives and friends. As time passed and the numbers of southern migrants to northern cities grew, the late summer holiday became as closely associated with "homecoming" as it was with church revivals. The break from fieldwork provided an opportunity for those who had left to come back and visit, renewing old associations, while those who had remained on farms visited friends living in the surrounding area.[25]

November and December leisure weeks were less church-oriented. Church services of the Christmas season were not community or district celebrations like those of July and August. Farmers had cash in hand from the sale of their cotton and other crops or from new loans, and families could spend at this time of year as they could at no other. In some parts of the rural South during the pre–World War I period, November or December also saw school "breaking," the Christmas recess of classes for farm children. Some communities marked the occasion with a meeting where children recited speeches, poems, Scripture, and other passages learned in their classes. In a South Carolina version of school breaking, the children were treated to a basketful of sugar cane joints after they had finished their recitals.[26]

Church recitals were not the only aspects of black children's schooling that fit cotton's calendar. Classes for rural children generally fell either in the winter months of light farm work or were divided between the early winter and summer work recess periods. "School ran five months," wrote Matthew Ward, who grew up in rural Tennessee in the early twentieth century. "It opened in November and the date depended upon how well the crops had been gathered. School closed early March or on the first of April. Sometimes there were enough children left by closing day for commencement services. . . . On closing day the women cooked up baskets and trunks of food. There were baseball games and the children went through examination demonstrations. . . . In the evening, before night, we would give speeches and dialogues. The men would miss the celebrations

because they would be working in the fields."[27] All children in
cotton-farming families felt the force of the crop's control over
their education. But even the dictates of the season were harsher
for black children than for white. Nate Shaw remembered how
white school administrators in Alabama at the turn of the
century ordered black schools to close when meager funds were
exhausted. "Soon as our school closed down cotton would be
ready to chop. We little colored children had to jump in the
white man's field and work for what we could get ... white
folks' schools runnin right on."[28]

As responsibility for the family's fortunes increased in step
with their age, the black children's attendance at school tapered
off. The proportion of black children in single age groups enrolled
in school throughout the South in 1910 showed steady increases
up to age eleven. Then the percentage of black children in
school began to drop, with a sharp decline after the age of
thirteen.[29] It was just at this point in their lives that black rural
youth turned to plowing, driving wagons, cooking meals, and
looking after younger siblings.

Cotton's seasons of work and rest influenced geographic mobility as well. One of the most common migration patterns that
emerged after the Civil War involved short distance moves from
one tenant farm to another, often within the same county.
These shifts of residence took place mostly after the cotton
harvest was completed and before the beginning of the next
growing season. A Mississippi landowner reported the hectic
movement of black families in his locality between October
1908 and January 1909: "In riding six miles along a public road
one day, I counted thirty-six wagon loads of household effects,
the owners seated on top, shifting from various plantations to
various other plantations." This circulation of rural blacks meant
that a family could cultivate a dozen or more different plots of
land and work for several different landlords. Occasionally a
change from one man's land to another's coincided with an
elevation to a higher tenure status, but more often it was
only a move to another small farm and another sharecropping
arrangement.[30]

Another pattern of geographic mobility among rural blacks
was seasonal movement from farms to industrial sites, towns,

or cities. Many rural blacks who migrated in this fashion got temporary jobs in expanding southern industries. They became wage earners during the periods when there was little fieldwork to do on the cotton crop, returning to their farms to plow, plant, or harvest. Though such temporary migration fit well into the cycle of fieldwork and leisure, it also bore the seeds of permanent cityward migration.

Some rural blacks seeking temporary wage work turned to small-scale industries that, because they were closely related to agriculture, operated seasonally. Fertilizer plants, cotton gins, and cottonseed presses were busiest both before and after the growing season, when labor from farm families in the surrounding areas was available for hire. An investigator reported that a fertilizer plant in Clarke County, Georgia, during World War I divided its annual work into two periods. One began in February and ended in April and the other went from May to January. The plant was busiest in the early spring months, hiring up to 155 workers to manufacture fertilizer and ship it to merchants and landlords. During the slack months of the year, much lower rates of production and lighter shipments took place. The payroll of unskilled labor, mostly blacks hired from the local area, was cut by 40 percent. "They are what are termed 'field hands,' or field laborers, and most of them, when they have completed the work of the busy season at the fertilizer plant, go back to the farm."[31]

Black men also sought temporary employment in other industries that were not so closely connected with southern agriculture and that offered relatively steady work year round. In the interludes of light farm work rural blacks moved to sawmills, logging camps, railroad construction and tie-cutting camps, turpentine camps, brickyards, coal mines, steel mills, and river or ocean docks. A historian of lumber workers found that part-time farming and part-time logging were common in Mississippi, northern Georgia, and South Carolina. Mississippi landowners lost their black hands to logging camps and sawmills during the summer lay-by period. But apparently the off-farm employment was strictly seasonal, because "the black man would choose cotton picking every time in preference to sawmill work. On the cotton plantation, rations were furnished, and with very little labor the Negro could make a crop." In Georgia a survey of "home employment"—industrial or semiindustrial jobs provided to black tenants and laborers by white landowners—showed that a decisive majority of landlords offered sawmill work during the July–August period.[32]

The seasonal shifting from agricultural to industrial or semiindustrial labor made work roles within black families more flexible and more complex. Some family members had to remain at home in the periods of light field labor while others were away earning wages, since there was still much work to do in the house, vegetable garden, and animal pens. In families with very young children, only the husband or wife could move in search of temporary jobs. But as sons and daughters reached their adolescence, their parents could take them along as extra hands or helpers at the seasonal jobs or assign them employment at neighboring farms and nearby towns. Gender as well as age determined where each family member worked, for how long, and at what wage rate. Beyond a certain point in his or her life cycle, however, each rural black was likely to spend the year at both farm and nonfarm labor, supplying a money income to the family when help on the farm was not needed, supplying field labor when making the crop demanded work from everyone.[33]

The black farmer's son could find seasonal jobs nearly everywhere his father could, though he might be given only a helper's tasks and a helper's wages until he was old enough to do a man's work. William H.'s father took him along to a brickyard in Alabama where the youngster set out the molded bricks to dry in the sun. Ben E.'s father frequently worked in Alabama coal mines, and the boy joined him as an underground helper when he grew big enough to do mining work. A boy could also transfer his ability to drive a team of horses to a paid job as a delivery wagon driver or simply hire out from his own family's farm to another farm as a plow hand.[34]

There seems to have been much less choice of wage work for young black women. In many families they and their mothers were the ones who maintained the household and farm while male members of the family were away at seasonal jobs. But an adolescent daughter could frequently find domestic employment, whether it was washing to take in at her own house or live-in housework or child care for a white family.[35] Cooking, cleaning, and washing could be as seasonal as mixing fertilizer. A 1921 study of black female domestics in Gainesville, Georgia, demonstrated that one-third of the women worked no longer than three months out of the year. "The term of service is much shorter in many cases, the servants remaining only a week or two and then leaving without offering an excuse. . . . They enter domestic service until the desired sum is secured and then return again to their homes. Others come in from the country to work during the time that they are not needed in the crops, but return again as soon as the busy season begins."[36]

The way in which seasonal tasks, work roles, and family resources combined also depended on the local economy and the jobs available to potential wage earners. The proximity of cities or towns to black farms could mean that parents and children lived under the same roof throughout the year, whether some members of the family worked off the farm seasonally or year round. The wider choice of occupations in the more densely populated areas of the South also allowed black rural families in these regions greater flexibility in assigning wage employment among members according to age and sex. In the more remote country districts the narrower range of options for increasing the black family's income could mean harder choices: accepting poorly paid jobs provided by the white landowner from whom the family rented land or migrating comparatively long distances over longer periods of time for better-paying seasonal work.[37]

However black families arranged to increase their income through wage earnings, there was in the framework of recurring seasonal work in southern industries or domestic service a logic from which northward migration developed. Work gangs at sawmills, lumber and turpentine camps, railroad labor camps, or fertilizer plants were transmitters of job information from men who had traveled widely to green farmhands who were taking their first job off the farm. In the course of even a brief work period in such areas, the green hands could learn where higher wages could be earned, housing was better, work was lighter, or amusement was livelier. Black women working in a white household similarly came in touch with more experienced cooks and laundresses in the same house as well as among the town's larger servant population.

Exchanges of information that took place during rural blacks' seasonal employment at work camps and in towns facilitated migration farther afield. Even if the black farmers returned to work in the fields again, they now possessed the rudiments of work experience, information, and social contacts necessary for movement farther from their homes. Where seasonal jobs added this leavening influence to the rural blacks' routine movements between agricultural and industrial labor, the potential arose for a deeper, more lasting break with cotton farming.

The implications of this transition from farm labor to wage work were particularly significant for rural black youth. Their employment off the farm was not only a pillar supporting their families' well-being, but also a gradual introduction to the requirements of earning their own living as well. A common pattern was for young blacks to save some of their wages as they grew older and eventually enter their own share tenancy or day labor arrangements with white landowners, marry, establish rural households, and begin families.[38] But another pattern was for seasonal nonfarm work to lead young blacks away from cotton farming altogether. Young men and women were especially susceptible to the attractions of different ways of living and working from those they had learned growing up. At this point in their lives, they had few responsibilities to limit experiments with new life-styles and occupations. They were more employable in many types of work and relished a greater desire for travel than those either younger or older. Thus industrial or domestic employment increased the potential for migration away from agriculture, particularly for those between the ages of sixteen and thirty.

Reaching a specific age was not as important for the realization of this potential among black youth as was the attainment of independence from their families. For many men and women, this was a long and difficult process. Even after they began to contribute wages to their families' annual income, many black teenagers remained in an indeterminate status between dependent children and family providers. If they took pride in their new roles as breadwinners, by the same measure they grew restless under their parents' guidance. This was true for Nate Shaw, who began plowing when he was nine years old and later worked seasonally on his father's orders at logging camps and at neighbors' farms. Shaw turned his wages over to his father, but discovered in himself a growing confidence and desire for independence. "I was feelin my man, gettin up close to grown. If a young fellow ever take on and feel like he's a man, he'll start it close to the time when he's eighteen, nineteen years old. He'll begin to feel himself and I begin to feel myself too." Increasingly impatient with the rigors of fieldwork, parental discipline, or the subsistence level of family incomes, young men sometimes simply ran away to support themselves in the same types of jobs they held during periods of light farm work.[39]

Teenage black women also expressed disenchantment with farm life and showed their readiness to move away from their families to support themselves. "When we picked cotton we had them big ol' baskets, put 'em in the wagon and bring 'em up to the house," said Pittsburgh migrant Jonnie F., who was raised in Alabama. "I would lift those hundred pound [baskets] just like my brother. I would just throw 'em on my back, child, and I would just dump 'em. It was fun then, you know, but when you commence to gettin' older and work, work, work, and stay the same . . . you know, you want a change." Her family moved to Montgomery, Alabama, but she went to Birmingham with a friend to find domestic service jobs. The narrow range of wage-earning jobs open to black women may have made early marriage or a move to a relative's household easier ways for them to escape parental authority and the routines of labor in their childhood homes.[40]

Other young blacks continued living with their parents beyond their teenage years, working at both farming and wage labor. But these men and women also faced the time when a new status within their families was either proclaimed by them or granted by their parents. For some, the passage from dependent son or daughter to independent contributor crystallized in emotional confrontations. Nate Shaw came back to his father's farm in August 1906 from his job at a local white farm. He was almost twenty-one and determined to strike out on his own.

"Papa, today I wound up on the last job you ever put me on and I got nothin out of it this year. . . . Soon I'll be thoroughly of age and I'll have to start from the stump. I aint got decent Sunday clothes; I aint got decent everyday clothes—I don't know what I'm goin to do. And I *may* marry." When Joe G. turned twenty-one, he was working at a sawmill and living with his parents in South Carolina. Following the payday custom, he handed his father his earnings from the sawmill, but his father promptly handed them back. Joe G. was stunned. "Papa, what does this mean?" His father said, " 'Now listen, son. You are 21 and you are supposed to take care of yourself. Your money is *yours*. Whatever you want me to have, you give it to me.' " In just the same way, John B.'s father returned his son's earnings to him one day. " 'Now this [money] is yours . . . you give me what you want me to have.' I remember it so clearly and can't forget it," John B. mused. "I was a man then—he called me a man."[41]

Probably few black parents demanded direct monetary contributions from their children after the age of twenty-one, but by that age many rural youths had already departed to begin their own work careers. A study of rural-urban migration in Virginia in the 1920s found that among a group of black migrants, roughly three-fifths either began nonfarm employment or had married and gone out on their own between the ages of sixteen and eighteen. More than four-fifths were independent by the time they were twenty. The median age of beginning their own work was between seventeen and eighteen for both black men and women, and almost equal percentages of each sex were working off their parents' farm by the age of twenty-two.[42]

When the annual cycle of farm labor and the individual life cycle came into phase, the lives of rural blacks could shift into a new trajectory. During a period of light farm work in their late teenage or early adult years, black youth were most likely to project their own plans and aspirations beyond their familiar rural communities. Many of them had, in effect, already tested the possibilities for new ways of living by working seasonally off their home farms. Now they could follow up on the tips they had accumulated from fellow employees, friends, and relatives and travel longer distances to new jobs.

The dynamics of this migration process before World War I

were largely confined within the South. But the labor demand from northern industries created by World War I opened new territory. During the war both landlords and industrial employers reported that instead of returning to their farms, rural blacks left seasonal nonfarm jobs to go to the North. Clyde V. Kiser discovered in his study of the movement of St. Helena Islanders to New York City that "the seasonal ebb and flow of individuals seeking temporary work constitute stages preliminary to permanent migration on the part of many individuals. Islanders are thus given their first contacts with outsiders. Many, caught up in seasonal tides, do not return, although they leave with the intention of staying only a few months."[43]

The combined influences of the annual farming cycle and the rural life cycle showed up among Pittsburgh's male black migrants. Among thirteen of the men interviewed for this study, northward migration was either an extension of their seasonal employment pattern in the South or a direct result of their work at a particular industrial site.[44] The black men arriving in Pittsburgh from World War I to the Depression were also more concentrated in the prime working years than were southern black males as a group. Forty-five percent of the migrants hired at one Pittsburgh iron mill from 1916 to 1930 were between the ages of fifteen and twenty-four when they reached the city, while only 21 percent of the South's rural black men fell into this age group. A 1917 survey of black migrants in Pittsburgh found that the men from eighteen to forty years of age made up 76 percent of the total. By comparison, in the rural South in 1910, black men from fifteen to forty-four comprised only 43 percent of their sex.[45]

There are two important qualifications to add to this analysis of the origins of black migration. First, although southern blacks who engaged in the seasonal-youth pattern of mobility typified the migrants to Pittsburgh from 1916 to 1930, they did not account for all the blacks traveling north in these years. In addition to the young, country-bred men and women there were indeed many migrants from southern towns and cities, many older migrants, as well as blacks from rural regions of the South where cotton was not the primary cash crop. The impetus to leave the South came from many different sources, affecting individuals from diverse backgrounds, circumstances, and localities.[46]

A second qualification follows logically from the first: the rural work/rest cycle and the life cycle cannot be considered "causes" of migration in the same sense as other influences operating on the black population. On one side, poverty, racial oppression, and general insecurity of life and property forced southern blacks to consider fundamental alterations in their condition. On the other side, there were new circumstances from around 1914 that became stimuli to migration: poor cotton harvests resulting from flooding and infestation by boll weevils, and demand for black labor in northern industries.[47] These factors in blacks' lives—the push and pull forces—were the proximate causes behind the rapid out-migration that began in 1916.[48]

The custom of seasonal migration and the coming of age among southern blacks, however, clarify how impoverished, semiliterate inhabitants of an economically backward region could respond quickly to changes both in their own rural settlements and in distant urban centers. The repeated shifts from farm to nonfarm work and the attainment of an independent status allowed rural blacks to link their routine lives to the urbanizing world of the South and the nation. By doing so, they readied themselves to grasp new opportunities when they arose, to exploit to their own advantage even the crises, reversals in their agricultural fortunes, or disruptions to their family lives. Consequently, rural blacks were already partially inducted into industrial and urban modes of labor by 1916, well prepared to seek the best-paying line of work they could find. In the mid-nineteenth century Karl Marx noted the same development among rural Britons: "Part of the agricultural population is . . . on the point of passing over into an urban or manufacturing proletariat, and on the lookout for circumstances favourable to this transformation."[49]

Industrialization, the disruption of agrarian societies, and rural-urban migration in fact occurred together not only in the southeastern United States but also throughout much of Europe from Ireland to Russia in the last century, as well as in Latin America, Africa, Asia, and the Mideast in this one. Everywhere that nascent capitalist market systems or centralized state bureaucracies have impinged on relatively stable agricultural groups, peasants have responded in varying ways that nonetheless have a unifying thread. For example, Italian rural laborers and tenant farmers from the Mezzogiorno between 1870 and 1920 traveled all over Europe and the Western Hemisphere seeking wages in construction. They usually returned to their homes after the building season ended. Scandinavians' migration mirrored southern blacks' movements away from farms, even in the employment at lumberyards and sawmills close to their origins that preceded movement over longer distances. The shuttling of rural Nigerians, Thais, Mexicans, and Egyptians between villages and burgeoning cities in their respective countries since World War II represents essentially the same process of maintaining at least a semblance of traditional rural life through transfusions of wages from the encroaching metropolis.[50]

As in many other parts of the world, the South's urbanization and industrialization nourished the process of cityward migration among rural blacks, allowing them to extend the geographic range of their movements gradually and bringing thousands of men and women more or less in contact with the cities and workshops beyond their places of origin. Though southern blacks remained largely a rural group on the eve of World War I, they had already contributed greatly to the growth of cities in the South. Between 1880 and 1910 the black populations of the major cities increased each decade by the following averages: Atlanta, 48.7 percent; Memphis, 57.2 percent; Birmingham (1890-1910), 131.5 percent; New Orleans, 15.8 percent; Richmond, 20 percent. While large cities in the South rapidly enlarged their black populations, the number of blacks in smaller southern cities also grew. Between 1880 and 1910 the black population of Mobile increased on an average of 23 percent each decade; Jacksonville, an average of 105 percent every ten years; Savannah, 29 percent per decade; Columbia, South Carolina, 28 percent; and Chattanooga, 63 percent.[51]

At the same time that blacks were entering southern cities, they were also moving into industrial occupations. Most jobs in newer industries of the South like textile manufacturing and railroad shop work were denied to blacks. But a narrow range of occupations specifically designated as "Negro jobs" provided work opportunities. The 66 percent increase in black nonfarm employment between 1890 and 1910 was funneled into railroad track construction and maintenance, coal mines, sawmills, and turpentine camps. By 1910 black men dominated this unskilled work. They also made up most of the dock workers in New Orleans, the tobacco workers in North Carolina, and the teamsters in major southern cities.[52] There were thousands of skilled black workers in southern towns and cities, but the black farmers seeking temporary jobs could find them most easily in the common labor positions of the rapidly growing sectors of the southern economy. Though physically exhausting and frequently very dangerous, these jobs provided wage earnings for short periods to rural blacks who could work only briefly.

Some southern blacks also moved to the North before 1916, despite their limited chances for good jobs in major industrial centers. Pittsburgh's black population more than doubled between 1890 and 1910, and that of major northern cities increased substantially between 1900 and 1910. Though the relative growth in these cities' black groups was impressive, the overall impact of northward migration from 1890 to 1910 on the distribution of the U.S. black population was not great. The proportion of blacks born in the South but living in the North and West rose from 3.5 percent in 1890 to 4.8 percent in 1910.[53] The real importance of this early northward movement lay more in the strategic position it gave the pre–World War I black migrants in northern cities in relation to those who followed them from 1916 to 1930. The earlier migrants in many instances became Pittsburgh gatekeepers to the southern blacks who arrived after them.

When viewed against this background of black urbanization and industrial employment in both the North and South, we can see that the mass migration beginning in 1916 was not a sudden, sharp departure from agriculture. It was instead an attempt to garner the benefits of new types of employment while maintaining foundations in the only way of life many blacks knew. The accumulated experience of thousands of southern blacks in seasonal cityward migration and temporary nonfarm employment showed up clearly in the ways that the grandchildren of the freedmen advanced toward Pittsburgh and other northern cities. Their lives in the rural South amounted to an education in migration and alternating seasons of farm and industrial labor. The rapid social changes set off by World War I did not immediately change all that they knew. Instead it quickly enlarged the field of geographic movement and work opportunities in which they could apply the lessons in seasonal migration that they had already mastered.

NOTES

1. Roger Ransom and Richard Sutch, *One Kind of Freedom: The Economic Consequences of Freedom* (Cambridge: Cambridge University Press, 1977), 64-67; Vernon L. Wharton, *The Negro in Mississippi*, in Studies in History and Political Science, ed. A. R. Newsome (Chapel Hill: University of North Carolina Press, 1947), 62-63; Joel Williamson, *After Slavery: The Negro in South Carolina during Reconstruction, 1861-1877* (Chapel Hill: University of North Carolina Press, 1965), 90-95; Robert Higgs, *Competition and Coercion: Blacks in the American Economy, 1865-1914* (Cambridge: Cambridge University Press, 1977), 45; Jay Mandle, *The Roots of Black Poverty: The Southern Plantation Economy after the Civil War* (Durham: Duke University Press, 1978), 17-20; W. E. B. Du Bois, *The Souls of Black Folk* (Chicago: A. C. McClurg, 1903), 147-48.

2. Peter Kolchin, *First Freedom: The Responses of Alabama's Blacks to Emancipation and Reconstruction* (Westport: Greenwood Press, 1972), 34-36, 39-40, 47-48; Mandle, *Roots of Black Poverty*, 20-21; Ransom and Sutch, *One Kind of Freedom*, 89-90; Williamson, *After Slavery*, 129-33; Wharton, *Negro in Mississippi*, 71-73; Higgs, *Competition and Coercion*, 49-50; Joseph D. Reid, Jr., "Sharecropping as an Understandable Market Response: The Post-Bellum South," *Journal of Economic History* 33 (Mar. 1973), 107-9.

3. Carl Kelsey, *The Negro Farmer* (Chicago: Jennings and Pye, 1903), 46-48; C. Vann Woodward, *Origins of the New South, 1877-1913* (Baton Rouge: Louisiana State University Press, 1951), 180-81; Williamson, *After Slavery*, 171-75; Higgs, *Competition and Coercion*, 55-56; Ransom and Sutch, *One Kind of Freedom*, 123; Robert P. Brooks, *The Agrarian Revolution in Georgia, 1865-1912* (Madison: University of Wisconsin Press, 1914), 32; M. B. Hammond, *The Cotton Industry*, Publications of the American Economic Association, New Series, no. 1 (New York, 1897), 141-51.

4. Lewis C. Gray, "Southern Agriculture, Plantation System, and the

Negro Problem," American Academy of Political and Social Science, *Annals* 40 (Mar. 1912), 96–97; Kelsey, *Negro Farmer,* 48.

5. Charles S. Johnson, Edwin R. Embree, and W. W. Alexander, *The Collapse of Cotton Tenancy* (Chapel Hill: University of North Carolina Press, 1935), 31–32; Ransom and Sutch, *One Kind of Freedom,* 127, 130, 132–40.

6. Kelsey, *Negro Farmer,* 48; Allison Davis, Burleigh B. Gardner, and Mary R. Gardner, *Deep South* (Chicago: University of Chicago Press, 1941), 329–31; Ransom and Sutch, *One Kind of Freedom,* 98–99; Reid, "Sharecropping," 114–19.

7. William Cohen, "Negro Involuntary Servitude in the South, 1865–1940: A Preliminary Analysis," *Journal of Southern History* 42 (Feb. 1976), 33–40, 55; Oscar Zeichner, "The Legal Status of the Agricultural Laborer in the South," *Political Science Quarterly* 55 (Sept. 1940), 422–28; Jonathan Wiener, *Social Origins of the New South: Alabama, 1860–1885* (Baton Rouge: Louisiana State University Press, 1978), 58–60; Thomas J. Edwards, "The Tenant System and Some Changes since Emancipation," in *The Negro's Progress in Fifty Years,* American Academy of Political and Social Science, *Annals* 49 (Sept. 1913), 43; Du Bois, *Souls of Black Folk,* 151–53; Johnson, Embree, and Alexander, *Collapse of Cotton Tenancy,* 18, 19.

8. U.S. Census Bureau, *Negroes in the United States, 1920–1932* (Washington: Government Printing Office, 1935), 578.

9. U.S. Census Bureau, *Negro Population in the United States, 1790–1915* (Washington: Government Printing Office, 1918), 638–40; Woodward, *Origins of the New South,* 205; Wharton, *Negro in Mississippi,* 61–62; Kelsey, *Negro Farmer,* 77.

10. U.S. Census Bureau, *Negro Population, 1790–1915,* 624.

11. Davis, Gardner, and Gardner, *Deep South,* 331–32; Brooks, *Agrarian Revolution,* 52, 59–60.

12. E. A. Boeger and E. A. Goldenweiser, *A Study of the Tenant System of Farming in the Yazoo-Mississippi Delta,* U.S. Department of Agriculture, Bulletin no. 337 (Washington: Government Printing Office, 1916), 11; E. C. Branson, "Farm Tenancy in the Cotton Belt: How Farm Tenants Live," *Journal of Social Forces* 1 (Mar. 1923), 219; Johnson, Embree, and Alexander, *Collapse of Cotton Tenancy,* 75–77; Rupert B. Vance, *All These People* (Chapel Hill: University of North Carolina Press, 1945), 229.

13. Boeger and Goldenweiser, *Study of the Tenant System,* 11; Edwards, "Tenant System," 42; Du Bois, *Souls of Black Folk,* 160–62.

14. Davis, Gardner, and Gardner, *Deep South,* 293–96; Ransom and Sutch, *One Kind of Freedom,* 85–87; Theodore Rosengarten, *All God's Dangers: The Life of Nate Shaw* (New York: Knopf, 1974), 305–30.

15. Gavin Wright, *Political Economy of the Cotton South* (New York: W. W. Norton, 1978), 159–60; Stanley L. Engerman, "Some

Factors in Southern Backwardness in the Nineteenth Century," in *Essays in Regional Economics,* ed. John F. Kain and John R. Meyer (Cambridge, Mass.: Harvard University Press, 1971), 303-6; Mandle, *Roots of Black Poverty,* 68-70; Brinley Thomas, *Migration and Urban Development* (London: Methuen, 1972), 152; Hammond, *Cotton Industry,* 170; C. Horace Hamilton, "Continuity and Change in Southern Migration," in *The South in Continuity and Change,* ed. John C. McKinney and Edgar T. Thompson (Durham: Duke University Press, 1965), 54.

16. Joseph B. Lyman, *Cotton Culture* (New York: Orange Judd, 1868), 16-35; Rupert B. Vance, *Human Factors in Cotton Culture* (Chapel Hill: University of North Carolina Press, 1929), 157-62; Jane Maguire, *On Shares: Ed Brown's Story* (New York: W. W. Norton, 1975), 44, 56-57; Davis, Gardner, and Gardner, *Deep South,* 325-27; interview: Charner C., Feb. 21, 1976.

17. Lyman, *Cotton Culture,* 36-45, 64-67; Vance, *Human Factors,* 166-69; Benjamin J. Free, *Seasonal Employment in Agriculture* (Washington: Works Progress Administration, 1938), 21, 23; Davis, Gardner, and Gardner, *Deep South,* 270-71.

18. W. T. Couch, "The Negro in the South," in *Culture in the South,* ed. W. T. Couch (Chapel Hill: University of North Carolina Press, 1935), 445; Charles S. Johnson, *Growing Up in the Black Belt* (Washington: American Council on Education, 1941), 100; W. E. B. Du Bois, "The Negro in the Black Belt: Some Social Sketches," U.S. Department of Labor, *Bulletin* 22 (May 1899), 402; Rosengarten, *All God's Dangers,* 15; Nell I. Painter, *The Narrative of Hosea Hudson* (Cambridge, Mass.: Harvard University Press, 1979), 8; interviews: Jean B., July 29, 1976, Gilbert M., Apr. 9, 1976, John B., Mar. 10, 1976.

19. Ruth Allen, *The Labor of Women in the Production of Cotton* (Austin: University of Texas Press, 1933), 194-95; interviews: Wesley M., Apr. 2, 1976, Jasper A., July 12, 1976, Julia D. (pseudonym), May 3, 1976, Callie N., June 23, 1976, Jonnie F., Apr. 23, 1976, Sallie S., June 18, 1976.

20. Allen, *Labor of Women,* 194; Rosengarten, *All God's Dangers,* 120-21, 191. The black family's restrictions on women's work to household chores began as soon as the slaves were freed. Ransom and Sutch, *One Kind of Freedom,* 62; Kolchin, *First Freedom,* 62; Williamson, *After Slavery,* 44-45.

21. Free, *Seasonal Employment,* 21, 23, and passim; Vance, *Human Factors,* 156, 164-65.

22. Davis, Gardner, and Gardner, *Deep South,* 379; Julia Peterkin, *Roll, Jordan, Roll* (New York: Robert O. Ballou, 1933), 237; Maguire, *On Shares,* 56-59 (emphasis in the original).

23. Vance, *Human Factors,* 169-71; Hortense Powdermaker, *After Freedom* (New York: Viking Press, 1939), 82-83; Davis, Gardner, and Gardner, *Deep South,* 379, 388; Maguire, *On Shares,* 57, 73, 144.

24. Matthew Ward, *Indignant Heart* (Detroit: New Books, 1952), 11-12; Maguire, *On Shares*, 43-44; Vance, *Human Factors*, 165; interview: Ed R., June 10, 1976.

25. W. B. Hill, *Rural Survey of Clarke County, Georgia, with Special Reference to the Negroes*, Bulletin of the University of Georgia, 15/Phelps-Stokes Fellowship Studies, 2 (Mar. 1915), 53.

26. Peterkin, *Roll, Jordan, Roll*, 249-50.

27. Ward, *Indignant Heart*, 5; Charles S. Johnson, *Shadow of the Plantation* (Chicago: University of Chicago Press, 1934), 134; Painter, *Narrative of Hosea Hudson*, 8; Blanche A. Beatty, "The Negro Child in the Rural Community," *Opportunity* 2 (Oct. 1924), 301; interview: Matthew J., May 28, 1976.

28. Rosengarten, *All God's Dangers*, 25.

29. U.S. Census Bureau, *Negro Population, 1790-1915*, 397.

30. Alfred H. Stone, "Negro Labor and the Boll Weevil," American Academy of Political and Social Science, *Annals* 33 (Mar. 1909), 170-71; Painter, *Narrative of Hosea Hudson*, 2-6; Johnson, *Shadow of the Plantation*, 117; Vance, *Human Factors*, 152.

31. Francis Long, *The Negroes of Clarke County, Georgia, during the Great War*, Bulletin of the University of Georgia, 19/Phelps-Stokes Fellowship Studies, 5 (1919), 38; T. J. Woofter, Jr., "Migration of Negroes from Georgia, 1916-1917," in U.S. Department of Labor, Division of Negro Economics, *Negro Migration in 1916-17* (Washington: Government Printing Office, 1919), 84.

32. Vernon H. Jensen, *Lumber and Labor* (New York: Farrar and Rinehart, 1945), 77-78; Clyde V. Kiser, *Sea Island to City* (New York: Columbia University Press, 1932), 149-50; Pete Daniel, *The Shadow of Slavery: Peonage in the South, 1901-1969* (Urbana: University of Illinois Press, 1972), 36-37; Woofter, "Migration of Negroes," 84; Rosengarten, *All God's Dangers*, 173; Kelsey, *Negro Farmer*, 50; Davis, Gardner, and Gardner, *Deep South*, 262; John W. Fanning, *Negro Migration*, Bulletin of the University of Georgia, 30/Phelps-Stokes Fellowship Studies, 9 (1930), 32.

33. Interviews: William H., June 17, 1976, Ben E., July 31, 1974; Couch, "Negro in the South," 444-45.

34. Rosengarten, *All God's Dangers*, 72-83; interviews: William H., June 17, 1976, Ben E., July 31, 1974.

35. Couch, "Negro in the South," 444-45; interviews: Callie N., June 23, 1976, Maria B., June 1, 1976, Queen W., Oct. 8, 1976.

36. Ruth Reed, *Negro Women of Gainesville, Georgia*, Bulletin of the University of Georgia, 22/Phelps-Stokes Fellowship Studies, 6 (1921), Table 11, 25. See also T. J. Woofter, Jr., *The Negroes of Athens, Georgia*, Bulletin of the University of Georgia, 14/Phelps-Stokes Fellowship Studies, 6(1913), 46.

37. Interviews: Sadie M., May 19, 1976, Wesley M., Apr. 2, 1976, William H., June 17, 1976, Gilbert M., Apr. 9, 1976.

38. Brooks, *Agrarian Revolution,* 60-61; Donald D. Scarborough, *An Economic Study of Negro Farmers as Owners, Tenants, and Croppers,* Bulletin of the University of Georgia, 25/Phelps-Stokes Fellowship Studies, 7 (1924), 34; Rosengarten, *All God's Dangers,* 82-83.

39. Rosengarten, *All God's Dangers,* 49; interviews: Jasper A., July 12, 1976, Gilbert M., Apr. 9, 1976.

40. Interviews: Jonnie F., Apr. 23, 1976, Julia D. (pseudonym), May 3, 1976.

41. Rosengarten, *All God's Dangers,* 82 (emphasis in the original); interviews: Joseph G., Nov. 26, 1973, John B., Mar. 10, 1976, William H., June 17, 1976.

42. Wilson Gee and John J. Corson, *Rural Depopulation in Certain Tidewater and Piedmont Areas of Virginia* (Charlottesville: University of Virginia Institute for Research in Social Sciences, 1929), 33.

43. Kiser, *Sea Island to City,* 154.

44. Interviews: Wesley M., Apr. 2, 1976, William H., June 17, 1976, Matthew J., May 28, 1976, Jasper A., July 12, 1976, Leroy M., July 9, 1974, Charner C., Feb. 21, 1976, Ed R., June 10, 1976, Clarence M., Aug. 5, 1974, Ben E., July 31, 1974, Caleb B., Apr. 9, 1976, Walter H., Oct. 25, 30, 1973, Joseph G., Nov. 26, 1973, John B., Mar. 10, 1976.

45. U.S. Census Bureau, *Negro Population, 1790-1915,* 182; A. M. Byers Company Personnel File, Archives of Industrial Society, Hillman Library, University of Pittsburgh; Abraham Epstein, *The Negro Migrant in Pittsburgh* (Pittsburgh: University of Pittsburgh, 1918), 18.

46. Florette Henri, *Black Migration: Movement North, 1900-1920* (Garden City: Anchor/Doubleday, 1975), 49-66.

47. Charles S. Johnson, "How Much Is the Migration a Flight from Persecution?" *Opportunity* 1 (Sept. 1923), 272-74; "The Negro Migration," ibid., 1 (Aug. 1923), 254-55.

48. Louise V. Kennedy, *The Negro Peasant Turns Cityward* (New York: Columbia University Press, 1930), 42-48; Emmett J. Scott, *Negro Migration during the War* (New York: Oxford University Press, 1920), 14; Woofter, "Migration of Negroes," 86-89; Charles H. Wesley, *Negro Labor in the United States, 1850-1925* (New York: Russell and Russell, 1927), 291-94; Henri, *Black Migration,* 75, and passim.

49. Karl Marx, *Capital* (London: Lawrence and Wishart, 1970), 1:642.

50. Robert F. Foerster, *The Italian Emigration of Our Time* (Cambridge, Mass: Harvard University Press, 1919), 36-37, 124; Timo Orta, "Finnish Emigration Prior to 1893: Economic, Demographic, and Social Backgrounds," *The Finnish Experience in the Western Great Lakes Region,* Migration Studies, no. 3 (Turku, Finland: Institute for Migration, 1975), 24, 26-27; Janet Abu-Lughod, "Migrant Adjustment to City Life: The Egyptian Case," in *Peasant Society,* ed. Jack Potter et al. (Boston: Little, Brown, 1967), 397-98; Joan M. Nelson, "Sojourners

Versus New Urbanites: Causes and Consequences of Temporary Versus Permanent Cityward Migration in Developing Countries," *Economic Development and Cultural Change* 24 (July 1976), 721-57; Nancy B. Graves and Theodore D. Graves, "Adaptive Strategies in Urban Migration," *Annual Review of Anthropology* 3 (1974), 119-20.

51. U.S. Census Bureau, *Negro Population, 1790-1915,* 95-105; U.S. Department of the Interior, Census Office, *Report on Population, 1890* (Washington: Government Printing Office, 1895), 1:451-83; Census Office, *Tenth Census, Population* (Washington: Government Printing Office, 1883), 416-25.

52. Wesley, *Negro Labor,* 248-52; Woodward, *Origins of the New South,* 360-61; Paul B. Worthman and James R. Green, "Black Workers in the New South, 1865-1915," in *Key Issues in the Afro-American Experience,* ed. Nathan I. Huggins, Martin Kilson, and Daniel M. Fox (New York: Harcourt, Brace, Jovanovich, 1971), 2:52-53.

53. U.S. Census Bureau, *Negro Population, 1790-1915,* 65, 93-102; U.S. Census Bureau, *Twelfth Census, Population,* Pt. 1 (Washington: Government Printing Office, 1901), 669, 675, 697; U.S. Census Bureau, *Thirteenth Census, Population: General Report and Analysis* (Washington: Government Printing Office, 1913), 242.

2

Reaching Pittsburgh

SOUTHERN BLACKS' MOVEMENT to Pittsburgh combined migration patterns from their rural environment with new ways of traveling. Even though they could adapt some of their customary types of movement to northward trips, Pittsburgh migrants faced difficult problems that required innovative responses. They had to provide for their dependents in the South during long absences. They needed to save or borrow money for train fare and for expenses in Pittsburgh. Above all, they needed information about Pittsburgh conditions. The city lured southern blacks with prospects of comparatively well-paid jobs and prosperous households, but few migrants had specific knowledge about the smoke-shrouded metropolis and its many satellite manufacturing towns.

Long before World War I Pittsburgh had become the center of a heavy manufacturing and mining region that took in the western Pennsylvania coal fields, the iron, steel, and coking plants, and a constellation of glass, brick, foundry, and electric machinery factories. Rivers, steep-sided valleys, and irregular hills dictated the industrial geography of the area. Into the city from the northeast flowed the Allegheny River, a transportation route for bituminous coal from Westmoreland and Armstrong counties. On its banks upstream from Pittsburgh hulked the modern Pittsburgh Plate Glass plant at Ford City and numerous metal manufacturers at Natrona Heights, Brackenridge, and Tarentum. On the Kiskiminitas River, a tributary of the Allegheny, stood large steel mills at Apollo and Vandergrift.

The Monongahela River threaded the hilly country south of

Pittsburgh to join the Allegheny at the center of the city. The Monongahela bore on its currents an immense barge traffic of coal, coke, and basic metals. From the American Wire and Steel mills at Monessen northward through the mill towns of Donora, Clairton, Glassport, and McKeesport, the river approached the outskirts of Pittsburgh. Then past the Carnegie Steel Company's works at Duquesne, Braddock, Rankin, and Homestead, the Monongahela finally entered the city limits where still more steel and iron plants lined its banks: the Jones and Laughlin Steel Company's Soho and South Side mills, the Oliver Iron and Steel Company plant, and the A. M. Byers Company iron mill among them.

The Ohio River, formed at the confluence of the Allegheny and Monongahela rivers in downtown Pittsburgh, wound away from the city on a northwesterly course. Its valley cradled still more heavy manufacturing plants, from the Lockhart Iron and Steel Company and Pressed Steel Car shops in McKees Rocks to the Aliquippa works of the Jones and Laughlin Steel Company, twenty-one miles downstream from Pittsburgh.[1] In the countless smaller stream valleys of the area were many more industries, coal mines, and railroad yards. Each of these cells of production in Pittsburgh's vast network was brought to the point of labor starvation by the spiraling demand for armaments and munitions during World War I and by the severing of the long-established labor supply from overseas. The war both increased the need for workers in Pittsburgh and disrupted the normal flow of men and women to the city's work places.[2]

The news of Pittsburgh jobs reached southern blacks through complex networks of communication, which first appeared during the pre–World War I period. Railroads, newspapers, and personal contacts between the earlier migrants and their native communities channeled news about Pittsburgh and other places to the South. As more and more southern blacks traveled north after 1915, the reticulation of communication lines speeded up rapidly. By the mid-1920s it seemed that even the inhabitants of the remotest rural hamlets of the South knew someone who had gone north, where to find printed notices of employment opportunities, or what rail lines could carry passengers to Pittsburgh.

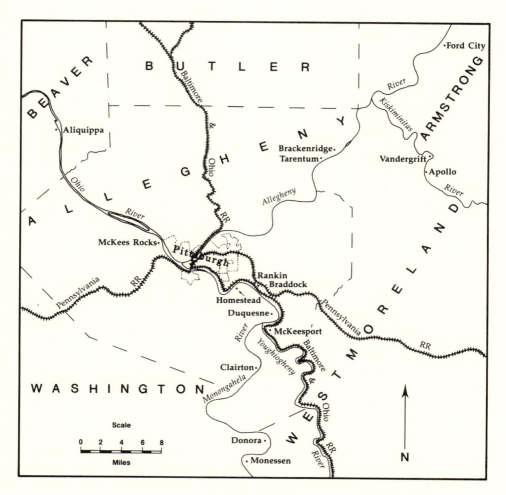

BEAVER

BUTLER

ARMSTRONG

·Ford City

Baltimore

&

Ohio

·Aliquippa

ALLEGHENY

Ohio

River

RR

Brackenridge·
Tarentum·

Allegheny

Kiskiminitas

River

Vandergrift·

·Apollo

River

McKees Rocks·

Pittsburgh

Rankin
·Braddock

Homestead

Duquesne·

·McKeesport

Pennsylvania

RR

Pennsylvania

RR

WESTMORELAND

River

Youghiogheny

Baltimore

&

Ohio

Clairton·

Monongahela

RR

WASHINGTON

Scale

0   2   4   6   8

Miles

Donora·

·Monessen

WES

Ohio

RR

River

N

The Pittsburgh District
Source: Pennsylvania State Highway Department, 1919

Railroads played an important part in blacks' migration to Pittsburgh, both as the chief means of transportation and as a vehicle of communication. From Florida, Georgia, the Carolinas, and Virginia three rail lines were the principal carriers to Richmond or to Washington, D.C.: the Atlantic Coast, the Southern, and the Seaboard Air Line railroads. At Washington migrants transferred to the Baltimore and Ohio for the rest of the journey to Pittsburgh. From the Gulf states, Tennessee, and Kentucky, the Louisville and Nashville Railroad and the Illinois Central linked southern cities and market towns to Cincinnati, St. Louis, and Louisville. Travel routes to Pittsburgh turned east from these points along the Baltimore and Ohio or the Pennsylvania Railroad lines. The railroads sent information as well as people between the North and the South, carrying letters, newspapers, and magazines from which southern blacks garnered information about Pittsburgh. Black railroad porters, dining car cooks, waiters, and trackhands traveling regularly on their jobs brought word of Pittsburgh to southern rail centers and to railroad work camps. The migrants themselves became the most effective transmitters of information. Returning by railroad to southern homes for visits, they verified the good news about Pittsburgh by their cash, new clothes, gifts for friends and relatives, and a whole new style of speech and manners.[3]

Newspapers and magazines swelled the flow of information between Pittsburgh and prospective migrants in the South. Pittsburgh's major black newspaper, the Pittsburgh *Courier*, printed "society" and "local events" columns. In these sections of the newspaper, blacks could read about personalities, weddings, club meetings, and even social visits among Pittsburgh's black families. The *Courier* circulated nationwide in the 1920s, bringing news about Pittsburgh's black community to towns and rural settlements hundreds of miles distant from the city. Other black newspapers and the journals of black fraternal and mutual benefit organizations also announced the need for black laborers in Pittsburgh in 1922, extending the reach of the existing information network many fold.[4] Southern blacks who first learned about Pittsburgh by word of mouth could soon read reports (or listen to them being read aloud) from the *Courier* and other sources. A semiliterate rural population, including many who had no kin or friends in the North, in this way accumulated knowledge about their destination from both printed and oral sources.

All prospective black migrants used this information to determine where, when, and how they were going to move, but they differed in what kind of information was most helpful for their planning. Wage rates, hours of work, and the availability of jobs were crucial for some, while travel costs and railroad connections were vital for others. Where they got their news could reflect what migrants needed to know before they could leave their southern homes. And their sources of information also frequently determined their routes and modes of travel. Thus there were distinct but overlapping migration patterns among the migrant population—male and female, single and married, young and old.

Wesley M.'s travels typified the young, unmarried men's migration to Pittsburgh. Keenly aware of better work opportunities and tired of field labor on his parents' South Carolina farm, he decided one day in 1924 to leave. "I was plowin' in the field and it was real hot. And I stayed with some of the boys who would leave home and . . . [come] back . . . and would have money, and they had clothes. I didn't have that. We all grew up together. And I said, 'Well, as long as I stay here I'm not going to get nowhere.' And I tied that mule to a tree and caught a train."

Wesley M. did not travel directly to Pittsburgh. The train he boarded in 1924 took him to a sawmill where one of his older brothers worked. After laboring as a water boy there for a few months, M. heard about higher wages at another sawmill in North Carolina. He moved there and got a job, but worked only four weeks when news of still better pay for black men in Youngstown, Ohio, set him to planning a longer journey to the North. With four friends from the North Carolina sawmill, M. went to Richmond, Virginia. There they met a labor agent for the Carnegie Steel Company who told them that the best place to find jobs was at the Carnegie mills in Homestead, Pennsylvania, ten miles south of Pittsburgh. Since the agent was not going to send another group of southern blacks to Homestead for three or four days, he offered M. a letter of introduction to the

Homestead mill's employment office. M. took the letter and caught a train to Homestead.[5]

Young, unmarried black men developed strategies for reaching Pittsburgh that were quite different from those of their female and older male counterparts. Less restricted in their geographic movement by marital, family, or work responsibilities, they frequently left home with little, if any, preparation. Some of them, like Wesley M., impulsively went in search of better pay; others simply ran away from domineering fathers. But even those who set out with their parents' blessings had seldom fixed their sights on a particular northern destination when they left their southern homes. They made their way to Pittsburgh by a series of short trips through the South or by several work stints in northern cities. This stepwise movement by itself frequently did not suffice to get southern blacks to Pittsburgh, so migrants commonly combined temporary jobs with other complementary strategies. Free railroad passes obtained from a Pittsburgh labor agent was one; another was traveling with a group of men rather than moving as individuals.

Matthew J.'s itinerary began in 1918 with a temporary job in the town closest to his father's South Carolina farm. From there he moved farther from his home to Lancaster, South Carolina, but only crossed a state border on the third move, which carried him to Charlotte, North Carolina. His next two trips brought him no further north. They seem to have been made only to get temporary work at places where higher wages were paid. In 1919 he came to Washington, D.C., where he lived for five years with his aunt while working as a construction laborer. A brother in Buffalo, New York, contacted J. and invited him to visit. Along the way to see his brother, however, he stopped in Pittsburgh to visit an uncle and remained there permanently, never reaching his brother's home.[6]

If Matthew J. was the most peripatetic migrant whose routes of travel we know, some version of his gradual advance to the North characterized the migration of most of the young, unmarried black men interviewed for this study. John B. left his parents' farm near Wilmington, North Carolina, in October 1915 and got to Pittsburgh in June 1917. Between his origin and his destination he worked both in an iron furnace in

Baden, North Carolina, and at a locomotive factory in Richmond. When Joseph G. headed north in 1923, he had already been employed at a sawmill near his father's Summerton, South Carolina, farm. He first went to Wilmington, North Carolina, with a group of friends to work in a fertilizer plant. After two months he went further north to Richmond, Virginia, in order to sign up with a labor agent who recruited there for Pittsburgh steel mills. Jasper A. went south instead of north when he left his home near Albany, Georgia—first to the lumber and creosote industries of Florida and later to Jacksonville, where he found a job as a painter. A. was painting oil storage tanks there in 1916 when he heard of a labor agent in the area who was hiring blacks for railroad work in Pennsylvania. He quit painting to sign up for the free trip to the North.[7]

Each temporary job along these routes led the migrants to the next leg of their journeys, though they seldom conceived the larger stepwise pattern in advance. Usually the first job in the series was close to their homes and fit the seasonal work cycle of the rural South so that the migrants could return to their families at the customary times of year. Earnings from a sawmill, fertilizer plant, or cotton seed mill paid for a trip farther from home—to a regional marketing or manufacturing center.

Many migrants at this stage were still searching primarily for better jobs in their own localities; moving to a northern city had not yet figured in their plans. But the South was teeming with men on their way to or from northern automobile factories, coal mines, or steel mills. The migrants who were just setting out on their travels met those veterans of the northward movement at roadhouses, work camps, pool halls, or barbershops and heard them talk about their experiences in Pittsburgh and other industrial centers. Once the uninitiated migrants raised their sights to a northern city, they began searching out labor recruiters, writing to relatives in the North seeking more information, or saving money for the train trip that would carry them out of the South.

Both the primary motivation and the logic behind the pattern of stepwise movement was expressed succinctly by Matthew J.: "I was looking for more money, and the further you go up the road, the more money you get."[8] Southern black men could plan their progress by using each temporary job on the route north to finance the next leg of their journeys. If they could not glean information from workmates about a likely destination in the North, then they could move a shorter distance to a better job in the South. As they found higher hourly wages on their way north, they were encouraged to continue until they reached cities like Pittsburgh or Detroit, where pay for unskilled work during World War I and the 1920s seemed fabulous compared to the prevailing wage rates in the South.

Black men often continued moving short distances from job to job after they reached the North. Frequently they arrived in Pittsburgh, found jobs, and shortly left the city to try out other places. Walter H. did not remain in Homestead for more than a few months after his first visit in 1923. He departed for a tour of industrial cities around the Midwest and East—Akron, Cleveland, Buffalo, and Erie—before he came back to Homestead. Many other men, both young and old, explored different northern cities before and after coming to the Pittsburgh area.[9] Some of the temporary migrants were actually passing through Pittsburgh en route to other destinations.[10] Since Pittsburgh did not straddle a major north-south rail line, it did not serve many migrants as a "jumping off" place for trips further north, east, or west. Unlike southern blacks in Chicago, St. Louis, Philadelphia, or New York, migrants in Pittsburgh, whether sojourners or aspiring residents, came to try out the city's work and community life.

Young, single female migrants developed different ways of coping with the difficulties of long-distance movement. None of the women interviewed for this study came north by working her way from place to place. Instead, they traveled the entire distance in one trip. Some came to Pittsburgh unaccompanied, while others journeyed with parents, siblings, or other relatives. Those who made the trip by themselves often knew someone in the city who could meet their train and help them get settled. On the other hand, almost half of the 642 individuals whom the black Traveler's Aid worker assisted in Pittsburgh between January and March 1919 were young women without friends or relatives in the city.[11]

What it could mean for a woman to come to Pittsburgh without friends, relatives, or a place to stay was described in the case of a black teenager: "Her six months here were full of bitter experiences, she was seduced in Virginia, followed the man here, jail, several courts, marriage and desertion." Finding lodgings in Pittsburgh represented a particularly hard problem for other single female migrants. During the first half of 1923, 165 black women found places to stay with black families in Pittsburgh through the auspices of the Urban League's room registry. Single mothers faced even harsher challenges. One woman with three children left her husband in Georgia during World War I to come to Pittsburgh. She ended up living in one damp room, using an outdoor water supply, trying to nurse her sick children back to health while she took in washing to earn money.[12] Despite these difficulties, some women migrants were undaunted. Julia D. was an unusually self-reliant southern migrant. She moved unaccompanied from Virginia to Homestead. Though her brother and some of her southern friends already lived in the area, she lodged with strangers in Homestead and soon found a job there as a restaurant cook.

Marriage foreshadowed migration for many black women. Their husbands moved from the South to Pittsburgh first, found jobs, looked for suitable living quarters, earned money for train fare, then sent a ticket south to waiting spouses. These careful, deliberate arrangements provided women migrants with a sponsor for their migration, a person through whom information about Pittsburgh reached the South, who met them at a train station, or who readied a rented apartment for them before they arrived. The married women were sometimes as young as the single women migrants. They differed from the latter mainly in moving to Pittsburgh to manage a new household.

Mrs. L., who grew up in Georgetown, South Carolina, first learned about the Pittsburgh area from a brother who had moved to the mill town of Homestead in the 1920s. In 1926 she married a South Carolina man who had also worked in Homestead a few years before. After the wedding, her husband returned to the mill town to find a job and a home for both of them. Six months later, she followed him and began housekeeping in quarters rented from her in-laws.[13] Carrie J.'s migration pattern paralleled that of Mrs. L.'s. Born in Devereaux, Georgia, in 1899, she left her parents' home after her first marriage. When

this marriage dissolved, she wed a second man who moved to
Cleveland in 1914. She waited to follow him until he had found
lodgings there. In 1919 Carrie J. and her husband moved to
Pittsburgh where her sister lived.[14]

Neither Mrs. L. nor Carrie J. had become an independent
wage earner before marriage. But even when southern black
women had supported themselves by holding domestic jobs
outside their parents' homes, they frequently depended on husbands or blood relatives for assistance in northward migration.
Maria B., who was single when she visited Pittsburgh in 1930,
did not return to the city to settle permanently until she was
married. During her initial visit she met one of her cousin's
male friends who courted her when she returned to her home
in Waynesburg, Virginia. Six months later the two were married,
and she went back to Pittsburgh to make a home.[15]

Like Maria B., Olive W. chose to settle in the North only after
she was married, even though she might have done so when she
was single. Olive W. grew up on her parents' farm in Alamo,
Georgia. She worked as a domestic in New Jersey through a
church program for southern adolescents. But when the program ended she went to live with her aunt in Baxley, Georgia,
and remained there until her marriage. In July 1919 she came
to Pittsburgh with her husband to begin a new life. Marriage
opened the possibility for migration for two other Pittsburgh
female migrants. Jonnie F.'s family moved from a farm in Bull-
ock County, Alabama, to Montgomery. From there, she went to
Birmingham to work as a domestic. Though a friend of hers
had moved to Pennsylvania and had written that it was "just
better" in the North, Jonnie F. did not migrate to Pittsburgh
until after she was married. Brought up in an elite black
family in Petersburg, Virginia, Lillyan P. finished high school
in 1913 and attended the Virginia Normal & National Industrial Institute. She taught school for four years near Norfolk
and then married in 1919. For the next six years she kept
house and raised children. Then in 1925 friends wrote to her
husband, urging him to bring his family north. She remembered that in March 1925 he went to Homestead "to see how
everything was. He wrote to me and asked if I would come to
visit him for a week, to look things over." Six months after

her husband had left Petersburg, Lillyan P. joined him in
Homestead.[16]

Even when black women relied on their husbands to prepare
a place for them in Pittsburgh, their role in the northward
movement was not passive. In some cases they vetoed destinations chosen by relatives and selected cities to which *they*
wanted to move. This was how Carrie J. came to Pittsburgh in
1919. She and her husband returned to Georgia from Cleveland
to be with her ailing mother. When her mother died, her
husband went to Cincinnati, found a job, and sent for her.
Carrie J. recalled what happened next: "I wrote him a letter
back. My older sister had come to Pittsburgh, and I took her as a
mother because I had lost my mother. And I wrote him back
and said, 'I don't want to stay in Cincinnati. I want to go to
Pittsburgh.' Next letter I got, he had got a job in Pittsburgh and
sent for me." Clearly Lillyan P. was reserving the same prerogative to overrule her husband's choice of Homestead as her new
home when she recalled that six months after he had moved
there, she took a train to the mill town, to "look things over." When
John T.'s wife followed him to Braddock, she disliked the grime
and dirty air so much that she returned to her home in Hender-
son, North Carolina, and tried hard to get him to join her there.[17]

Black women's active role in migration extended far beyond
sharing the choices of destinations. Once they set up housekeeping in Pittsburgh, they encouraged other members of their
families to move north. As city dwellers and housekeepers, the
female migrants could offer information about Pittsburgh and a
place to stay when the newcomers arrived. Several years after
she moved north, Maria B. lodged two of her brothers until,
with her husband's help, they found jobs. Henry B.'s sister, who
lived in the Hazelwood section of Pittsburgh, invited him to live
with her family until he could find work in the city. Ed R.'s
mother was the first member of his family to migrate. She lived
with R.'s stepfather in the industrial suburb of Braddock when
R. himself decided to move to the Pittsburgh area. It was his
mother who told him how to make travel arrangements.[18] Black
women thus became links in the migration chains that drew
some southern black families to Pittsburgh.

Chain migration, in which each family member followed a

relative to the North and then provided assistance to other relatives who moved later, was ideally suited to the problems that southern blacks faced in journeying to Pittsburgh. Not only could family members provide reliable information to relatives in the South, they could also offer a home for siblings, sons and daughters, cousins, and in-laws. Through careful economizing, the family members in the North could send part of their earnings back to the South to support relatives and to pay the way for other relatives. By such strategies black families maximized their scant resources to shepherd their members to Pittsburgh.

Chain migration to Pittsburgh often proceeded from the oldest family members to the youngest. Lee C. came from Richmond, Virginia, to Braddock after his older brother had settled there. Julia D.'s two younger brothers followed her to Homestead. After Sarah M.'s family made a home in Pittsburgh in 1917, her mother's younger brother came to join them, find work, and settle in the North, too. But there were also many cases of older relatives succeeding younger ones to Pittsburgh. Callie N.'s father went to Pittsburgh in 1920 in the footsteps of his own children. Richard C.'s mother came north from Virginia to be with him and his brother in the city. Hezekiah M.'s younger sister and brother-in-law gave him a place to stay when he moved there from West Virginia.[19]

The community networks of southern blacks supported chain migration as much as kinship networks did. Friends, neighbors, workmates, and fellow church or lodge members from the South helped each other travel north the same way relatives did—passing along information about Pittsburgh and offering temporary living quarters in the city to arriving friends and associates. Some black men journeyed together to Pittsburgh, but community bonds and friendships more often came into play by individuals migrating to join friends who had moved to Pittsburgh already. Charner C. and Willie S. each moved to Pittsburgh initially to visit friends from their southern homes. Lucille S.'s father came to Pittsburgh because he knew friends from his native Lumpkin, Georgia, who had jobs at a Jones and Laughlin Steel Company mill.[20]

Kinship and community networks quickly intertwined in the

migration chains that linked Pittsburgh with hundreds of southern towns and rural settlements. One family's northward movement quickly drew the family's friends to Pittsburgh, and the friends' relatives joined the migration soon after. Migration flows from particular places in the South to Pittsburgh neighborhoods sometimes shaped the migrants' patterns of settlement as well as their patterns of movement. Seeking the comfort of old associations in their new environment, the families that had been neighbors in the South became neighbors, if not roommates or housemates, in the North. The sharing of information and careful maintenance of social bonds sometimes led to a clustering of southern blacks in northern cities, based on a common place of origin.[21]

Men as well as women reaped benefits from chain migration to Pittsburgh, especially older, married men. For those who were heads of households, migration incurred risks of the kind that a man in Burton, South Carolina, explained to a Pittsburgh contact: "I am a Blacksmith by trade. one of the all round type. . . . I am 55 years old, own property in this locality and have a wife . . . I do not care to move family before I can locate myself, by coming and spend at least 6 months."[22] Middle-aged black men with families to support and steady, relatively secure jobs thought carefully about the possible gains and losses in migration before they moved.

Fearful of abandoning their families for too long while they searched for work, older men needed prior knowledge of which Pittsburgh companies were employing migrants, how much they were paying, and how much of his wages a man could save from a given job. If a northern relative or friend could provide information, then the older male migrant headed north much as the women did — to join family members or acquaintances in Pittsburgh. William H., who grew up in Pollard, Alabama, worked around sawmills and lumberyards long enough to become a lumber grader. In the early 1920s his wife's aunt and uncle were living in the western Pennsylvania coal fields. They invited him to bring his wife north and join them. H. agreed and set out in 1924, leaving his wife in Mobile until he could find work and get settled. In a similar fashion James S. turned to his wife's parents for help in moving to Pittsburgh. S. grew up around

Albany, Georgia, and as an adult worked on railroad track gangs. Later he got a job as a railroad camp cook. "My reason [for coming to Pittsburgh] was my in-laws were already here. They sent for me." In 1924, one year after his in-laws had moved north, S. and his wife traveled together to join them in Pittsburgh.[23]

Unlike female migrants, however, southern black men reached far beyond kinship networks for information about Pittsburgh and for various types of assistance in migrating and settling in the city. Heads of households who had no relatives in the city wrote for information. Some sent inquiries to the Pittsburgh Urban League. J. W. Mitchell sent a series of questions: "I have a very large family and would like very much to come north if I could get a good job for all of my folks. . . . What do they pay per day in those plants now. can wommen find work to do up there at a living wag. What does house rent and fuel cost per month." Another man explained his situation to the Urban League in this way: "I am a married man and would like to settle down in some place in the north where I can make a respectable living."[24] Officials of the Urban League of Pittsburgh encouraged male migrants to come north by themselves first and to send for their families later. "Be sure to advise the men not to bring their families until they have come here and made provisions for them," wrote John T. Clark, executive secretary of the League to a contact in Houston, Texas.[25]

Information in Pittsburgh newspapers and in letters from the Pittsburgh Urban League encouraged southern black men to arrange their northward journeys at particular times of the year. The Pittsburgh *Courier* quoted an official of the Pennsylvania State Employment Department in 1923 concerning the best time to move to the city: "Tell colored people that under no circumstances come to Pittsburgh looking for a job before next April 1, no matter what kind of advertisements are seen. . . . May is the best month of the year to come North. Then there is the possibility of work all summer, but in the winter everything gets slow and there is little chance for newcomers to find something to do."[26] The Urban League drafted a circular to mail to individuals in the South who requested information about Pittsburgh, the weather conditions, work, and housing.[27]

One reply to this circular revealed the vital importance of the information disseminated by the Urban League. "Your letter rec'd and I was pleased to get the information," wrote William Ramsey from Aiken, South Carolina. "No I will not try to come up there now as I know that the weather is quite cold. I have planned to make the trip about April the first." Other messages from black southerners asked for weather reports or explained the part that northern winters played in the formulation of migration plans. "Pleas write soon," began the request from J. H. Cullen of Greenwood, South Carolina, "and if it is not to cold I will come in short and if it is to cold I will awaite untell about the first of April." Willis Chatman, a black farmer in Lindale, Georgia, explained the contingencies in his travel plans: "Of course I dont ceare to leave here untell Spring but if I can get and inside Job for the winter I will get rady and come in short."28

The older male migrants' patterns of movement had elements in common both with married women and younger men's migration. Like the women, many older men carefully sifted information about Pittsburgh before moving directly to the city. But like many young, single men, they gathered information from relatives and friends as well as strangers. Though older men usually could not take the time to work at several temporary jobs on their way north, they did resemble young men in two other strategies to which they resorted: group migration and employer-sponsored, free transportation to Pittsburgh.

It was not unusual for southern black men of all ages to travel with one or more friends, relatives, or workmates. Several difficulties of migrating alone for long distances were mitigated by group travel. Comrades of the road maintained each other's courage and spirits—an important contribution to migrants leaving homes on long journeys for the first time. The group's combined work experience and personal contacts exceeded those of any individual member, and its choice of likely places to look for work was broader and better informed. In a group the members' individual resources could be pooled so that all could reach the same destination and remain together.

John T. left his wife tending his small cleaning and tailoring shop to go north with a friend. Departing from Durham, North

Carolina, in 1924, the two men reached Columbus, Ohio, where they failed to find work. On the verge of giving up their migration plans, T.'s friend suggested that they try Pittsburgh where a relative of the friend's could at least offer free housing. T. found that in order to carry out his friend's strategy, he would have to pay both of their fares to Pittsburgh. Yet the plan worked, and both men found jobs. Lee T. had worked his way from South Carolina to Petersburg, Virginia, where he labored on a street-car track gang. When a group of men from this job went to look for work in Pittsburgh in 1919, T. joined them and used his own savings to pay all of their train fares. In 1917 Jean B. left his native southern sawmill village with his stepfather, cousin, and several friends. They took a train north, some disembarking in Youngstown and Middletown, Ohio, while others continued to Pittsburgh.[29]

Traveling north in a group was also a cooperative undertaking, similar in this respect to the chain migration of family members. Migrants planning to travel in a group could make decisions collectively. Some agreed, for example, to select one of their number to write for information, purchase railroad tickets, and devise a timetable for migration. Albert Johnson of Le Compte, Louisiana, explained this arrangement to Pittsburgh Urban League officials in 1923: "Sir, in reading the odd Fellows Journal I saw where labor was needed in different plants and I was chosen by my brethren to try to find the Real straight. . . . All who chosen me for writer is men of family." John D. Maxwell was another writer nominated by his peers. "I hearby wish to state that I am Represent a body of about 200 laboring men," he informed the Urban League of Pittsburgh, "who would like to except that Pittsburgh offer and would come ameditly if you would send Transportation."[30]

Prominent northern blacks who favored northward migration advocated group movement on a mass scale, but more obscure individuals in the South also tried their hands at leading groups of southern blacks to Pittsburgh. These local organizers described themselves alternately as members of migrant groups and as aspiring labor agents. J. R. Hill wrote from Philadelphia to the Urban League of Pittsburgh in 1923, "I write to ask you if you will assist a few dependable men in getting over there.... I have letters from quite a number of friends from the South asking me to look up jobs for them." R. L. Quarles in Houston assured the Urban League of his reliability as a supplier of migrant labor: "i can get so many moor from here for i have all way stood good in Houston among my people and they can trust me." Others based their promises to deliver black workers to the North on their knowledge of Pittsburgh conditions or the authority that they had over other prospective migrants. E. A. Massey in Durham, North Carolina, explained: "I have shown many of my friends your letter & have also explained the different works which you have. I have more than 25 men that would love to come up & be in the employment of your firm & they all have ask me to advise or help them to go there?" And from Savannah, Georgia, W. J. Waites wrote to Pittsburgh in 1923, "Now these 1,000 men you wont. I done got them waiting . . . I work lots hands everyday in the fertilizer plant. I am the leader, sir, over them all."[31]

As a migration strategy, group movement displayed some of the characteristics of chain migration. Like the black men and women who moved north in the footsteps of a family member, those who migrated with a gang from their work place or in a group of neighbors tried to carry with them a part of their native social environment. Joseph G. reached Homestead via sawmill and fertilizer factory jobs in the Carolinas. He traveled with four other men from his sawmill gang all the way to western Pennsylvania. When James Buggs of Georgetown, South Carolina, tried to arrange the migration of several of his neighbors to Pittsburgh in 1923, he explained: "We will like to get some under Stand of the Job before we come all ar married men and work mens we work together farming." Though the migrant group could disperse soon after reaching Pittsburgh—as Joseph G.'s did—or gradually lose members en route to the North like Jean B.'s, it might still have cushioned the new experience of long-distance travel for those who set out together from the South.[32]

A different kind of group migration developed from the recruitment of black labor for Pittsburgh industries. Employers who were struggling to fill their general or specialized work force requirements retained labor agents. In the early 1920s, for example, the Standard Steel Car Company had an agent bring a group of black riveters from Norfolk, Virginia, to Pittsburgh. The Pennsylvania Railroad during World War I employed recruiters to scour many parts of the South for laborers to work on its lines between Philadelphia and Pittsburgh. The Carnegie Steel Company's plants in and around Pittsburgh each had its own recruiting personnel, methods, and southern sources. In 1916 the company's Clairton Coke Works brought between 150 and 200 blacks from Charlottesville, Virginia, while the Homestead Works had an office in Richmond, Virginia, where an agent signed up men for employment in the steel mill. In most cases the blacks who received the free train tickets from northern recruiters signed a contract to work for the Pittsburgh employers and to repay the cost of transportation through deductions from their wages.[33]

Agents for Pittsburgh mills and factories most actively recruited blacks in the South when labor demand was at a peak, relying on routine out-migration to provide their labor needs at other times. Thus we hear of labor agents from Pittsburgh signing up southern blacks in 1916–19 and 1922–23, but seldom in other years. The contribution of labor recruitment to the total volume of black migration even in these periods of high labor demand may not have been large. In the spring of 1917, for example, only seventy-nine of a group of 474 Pittsburgh migrants said that employers paid their way to Pittsburgh.[34]

Pittsburgh labor agents offered vital assistance to southern blacks seeking to move north. Agents posted announcements of northern jobs, held meetings, discussed their needs with leaders in southern black communities, and distributed train passes to anyone interested in working in the mines, mills, or factories they represented. C. H. Johnson of Millhaven, Georgia, indirectly acknowledged the importance of labor agents when he wrote to inquire about Pittsburgh jobs: "I am a farmer down here on Savannah River. . . . The labor agents don't come in this neck. I want to get in tuch with you along this line."[35] Employer-sponsored migration lacked the collective, cooperative qualities of southern blacks' own chain or group migration, but it offered several important attractions: free travel, information about Pittsburgh, and guaranteed employment and housing.

Although contemporary observers as well as some later students of the migration agreed that these were powerful inducements for southern blacks to sign up with a labor agent, disagreement exists on the recruiters' part in the northward movement. One Pittsburgh investigator portrayed agents wielding great powers of persuasion over the migrants: "Undoubtedly many Negroes have come . . . in response to the seductive arts of labor agents. . . . These emissaries, both in the North and in the South, made glowing promises of high wages, social equality, and better living conditions above the Mason-Dixon Line." Contributors to the U.S. Department of Labor's study, *Negro Migration in 1916–17,* cited instances of labor agents initiating migration from southern states and localities to Pittsburgh. But more recent analyses of the migration have deemphasized the recruiters' activities as a factor in motivating southern blacks to move north.[36]

Pittsburgh migrants' experiences shed some light on the part that labor agents played in the migration, suggesting that the relationship between southern blacks and Pittsburgh recruiters was more complex than has been previously shown. Far from regarding labor recruiters as men who were leading them to the "Land of Promise," migrants often cast suspicious glances at the agents and their travel plans. During World War I cases of agents who exploited southern blacks by charging money for the train passes were well known. The laws and local ordinances passed in the South during periods of peak migration that limited labor agents' activities provided another reason for caution. If agents could be arrested and jailed or fined for recruiting black labor, a much worse fate at the hands of white justice might await a migrant known to have dealt with an agent.[37] The long history of northern employers recruiting unwitting southern blacks as strikebreakers was also on the minds of some migrants who wrote to the Pittsburgh Urban League asking for free train tickets. "[L]et me know what kind of work is this," Henry Bradly demanded in December 1922. "It ant no striek is it now[?]" When James Byrd offered to recruit black workers and send them to Pittsburgh, he stated his conditions: "I can furnish you with real mens for work up thair providing the Transportation are paid by you also providing thair is no Labore trouble."[38]

Many migrants viewed free train passes simply as one way among others of reaching the North. The term *transportation* by which migrants referred to employer-sponsored travel suggested a view of labor recruitment schemes as a means toward an end. A black man in Ivor, Virginia, was more explicit when he declared in 1923, "I myself am not particular about the *transportation proposition,* but when a man tries to save car fare and fails, and sees a free way open for a chance to go out and then pay [later] it is a bit tempting."[39]

Migrants who signed up for transportation were as a group neither the wildly excited nor the docile enlistees in the armies of northern labor that contemporary descriptions alternately portrayed. Some manipulated the free travel schemes for their own ends. Instead of faithfully showing up to work at the northern destination stipulated in their contracts, some southern blacks left the trains when they chose to and disappeared into the crowds in railroad stations, intent on finding even better paid employment than the agent had offered them.[40] When employers responded to such violations of the terms of recruitment schemes by forcing migrants to turn over their belongings as security, southern blacks still refused to restrict their movement. In 1919 John B. got a railroad pass in Richmond from an agent for the Jones and Laughlin Steel Company. The train took him to the company's mills in Aliquippa, Pennsylvania, about twenty miles from Pittsburgh. There the company locked up his suitcase and put him to work on a pick and shovel gang. Unhappy with his work assignment, B. quit his job and went to Homestead to find other work, leaving his baggage in the perpetual care of Jones and Laughlin.[41]

In these ways Pittsburgh migrants made as good use of labor agents as the agents and employers made of them. Free tickets and guarantees of work were crucial for southern blacks who had no relatives or friends in the city. Indeed, none of the men interviewed for this study who relied on labor agents during his northward movement had marital or blood relations in Pittsburgh. But all of them had already left their homes and had begun to search for jobs when they learned of the possibility of employer-paid transportation. The labor agents with whom these men dealt convinced some of them to change their original destinations and go to Pittsburgh. But for each migrant, the train ride paid by a city firm was only the last leg of their journey north.

When we put this evidence on labor agents' roles into the context of southern blacks' patterns of movement, we can reach a number of broader conclusions about the ways migrants traveled to Pittsburgh. First, free transportation provided by labor agents was only one of several ways to travel long distances. Second, most southern blacks planned and managed their own northward movement, using labor agents when they found it expedient. Third, they fit the benefits of labor recruitment schemes into strategies of movement that they developed largely from information transmitted by other black migrants along the lines of communication between the North and the South. Finally, it was the migrants' careful and deliberate planning, rather than spur-of-the-moment decisions to leave the South, that characterized their journeys.

Southern blacks trying to reach Pittsburgh developed several ways of overcoming the hurdles of distance, transportation costs, loneliness, and ignorance of northern urban life. Some of the migrants' solutions for the problems of long-distance migration, such as chain migration, drew on resources within their own families and communities. Other solutions, like temporary employment in several places between the South and the North, were adaptations from their southern migration patterns. Between their places of origin and Pittsburgh, however, most of the migrants had to resort to new strategies in order to reach the North. Younger, unmarried southern blacks did most of this experimenting, but Pittsburgh migrants generally had prepared themselves to adapt to new conditions and experiences by the time they disembarked from their trains in the city.

NOTES

1. Frank C. Harper, *Pittsburgh: Forge of the Universe* (New York: Comet Press Books, 1957), 195–201, 217–18, 236–37; Frank C. Harper, *Pittsburgh of Today: Its Resources and People*, 2 (New York: American Historical Society, 1931), 537–48, 574–98; Leland D. Baldwin,

Pittsburgh: Story of a City (Pittsburgh: University of Pittsburgh Press, 1937), 331-34, 341-45; John N. Boucher, *A Century and a Half of Pittsburgh and Her People,* 2 (New York: Lewis Publishing, 1908), 51-62, 331-34.

2. Harper, *Pittsburgh: Forge of the Universe,* 251-52; *Iron Age* 98 (Oct. 26, 1916), 948-49; H. Cole Estep, "Knocking Out a Billion Dollar Loss," *Iron Trade Review* 60 (Jan. 4, 1917), 5-11; E. L. Shaner, "Filling the Thinning Ranks of Labor," ibid., 60 (June 28, 1917), 1391-95.

3. Interviews: Richard C., Aug. 8, 1974, Wesley M., Apr. 2, 1976, Elonzo H., Oct. 23, 1973, Ed R., June 10, 1976.

4. Andrew Buni, *Robert L. Vann of the Pittsburgh Courier: Politics and Black Journalism* (Pittsburgh: University of Pittsburgh Press, 1974), 80-81; Albert Johnson to John T. Clark, Jan. 30, 1923, John Green to John T. Clark, Dec. 16, 1922, Carter G. Woodson Collection, John T. Clark Letters, Library of Congress, Washington, D.C. (hereafter cited as Clark Letters); Louise V. Kennedy, *The Negro Peasant Turns Cityward* (New York: Columbia University Press, 1930), 52-56; U.S. Department of Labor, Bureau of Negro Economics, *Negro Migration in 1916-17* (Washington: Government Printing Office, 1919), 66, 86-87, 100-101; John T. Clark, "The Migrant in Pittsburgh," *Opportunity* 1 (Oct. 1923), 303.

5. Interview: Wesley M., Apr. 2, 1976.

6. Interview: Matthew J., May 28, 1976.

7. Interviews: John B., Mar. 10, 1976, Joseph G., Nov. 26, 1973, Jasper A., July 12, 1976.

8. Interview: Matthew J., May 28, 1976.

9. Interview: Walter H., Oct. 25, 30, 1973; John Trice to John T. Clark, Dec. 14, 1922, John Jackson to John T. Clark, Dec. 17, 1922, Marcellous Hall to John T. Clark, Mar. 5, 1923, E. A. Brown to John T. Clark, Dec. 1922, Clark Letters.

10. Interview: Ed R., June 10, 1976; Urban League of Pittsburgh, *Bulletin* 2 (May 1919).

11. Ruth Stevenson, "The Pittsburgh Urban League" (M.A. thesis, University of Pittsburgh, 1936), 86.

12. Urban League of Pittsburgh, *Bulletin* 2 (May 1919); Clark, "Migrant in Pittsburgh," 304; interview: Julia D. (pseudonym), May 3, 1976; Abraham Epstein, *The Negro Migrant in Pittsburgh* (Pittsburgh: University of Pittsburgh, 1918), 65.

13. Interview: Mrs. Abraham L., Mar. 11, 1976.

14. Interview: Carrie J., July 23, 1976.

15. Interview: Maria B., June 1, 1976.

16. Interviews: Olive W., July 23, 1976, Jonnie F., Apr. 23, 1976, Lillyan P., Nov. 9, 10, 1973.

17. Interviews: Carrie J., July 23, 1976, Lillyan P., Nov. 9, 10, 1973, John T., Nov. 1, 23, 1973.

18. Interviews: Maria B., June 1, 1976, Henry B., Aug. 2, 1974, Ed R., June 10, 1976.

19. Interviews: Lee C., June 9, 1976, Julia D. (pseudonym), May 3, 1976, Sarah M. (pseudonym), Sept. 2, 1976, Callie N., June 23, 1976, Richard C., Aug. 8, 1974, Hezekiah M., Oct. 8, 1976.

20. Interviews: Charner C., Feb. 21, 1976, Willie S., July 15, 1974, Lucille S., Jan. 10, 1977.

21. Curtis C. Roseman, "Channelization of Information Flows from the Rural South to the Industrial Midwest," Association of American Geographers, *Proceedings* 3 (1971), 140–46; Emmett J. Scott, *Negro Migration during the War* (New York: Oxford University Press, 1920), 96; interviews: Caleb B., Apr. 9, 1976, Maria S., May 13, 1976, Walter H., Oct. 25, 30, 1973.

22. Robert S. Simmons to John T. Clark, Dec. 25, 1922, Clark Letters.

23. Interviews: William H., June 17, 1976, James S., June 7, 14, 1974.

24. J. W. Mitchell to John T. Clark, Dec. 12, 1922, John Trice to John T. Clark, Dec. 14, 1922, Clark Letters.

25. John T. Clark to R. L. Quarles, Jan. 6, 1923, Clark Letters.

26. Pittsburgh *Courier,* Jan. 24, 1923, 1.

27. Draft letter, Dec. 14, 1922, Urban League of Pittsburgh (ULP) Records, Archives of Industrial Society, Hillman Library, University of Pittsburgh.

28. William Ramsey to John T. Clark, Jan. 22, 1923, J. H. Cullen to John T. Clark, Jan. 19, 1923, Willis Chatman to John T. Clark, Jan. 21, 1923, Clark Letters.

29. Interviews: John T., Nov. 1, 23, 1973, Lee T., May 26, 1976, Jean B., July 29, 1976.

30. Albert Johnson to John T. Clark, Jan. 30, 1923, John D. Maxwell to John T. Clark, Mar. 3, 1923, Clark Letters.

31. J. R. Hill to John T. Clark, Mar. 3, 1923, R. L. Quarles to John T. Clark, Dec. 26, 1922, E. A. Massey to John T. Clark, Feb. 26, 1923, W. J. Waites to John T. Clark, Mar. 6, 1923, Clark Letters; Florette Henri, *Black Migration: Movement North, 1900–1920* (Garden City: Anchor/Doubleday, 1975), 63.

32. Interviews: Joseph G., Nov. 26, 1973, Jean B., July 29, 1976; James Buggs to John T. Clark, Jan. 18, 1923, Clark Letters.

33. Ira De A. Reid, "The Negro in the Major Industries and Building Trades of Pittsburgh" (M.A. thesis, University of Pittsburgh, 1925), 15; Horace R. Cayton and George S. Mitchell, *Black Workers and the New Unions* (Chapel Hill: University of North Carolina Press, 1939), 8; Epstein, *Negro Migrant in Pittsburgh,* 21; interview: Charles B., July 16, 1976. An example of a labor contract is in Epstein, *Negro Migrant in Pittsburgh,* 35.

34. Epstein, *Negro Migrant in Pittsburgh,* 21, 26; Rollin L. Hartt, "When the Negro Comes North: I. An Exodus and Its Causes," *World's Work* 48 (May 1924), 84; Scott, *Negro Migration,* 135.

35. C. H. Johnson to J. T. Clark, Mar. 5, 1923, Clark Letters.

36. Epstein, *Negro Migrant in Pittsburgh,* 25; U.S. Department of Labor, *Negro Migration in 1916-17,* 64, 86, 121; Henri, *Black Migration,* 80.

37. U.S. Department of Labor, *Negro Migration in 1916-17,* 120; Jonathan Wiener, *Social Origins of the New South: Alabama, 1860-1885* (Baton Rouge: Louisiana State University Press, 1978), 58-59; William Cohen, "Negro Involuntary Servitude in the South, 1865-1940: A Preliminary Analysis," *Journal of Southern History* 42 (Feb. 1976), 39-40.

38. Henry Bradly to John T. Clark, Dec. 11, 1922, James Byrd to John T. Clark, Jan. 22, 1923, Clark Letters.

39. Unknown author to Urban League of Pittsburgh, Jan. 17, 1923 (emphasis in the original), ULP Records.

40. Interview: Jasper A., July 12, 1976; Henri, *Black Migration,* 61; Epstein, *Negro Migrant in Pittsburgh,* 21.

41. Interview: John B., Mar. 10, 1976.

3

Places in the City

WHEN THEY ARRIVED in Pittsburgh, the black migrants confronted the urban job and housing markets that mediated their adjustment to northern life. The first hours in the city and its environs were disorienting and discouraging for some newcomers. Wesley M. became confused on the streetcars trying to find Homestead. He rode back and forth between Braddock and Pittsburgh several times before a conductor told him that the car had been traveling through Homestead on each trip. The mill districts and urban neighborhoods looked unappealing to many southern blacks, and the jobs for which some had ventured north turned out to be quite different from the written or verbal descriptions they had received before reaching Pittsburgh.[1]

Beyond these initial reactions to the look and feel of Pittsburgh, however, black migrants quickly had to find opportunities to support themselves. Most newcomers had little savings; their migration plans could be scuttled within a few days if they did not find employment and lodging. Their success in obtaining the necessities of life depended partly on the particular time they reached the city. The housing and job markets absorbed the migrants at rates that varied greatly between World War I and the Depression. The number of southern blacks seeking footholds in the industrial environment also fluctuated widely, creating stiff competition at certain times for the work and shelter the city offered.

The pace of black population growth in Pittsburgh and its environs reflected the demand for black labor; consequently,

the number of blacks coming to Pittsburgh, instead of growing
steadily, rose and fell with economic conditions. One estimate
in 1917, based on a survey of firms hiring blacks, put the
increase in the previous two years in the number of black
workers at 9,750. Dependents living with these black workers
raised the estimate of total in-migration to 18,550.[2] The high
point of black employment during the World War I years was
reached in 1918, when the Pennsylvania Department of Internal Affairs found 15,797 blacks working in Allegheny County.
This figure represented a 100 percent increase since 1916.[3]

Thereafter the flow of migrants receded, slowly through 1919
(except in September and October, when the steelworkers' strike
encouraged a new influx), then quite rapidly in 1920 and 1921.
The number of blacks employed in Pittsburgh shrank 43 percent between 1920 and 1921; in Allegheny County the relative
decrease was 40 percent. The average loss in black employment
in eleven mill towns around Pittsburgh was 51 percent.[4] Though
the U.S. Census of 1920 showed nearly a 50 percent increase in
black population of Pittsburgh since 1910 (table 1), the decline
in the number of blacks in Allegheny County from 1919 to 1921
suggested that the census figures for Pittsburgh were deceptive
as a measure of recent changes in the area's black population.
On one hand, many more blacks lived and worked in the Pittsburgh area during World War I than were there in 1920. On the
other hand, far fewer blacks remained in the area just one year
after the 1920 data were collected.

During the years from 1922 to 1930 fluctuating labor demand
in Pittsburgh caused sharp changes in the tempo of black
migration. From late 1922 until the fall of 1923, migration
revived vigorously, but then slowed again in 1924. The following year a new survey found that the number of blacks in the
city itself was about 25 percent greater than it had been in 1920.
But in some of the neighboring mill towns, the 1922–23 spurt in
the number of arrivals resulted in much greater growth. Clairton's
black population rose by nearly 100 percent between 1920 and
1925; Homestead's, by 165 percent. In seven mill towns around
Pittsburgh the combined black population grew by 95 percent
in this period.[5] By 1930 Pittsburgh blacks numbered 54,983, a
45.8 percent increase over the black population in 1920, and

Table 1
Black Population of Pittsburgh and Allegheny County, 1890–1930,
with Estimates of Increase in Pittsburgh due to
In-Migration, 1910–20 and 1920–30

| Year | Black Population | |
	Pittsburgh	Allegheny County
1890	10,357	13,501
1900	20,355	27,753
1910	25,623	34,217
1920	37,725	53,517
1930	54,983	83,326

| Years | Pittsburgh | |
	In-Migration	Percent of Total Population Growth due to In-Migration
1910–20	10,478	87
1920–30	10,633	62
Total, 1910–30	21,111	72

Source: U.S. Department of the Interior, Census Office, *Eleventh Census, Population,* Pt. 1 (1895), 476, 478; U.S. Census Office, *Twelfth Census, Population,* Pt. 1 (1901), 554, 637, 639; *Thirteenth Census, Population: General Report and Analysis* (1913), 242; *Fourteenth Census, Population: General Report and Analytical Tables* (1922), 1358; *Fifteenth Census, Population: Reports by States,* Pt. 2 (1932), 660; U.S. Census Bureau, *Negro Population, 1790–1915* (1918), 103; U.S. Census Bureau, *Negro Population, 1920–32* (1935), 64.

Note: Pittsburgh's black population for 1890 and 1900 includes the black population of Allegheny City, which was incorporated into Pittsburgh in 1908. In-migration estimates were derived by averaging the results from forward and reverse survival rate methods, applied to age cohorts 10–34 and 20–44.

more than double the number in the city in 1910. In the same twenty-year period the city's total population grew by less than 25 percent.

Beneath the shifting tempo in the growth of black population, there was a large net increase between 1910 and 1930: 49,109 in Allegheny County and 29,360 in Pittsburgh itself. About 21,000 of Pittsburgh's black population gain was attributable to in-migration, a proportion of nearly three-fourths for the twenty-year period (table 1). How many of the newcomers were south-

ern cannot be calculated, though the large contingents of blacks
living in Pittsburgh in 1930 who were born in southern states
indicated that movement to the city from below the Mason-
Dixon line accounted for most of the black population growth.

The increase in Pittsburgh's black population between 1910
and 1930, both relative and absolute, was smaller than that in
most other northern industrial centers.[6] In novelists Arna
Bontemps and Jack Conroy's felicitous phrase, Pittsburgh was
one of the lesser moons of the migrant tides.[7] But despite the
comparatively small size of its migrant population, Pittsburgh's
housing and job markets felt the presence of southern newcomers quite as much as New York's Harlem, Chicago's South
Side, or Cleveland's East Side.

The attractions of the Pittsburgh area for southern blacks did
not include the boardinghouses, apartments, or single-family
residences that were available to them. They came in the first
instance for jobs, yet they needed shelter as soon as they arrived.
The migrants found lodgings mainly in two areas: the Hill
District in Pittsburgh itself, and roominghouse districts of the
mill towns surrounding the city. Within racially segregated
residential areas, the migrants formed enclaves, occupying the
most dilapidated, poorly equipped, unsanitary structures.

Before the arrival of the southern blacks during World War I,
Pittsburgh blacks lived in every ward of the city. But they had
begun to concentrate in an old residential section adjacent to
the downtown business area. Known as the Hill District, it
encompassed the city's Third and Fifth wards. The Third Ward
became home to a small but concentrated black population in
the late nineteenth century. The Hill District as a whole, however,
sheltered at this time most of the city's Russians, Syrians, and
Roumanians as well. Somewhat more than two-fifths (42 percent)
of Pittsburgh's blacks lived here in 1910. Other established
black neighborhoods were in Lawrenceville (Sixth Ward), the
Strip District (Twelfth Ward), Second Avenue downtown (First
Ward), North Side (Twenty-first Ward), and East Liberty (Seventh
and Eighth wards).[8]

Residential segregation of blacks in Pittsburgh increased during the 1916–30 period, but this increase began from a relatively low level of segregation in the early twentieth century.

The city's Fifth Ward was only 25 percent black in 1910, while the Third Ward was 17.4 percent black. Blacks formed no more than 10 percent of the population in any other city ward.[9] In 1907 Helen Tucker, a member of the Pittsburgh Survey staff, found small knots of black population in Pittsburgh, but no extensive black neighborhoods: "In general, though living in certain localities, they are not segregated. This does not mean that there are not some Negro streets, but very often a row of from three to seven houses will be found in which Negroes are living, while the rest of the street is filled with white people."[10]

Even after the rapid black population growth of the World War I period and the 1920s and the convergence of blacks on the Hill District, Pittsburgh still had a relatively dispersed black population. What the immigration of southern blacks brought about in Pittsburgh was not a single, contiguous ghetto, but several neighborhoods where the number and percentage of black residences grew sharply. Less than half of all blacks lived in the Hill District in 1930, but new black neighborhoods had formed in Beltzhoover (on the bluffs along the western side of the Monongahela River) and Homewood in the Brushton neighborhood in the city's East End, far from the older center of black population. The percentage of Fifth Ward inhabitants who were black increased from 25 to 54 percent between 1910 and 1920. The proportion of blacks in the Third Ward grew from 17 to 40 percent in the same period. The Thirteenth Ward in Pittsburgh's eastern quadrant saw the percentage of black residents leap from around 3 to more than 17 percent in these twenty years.[11]

The first southern blacks to arrive in Pittsburgh during the Great Migration often roomed in buildings with Italian or Greek men or rented rooms on a street that was home to Jewish or Polish families. But migrants reaching the city in later years more likely found lodgings only in neighborhoods that were largely inhabited by blacks. The number of blacks in the Third and Fifth wards grew by 13,814 while the foreign-born population in these sections fell by 7,613.[12] Enumerations of Jewish schoolchildren in Pittsburgh during the 1920s indicated a drop of one-third in the Hill District compared to a citywide decrease of Jewish pupils of only 2.6 percent. The more prosperous European immigrants and their children moved out of the Hill

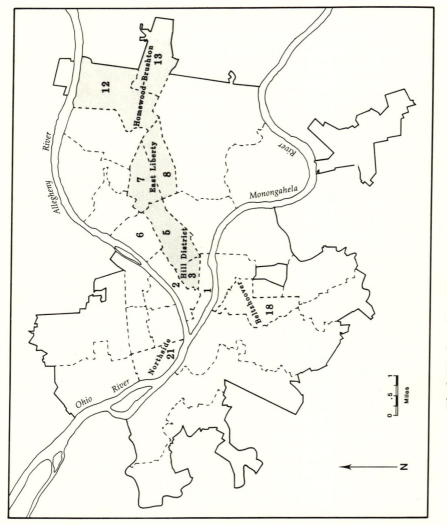
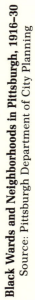

Black Wards and Neighborhoods in Pittsburgh, 1916–30
Source: Pittsburgh Department of City Planning

District to newer dwellings, mostly on the eastern edges of the city, leaving the decaying structures behind for the black newcomers.[13] Southern blacks who moved into the mill towns and factory districts in the vicinity of Pittsburgh more likely had immigrant and American white neighbors, but those in the city settled in neighborhoods that became more exclusively black with each passing year.

Working-class housing in early twentieth-century Pittsburgh and its satellite industrial towns was notoriously bad. The housing for black workers—already beneath the standard for Allegheny County—worsened during the rapid in-migration. Overcrowding in black homes, noticed by investigators before World War I, became much worse. The severe shortage of rental units that blacks could occupy in the Pittsburgh area also gave rise to several new types of housing for the incoming southern blacks: railroad cars converted to bunkhouses; basement dwellings; boathouses on the Monongahela River; warehouses; make-shift shelters hastily built in previously uninhabited ravines and hollows.[14]

Such accommodations barely afforded shelter for the migrants, but the tenements, apartments, and roominghouses were also grossly inadequate. "The conditions . . . often beggar description," wrote Abraham Epstein, a University of Pittsburgh economics student in 1917. "In many instances, houses . . . are dilapidated dwellings with the paper torn off, the plaster sagging from the naked lath, the windows broken, the ceiling low and damp, and the whole room dark, stuffy and unsanitary." There was little change in the standard of black housing during the 1920s. A housing study in the Hill District in 1929 revealed that more than 10 percent of the dwellings studied were "unfit for habitation." The defects found in the investigation indicated long periods of neglect by landlords: "leaky roofs, broken window panes, holes in flooring, broken panels in doors, defective flues." Pittsburgh's black housing often lacked modern sanitary facilities. In the mid-1920s only 20 percent of black houses had bathtubs and only 50 percent had inside toilets, while 30 percent had nothing better than outside water closets and 20 percent no more than privies. This situation represented little, if any, improvement over conditions in the migrants' living quarters during the World War I influx.[15]

Such housing was not unfamiliar to Pittsburgh's poorer white workers, but a larger proportion of structures inhabited by blacks were substandard. Throughout Allegheny County, roughly one-fifth of the rental units in 1935 fell into the "in need of major repairs" and "unfit" categories. But one-third of Hill District buildings (33.7 percent) and more than one-half (56.7 percent) of Strip District houses were so classified. Thirty-three percent of rented dwellings in Allegheny County were found "in good condition" in 1935, but only 23 percent of all dwellings in the Hill, and a mere 7 percent in the Strip District could be described this way.[16]

The shortage of housing for blacks in Pittsburgh, coupled with the arrival of thousands of southern migrants, created severe overcrowding in the black residential sections. Nearly two-thirds of the black men in a World War I study slept in bedrooms with three or more roomers. Abram Harris, a graduate student at the University of Pittsburgh, found an average of four people per room in Pittsburgh's black residences.[17] While the wartime conditions under which the male migrants slept two, three, and even four to a bed on double shifts did not last into the 1920s, the migration packed black homes to overflowing from 1916 to the Depression.

Pittsburgh manufacturers arranged two kinds of housing for the southern black men whom they recruited. They built segregated black migrant camps and bunkhouses during World War I in Braddock, Homestead, Duquesne, McKees Rocks, and many other locations in Allegheny County. The black laborers slept on cots or bunks, ate in company dining halls, and used toilets and washrooms on the premises. Some firms hired black managers to supervise the migrant accommodations.[18]

Many firms employing large numbers of southern blacks also arranged lodging in private boardinghouses operated by black families who lived in the neighborhoods surrounding their mills. Companies surveyed black households to find the families who would lodge one or more of the men being transported from the South. In Homestead families who wanted to put up mill workers told company representatives how many men they could room. The Carnegie Steel Company assigned each southerner it transported to one of the black households in the mill town. Once the migrants had completed the process of enrolling themselves in the employment office, they fanned out from the mill in small groups. Black personnel agents led each of the groups around Homestead, showing the new workers where the boardinghouses to which they were assigned were located.[19]

A common practice was for the migrants' employer to deduct from pay envelopes the money that each lodger owed to his boarding family. On mill town paydays the black housewives trooped to the payroll offices to pick up their room-and-board money, a ritual that immigrant boarding mistresses had followed for years.[20] Transient black migrants took advantage of this arrangement by quitting their Pittsburgh jobs between paydays without telling their boarding family. Before it was discovered that the company had stopped the room-and-board deductions for the men who had quit, the transients had eaten several free meals with the boarding family and occupied a room in their house, gratis.[21]

Other black families took in thousands more migrants to share the few small rooms they occupied. In Epstein's 1917 survey four-fifths of the migrant families with three or more rooms kept boarders. A random sample of 227 Hill District dwellings rented by blacks in 1929 showed that almost one-third of the homes included one or more lodgers, the majority of them male roomers. Southern black men generally preferred lodging with a black family to living at a company bunkhouse. The migrants deserted Carnegie Steel's four bunkhouses in Homestead at the first opportunity. "As soon as the men can find another place to live they move to boarding houses and private homes," reported Ira Reid, a black investigator of Pittsburgh's black wage earners and their communities.[22]

The migrants' housing preferences in Pittsburgh led to the clustering of southern blacks in subcommunities within the black neighborhoods. Many men liked to live close to their workplaces to save car fare and avoid a long walk to and from their jobs. This was one of the reasons why some migrants at first tolerated the company-built bunkhouses, boardinghomes, and railroad camps. While less than 1 percent of Pittsburgh blacks lived in the Seventeenth Ward on the city's South Side,

nearly one-quarter of a sample of southern migrants employed
at the Byers mill lodged there, a short walk from their work.[23] A
small number of black boardinghouses, sheltering a mostly
southern migrant population, could be found in the shadows of
many large mills and factories in Allegheny County from 1916
to 1930. And some companies constructed their crude bunkhouses for the new black workers in the very midst of the
warehouses and rail yards on their own property.[24]

Chain migration of southern black families and lodging
arrangements in Pittsburgh reinforced the tendency for migrants
to room together in Pittsburgh or near each other. The common pattern was for each family member to live at least temporarily with relatives or friends residing in the Pittsburgh area.
Harvey C. joined his parents and brother in Homestead in 1918;
Ed R. moved in with his mother and stepfather; James S. and
his wife at first lived with her parents in Pittsburgh. The movement of groups of southern working men produced a similar
result. For example, the gang in which Jean B. traveled from
Mobile, Alabama, to Pittsburgh roomed together when they
reached the city. Networks of friends that helped to speed the
exchange of information between north and south also brought
southern blacks together under the same Pittsburgh roofs.[25]

Residential grouping of migrants came about in other ways.
The boardinghouses to which southern migrants were assigned
by the companies that brought them to Pittsburgh frequently
had owners or managers who were themselves recent migrants.
"In Ford City, it appears that the Colored people who operate
the boarding houses are the families who have recently come
North," the black welfare agent at the Pittsburgh Plate Glass
Company reported in 1918. Lodgings for the migrants in Homestead in 1918 were "run by colored families who have lived in
these localities for some years prior to the migration. In several
instances, however, these lodging houses are kept by the wives
of the men who have recently migrated North." One of these
boardinghouse mistresses in Homestead was Maria S. She and
her husband came from Louisville, Kentucky, in 1918 and eventually found a six-room house on Sixth Avenue. Her husband
helped his employer, the Harbison-Walker Refractory Brick
Company, secure black laborers by inviting his friends from

Louisville to come to Homestead, work at the brick factory, and lodge at his house. In Braddock Lee C.'s brother opened an eleven-room lodging house when he came to the mill town during World War I and put up many fellow southerners there during the 1920s.[26]

Southern men sometimes made cooperative rooming arrangements by renting a house and maintaining it together. When Walter H. returned to Homestead from his family's Virginia farm in 1923, he first roomed at a boardinghouse on Lynch Street, operated by a black man named Hoskins. H. was one of three men sleeping in one room in the Hoskins boardinghouse. The three boarders decided after a short time that the rate of $9.00 each per week for room and board was too high for the crowded space. They first arranged with Hoskins to pay only a room fee and to cook for themselves. Later they moved from the boardinghouse on Lynch Street to a house on Cherry Way in Homestead, which they rented and occupied together for several years.[27]

The residential grouping of southern blacks, coupled with the emergence of new black residential areas in Pittsburgh and its environs, created differences among black neighborhoods of dwellings, occupants, and life-styles. A residential separation among blacks developed in Homestead, ten miles upstream from Pittsburgh on the Monongahela River, where the mills of Carnegie Steel Company's Homestead Works dominated the valley and the lives of the townfolk.

Adjacent to the mills were the courts and alleys of the poorer section of town. Europeans preceded southern blacks to the boardinghouses and bunkhouses of this neighborhood.[28] After 1916 an increasing proportion of the workers housed here were black, though whites never completely abandoned the area. Sixth Avenue, with its taverns, restaurants, shops, and brothels, was the main thoroughfare. Homestead blacks commonly referred to this section by the mills as the Ward.[29]

Further from the river's edge a steep hill rose high above the streets of the Ward. Here Andrew Carnegie, following a housing pattern well established even by the late nineteenth century, built both the mill superintendent's mansion, a public library, and single-family homes for skilled mechanics. There were few commercial establishments of any kind.[30] To distinguish this neighborhood of uncrowded streets and tidy homes from the teeming Ward, black Homesteaders used the name "Hilltop."[31]

The citizens of Homestead were socially divided even before a large number of blacks settled in the town. To a certain degree, Homestead's housing pattern provided one direction of cleavage for the black population to follow. The homes of skilled black workers in the Hilltop section, among those of the black shopowners and professionals, were as much perquisites of their occupational status as the single-family dwellings of white mechanics. Some migrant mill workers lodged with black families in the Hilltop neighborhood, in nearby towns, or even in Pittsburgh itself, but the majority of southern migrants who found jobs in Homestead's mills and factories packed into the boardinghouses of the Ward.

Homestead's social ecology reinforced the differences between its inhabitants. Though most black Homesteaders depended for their livelihood on the steel works, the older black residents of Hilltop could look down on the newcomers in the Ward in more ways than one. Many inhabitants of the Ward, whether lodged temporarily or putting down roots, were strangers in Homestead. Though they might work with a Hilltop resident at a steel furnace, they kept to the Ward in their free time and seldom met their workmates outside the mill. The Ward enjoyed a reputation for gambling and prostitution that overshadowed Pittsburgh's larger black districts. Pay day in the Ward attracted itinerant merchants, pool sharks, and high rollers from near and far. The Ward was raucous and rough, and Hilltop parents sometimes forbade their children to go there at all.[32]

Southern blacks differed widely in their general reactions to Pittsburgh and its neighboring manufacturing towns, but they condemned practically with one voice the housing conditions they found. The dirt of the mill districts shocked many of the migrants who had grown up in the midst of rural poverty. "Man, it was ugly, dirty!" recalled Harrison G. "The streets were nothing but dirt streets." The pall of smoke that hung over the whole area grew thickest when the mills were running around the clock, labor was in greatest demand, and southern blacks could find jobs with little trouble. But the laden atmosphere at such times made Pittsburgh living conditions practically unbearable, burdening especially the female migrants who struggled to keep their homes clean. "When I first came to Pittsburgh, I really didn't like it," Queen W. admitted. "Because it was too hilly and it was too smoky." John T. said, "The South is clean. Everything is white, beautiful. . . . Everything was black and smoky . . . here." His wife took one look at Braddock in the rain and returned to her North Carolina home.[33]

A female migrant from Georgia who was living with her family in a one-room Pittsburgh apartment during World War I told Abraham Epstein, "I never lived in such houses in my life. We had four rooms in my home." Laura L. came from Virginia to join her husband in 1923, but shunned the "slum" area of the mill town where many migrants stayed. "I wanted no part of it," she stated flatly. Lillyan P. needed help to find the apartment house in which her husband had rented rooms in preparation for her arrival in Homestead in 1925. Her train got to town before her husband's shift in the mill ended, so she asked directions from a newsboy at the railroad station. When the newsboy brought her to an address in the boardinghouse section of the mill town where trash cans stood by the doors, she asked her guide: "Is this the back entrance?" "No," he said. "It's the front." Overcoming her dismay at these surroundings, so unlike anything she had seen in her native Petersburg, she said to herself the words of the biblical Ruth as she entered the house to wait for her husband: "Where you go, I will go, and where you lodge, I will lodge."[34]

Rents for the dwellings that seemed so inferior to southern blacks were comparatively high. The average weekly wage for the migrants in Pittsburgh in 1917 was about $21.00. A boardinghouse room in that year went for between $1.50 and $1.75 per week, while board usually cost between $5.00 and $7.00 per week. Southern black families occupying one or two rooms most often paid between $10 and $15 per month. But owners of houses and apartments in Pittsburgh's black neighborhoods took advantage of the heavy demand for lodging at certain times. There were cases in which landlords pitted migrants against each other by offering rooms to the highest bidders. Other owners demanded high rents for shabby lodgings.[35] In the mid- to late 1920s blacks' housing costs in Pittsburgh rose above the levels reached in the late teens. The Pennsylvania Department of Welfare found that blacks paid higher rents than whites in Pittsburgh itself, but slightly less than whites in the nearby mill towns. A study conducted in 1926 by a Pittsburgh banking firm indicated that Pittsburgh's renting families as a whole spent about one-seventh of their income on rent. The 1929 housing survey, however, showed that rents for 227 black families in the Hill District consumed close to one-fourth of their income.[36]

High rents for poor housing were a source of the migrants' discontent in Pittsburgh from World War I through the 1920s. This dissatisfaction was manifested in transiency and high rates of residential turnover in the squalid neighborhoods that were filled to overflowing with new arrivals from the South. "Few of these people intend to remain here unless they can get a better place to stay," claimed Epstein in 1917. He added: "We might cite dozens of incidents of men who have either had their families here or intended to bring them, but have gone to other cities where they hoped to find better accommodations." The head of the Urban League of Pittsburgh in 1920 wrote, "We find itinerancy more a matter of district than of family. . . . in one section called the Second Avenue section . . . there is a complete family turnover on an average every two months. . . . The district where there is a great deal of moving about and unsteadiness is perhaps the most neglected and the only District in which the Newcomer can find accommodations which is most distressing to the crudest Negro families of the South."[37]

The failure of Pittsburgh housing to meet migrants' customary standards, let alone their hopes for better conditions, contributed to employers' problems in retaining their southern black employees. That some newcomers could find lodging only at long distances from their places of work was one factor increasing migrants' absences from jobs. Few Pittsburgh area firms built single-family houses for the new workers, counting instead on the rundown structures that once had sheltered earlier mill recruits. In 1920 the secretary of the Employers Association of Pittsburgh admitted that the organization's employment office was turning away roughly 250 blacks every week because member firms had no housing where they could be lodged. "The improvement in the housing situation since the war has been so slight," Ira Reid found in 1925, "that the problems remains [*sic*] until the present time the most acute phase of the labor supply problems."[38]

Though finding a place to sleep was the migrants' first need after arriving in the Pittsburgh area, getting a job was ultimately more important. When Matthew J. reached Braddock, he went to New Hope Baptist church on Sixth Avenue to ask for a recommendation for a good, clean boardinghouse. He paid for a room for two weeks in advance, thinking that if he did not get hired by that time, he would leave the area for another destination. Harrison G. followed his father's advice about lodgings and jobs in northern cities. "My daddy would always tell me when I would leave, 'Now when you go into a big town, first thing you do is get you a room; if it looks like you're going to be around for two or three days, get a job.' I said, 'Why hurry?' And he said, 'Well, that will keep you from mischief. . . . Big cities [can] ruin you.' "[39] The availability of jobs for blacks in the Pittsburgh area was susceptible to sudden changes, however. Southern black men and women who heard of work in Pittsburgh had to take their chances that there would still be employment when they reached the city.

Male and female migrants fit Pittsburgh jobs into their migration strategies in different ways. Whether single or married, the southern women's first jobs in Pittsburgh were frequently unpaid and located within the walls of their new homes. Unpacking belongings, looking after children or younger siblings, shopping, and cooking—all the tasks of "setting up housekeeping"—absorbed the female migrants' first days and weeks. After their rooms were in order, most of the southern black women had to seek paid work to earn wages and contribute to the support of their husband, children, or relatives. By the time they began looking for work, they already knew their neighborhoods, other black women who had jobs, and the larger employers of black females. Unlike the male migrants' search for employment, women's efforts to find work were not as often compressed into the few days or weeks immediately following their arrival in the Pittsburgh area.[40]

Whatever larger goals southern black men cherished in traveling north, finding a Pittsburgh job was basic to their long-term plans. Consequently, their fortunes tended to rise and fall with the sharp fluctuations in labor demand from 1916 to 1930. For those who had been transported to work for a particular employer, the problem was not simply getting hired, but finding suitable work. The majority of black men arriving in western Pennsylvania had to find jobs—any jobs—to succeed in their migration.

Migrants were aided in the periods of high labor demand by agencies that sought to find black workers for Pittsburgh jobs. The U.S. Employment Service during World War I had an office in the city that maintained job listings. It worked in conjunction with the Pittsburgh Urban League for a time. The League was founded in 1918 and dedicated itself at first to placing southern migrants in city jobs. It circulated an announcement of Pittsburgh job openings in December 1922 in the national black press. It had direct ties to the employment offices of the city's major industrial employers and indirect ones with many smaller firms, downtown department stores, and construction contractors.[41]

With efforts from all quarters aimed at drawing southern black labor to Pittsburgh mills from 1916 to 1919 and in 1922-23, the migrants looking for steel industry jobs had no trouble finding work. In fact, those who came on "transportation" from the South had jobs guaranteed to them before they reached the city. The passenger cars of new recruits drew up to the gates of steel mills, and company representatives greeted the southern blacks as they disembarked. The new recruits lined up in military formation and marched from the train siding into the mill yard. The first stop was sometimes the plant's cafeteria, where the transportation men ate meals. Before the black men left the companies' premises, the personnel agent carefully explained where and when they should report for work. The southerners' first shift could start the evening of the same day they arrived.[42]

The migrants who reached Pittsburgh without assistance from an employer also enjoyed easy access to industrial jobs during the boom periods. One avenue to employment was through relatives or friends who had arrived in the city earlier and explored the local factory districts, employment offices, and streetcar lines that connected all of the large manufacturing towns and districts. Henry B. found work at the Jones and Laughlin mill in Hazelwood by following the advice of his brother-in-law. When Harvey C. came to Homestead to live with his parents and siblings, he followed his father and brother to work at the Homestead mill. Both Matthew J. and Gilbert M. went to employment offices suggested by their uncles whom they were visiting. Other Pittsburgh migrants were guided to jobs by friends and acquaintances. Charner C. came from Detroit to Homestead to visit a boyhood friend from South Carolina. Gossiping with his friend and a group of black steelworkers, C. learned that the Homestead mill was hiring large numbers of men, so he went to the employment office and quickly got a job. William H. reached the Pittsburgh area intending to look for a coal mine job in a mining town where his in-laws lived. But he unexpectedly discovered a friend in the city who advised him of a factory job that H. applied for and got.[43]

In many cases, particularly where relatives helped migrants find work, the assistance was merely an extension of the aid migrants got in moving to Pittsburgh from the South. Kinship support of the migrants shifted from providing lodging and meals to helping newcomers find work. But friends and relatives in Pittsburgh seldom did more for the men and women interviewed for this study than advise migrants where to ask for jobs. Unlike the kinship networks among European immigrants in Pittsburgh, which powerfully influenced the hiring of foreign-born newcomers, the southern blacks' families and friends apparently had less leverage inside the workplace. In offering information about Pittsburgh jobs, the migrants' relatives were doing all they could.

The Slavic and Italian immigrant families who had lived and worked in Pittsburgh for three decades were veteran industrial workers and urbanites compared to the southern black newcomers. The employment practice of the late nineteenth and early twentieth centuries of assigning immigrants to jobs based on their ethnicity allowed the immigrants to build up solid family, community, and ethnic groups within particular departments of mills and factories. Each newly arrived member of the immigrant family could count on his group to intervene directly in the job search on his behalf.[44]

For several reasons, southern blacks during World War I and the 1920s could not duplicate the immigrants' support of relatives and friends. The most obvious reason was that most Pittsburgh blacks who had lived in the area before 1916 did not work in the mills to which the new migrants were attracted. They had more often found work in domestic service, in the older, smaller iron mills, or nonmanufacturing industry. Changes in managerial practice during the arrival and settlement of southern blacks in Pittsburgh also undercut the formation of black kinship networks inside workplaces. Employment offices at mills and factories gradually consolidated the function of hiring new employees that once had been the prerogative of department supervisors, shift foremen, and gang bosses. Even the migrants' relatives who could put in a good word with a foreman had less influence than their immigrant counterparts did in an earlier period. For black migrants, it was the employment manger — the "hiring boss" — who was the crucial figure in getting a job, not the gang leader with whom immigrants had dealt successfully. Further, Pittsburgh companies by and large did not follow a Jim Crow policy in assigning blacks to departments. Although confined mostly to unskilled positions, blacks were often posted widely throughout mills and factories. Thus blacks seldom could approach their supervisors as the majority in a particular section of a mill to speak in favor of a newly arrived jobseeker.[45]

The information about jobs that some Pittsburgh migrants got from family and friends may not even have been crucial in their getting jobs. On the one hand, information was readily available from many other sources to those who came to the city in the periods of high employment. Tenements, pool halls, barbershops, employment agencies, and street corners hummed with news of which plants were hiring men, which companies paid the best wages, and which had the best housing for migrants. Some men who explored the avenues along river banks where mills and factories stood never even had to enter an employment office to ask for work. "Some of the mills would need labor so bad," said Willie S., "they'd have a man sometimes standing right at the mill. When you'd pass on the street he'd inform you . . . he was going to hire so and so many today. And you could go in and be interviewed and you may get a job. . . . It was very easy — *very easy* to get a job."[46]

On the other hand, information on which firms paid well or poorly, or which employers had good safety records counted for little. As the 1920s wore on, mounting unemployment and underemployment in Pittsburgh mills and factories cast a pall over southern blacks' efforts to find jobs. The public and private agencies that formerly supported the migrants' job searches either gave up such service or grew less effective in placing newcomers. The Urban League of Pittsburgh found itself in 1927 and 1928 with more black job seekers than listings — just the opposite situation from that of a decade before. The industrial firms, no longer needing continual additions of southern blacks to their crews, dropped their recruitment programs. Where the migrants of the prosperous years had mingled with other southerners brought to Pittsburgh on transportation, the migrants in the lean years paced the streets in crowds of unemployed workers.[47]

"I had $2.50 left — that's all," recalled John T., who had come to the Pittsburgh area in 1924 from Henderson, North Carolina. He was a tailor and clothes presser by trade. Deeply religious, he had traveled north with a friend, looking for high wages with which to support both his wife and his training for the ministry. He and his friend had already tried to find work in another town and had come to Pittsburgh to try their luck. Early one morning shortly after arriving in Pittsburgh, they made a final effort to find work at the Westinghouse factory in East Pittsburgh.

> There was eighty some men standing in line. Me and him was the only colored. . . . When I got close to the man by the door, he looked and saw me. "Stand aside," [he said]. I stepped aside. Man, I'd been standing up there and I'd seen them turning down folks like *that!* I knowed there was no chance for me, and how I prayed! I just *believed* I was going to work. So I walked up to the desk.
>
> He looked at me, says, "What do you want?" I said, "I want to go to work this morning." That man sat there pecking on his desk [with a pencil] four or five minutes,

says, "I don't need no laborers." I said, "I'm not particular about laboring." "Can you write?" I told him, "Yeah, I can write."

He kept tapping on his desk. . . . Man, I was praying all the time, "Lord, don't let him say no." He said, "I'm going to give you a *good* job. If you're good at it, and stick with it, you can make good."[48]

This story, and similar ones told by other Pittsburgh migrants, throw black men's job searches into sharp relief. Clearly the skill required to find work in a depressed labor market was quite different from that appropriate to full employment conditions. It was enough for a migrant during the war or in 1922–23 to get plenty of reliable information about jobs. But when the newcomers had to compete for work with many unemployed job hunters, quick wits, determination, and even bravado could be decisive in bearing up beneath a hiring boss's scrutiny.

Black men in the Pittsburgh area often took part in a hiring process similar to the "shape-up" among longshoremen at ocean ports. Jobseekers stood around the walls in factory and steel mill employment offices while the manager looked them over prior to selecting the few that would be hired that day. Construction laborers gathered at building sites with their hods, anxious for a foreman to beckon to them.[49] It was a harrowing moment toward which their migration in periods of low employment had led. Many, feeling helpless to affect the manager's selection, simply drew themselves up to full height and awaited judgment. Others tried to think of some gesture, some words that might strengthen their chance of being hired.

"Can you take heat?" one foreman asked a newcomer in Jones and Laughlin Steel Company's office one day. The black migrant replied coolly, "I can take heat and most anything about doing a job." "I got a job," another employment manager told a black migrant to the mills one snowy February day, "but it's outside." The migrant retorted, "If there's anybody else out there, I can go out there, too." One boss tried harder to shake a newcomer's confidence. "Boy, you're pretty young. Do you know how to work?" "I can do anything you can do," the black man shot back.[50]

In these face-to-face meetings between southern blacks and company representatives, there was a pattern of question-and-response, a mode of verbal exchange that resembled nothing so much as the posturing of opponents before a boxing match. Between the newly arrived southern black intent on finding a job on one side and the scowling hiring boss on the other side, there developed a sort of ritual squaring off between contestants. No matter how brief the actual conversations were, some migrants managed to communicate their qualifications for work as well as their determination to be employed. Unlike the situation in a boxing match, however, the man behind the employment desk during the lean years of the migration had a near monopoly of power over the black applicants. Yet migrants, prodded by their urgent need for work, could briefly take the initiative to display their mettle while the boss looked them over. John T. simply said he was "not particular about laboring," nudging the employment manager to reveal other available positions. Other migrants' narratives include some statement that they made *after* being refused for work, the final words by which they pressed the company agent to change his mind.

"When I walked into the office there, the man was saying [to the job applicants], 'that's all!' and I said one word, I said, 'Well, everywhere I go that's all I've heard someone say—'that's all.'" The bitterness of these words drew the boss's attention to the migrant job seeker. Other recent arrivals in Pittsburgh, having been rejected for employment, came back with blunt questions— "A big place like this, and you don't have any jobs?" one man asked in disbelief in a steel mill employment office. Seizing on any opening that the confrontation with the manager provided, these migrants deftly maneuvered their way closer to the jobs they had come north to find.[51]

Certainly there were many migrants who found themselves back on the streets after such exchanges with company representatives. But those who answered sharply and finally got jobs exulted in their success. In these cases, there was more than a personal victory involved, for every encounter in an employment office embodied at least part of the struggle of poor blacks against the obstacles raised by white representatives of powerful corporations. Ben E. chuckled when he remembered how he and his father were selected by an employment agent from a group of eighteen jobseekers at the American Wire and Steel mills, though he was too young and his father too old to be on the company's payroll.[52] Harrison G. overcame the resistance of a personnel office guard when he won a job at Jones and Laughlin Steel Company.

> The old beat house cop on the inside said I had to wait [in line]. . . . "That's the rule." I said, "Well, I wouldn't get in line nohow and I don't have time. If I want this job here, I'm going on to work anyhow. *I mean it.*". . . The employment manager . . . said to the . . . [cop], "Bring that fellow over here. . . . This guy is comin' to work. He's the kind of man we want.". . . This old cop was saying, "Breaking the rules." [The employment manager] said, "Rules is made to break."[53]

If migrants' job searches in Pittsburgh pitted them against the arbitrary authority of white bosses, it is not surprising that their narratives echo major themes of Afro-American culture. Slaves' stories featured tricksters who outwitted more powerful opponents through cunning or deceit. In the twentieth century blacks retold these tales, using the same characters and situations, but showing more direct confrontations between the antagonists. There were many differences between these traditional tales and the migrants' stories—in the black characters themselves, their foes, the situations portrayed, and the relationships between the principal figures. Yet, when the migrants told how they found work in Pittsburgh during hard times, they drew on the same David-and-Goliath theme, aligning themselves with the black folk heroes who won against great odds.[54]

Getting jobs and lodgings in the Pittsburgh area might be considered the last step in the migrants' northward journeys rather than the first phase of their urban lives. Many of the men and some of the women had traveled to other cities, had sought and found places, and soon after departed again. Nothing on the surface of their initial experiences in Pittsburgh distinguished their movement north from earlier forays into industrial labor. Certainly patterns of residential concentration, work, family, and social life did not crystallize in the first weeks of southern blacks' stay in the Pittsburgh area.

But beneath the fluid movements that marked southern blacks' first brush with northern urban life, there were changes in the fundamental conditions of their migration. Longer distances separated the migrants from their birthplaces, straining their close ties to southern homes. Most blacks had remained essentially a rural people in the South, regardless of how long they labored for wages or how frequently they had moved from farms to work camps. But when they reached Pittsburgh and found perches on its mammoth industrial edifice, the migrants were exposed to the social forces exerted by full-time industrial labor and by residence in a northern city. The nature of this labor, and the social relations shaping blacks' status as northern urban workers, began to work on Pittsburgh's migrants. They had been seasonal auxiliaries to southern industry; now they began the transformation to northern employers' pool of unskilled labor.

NOTES

1. Interviews: Wesley M., Apr. 2, 1976, John B., Mar. 10, 1976, Harrison G., Aug. 23, 1974, Jerome G., Aug. 1, 1974; Abraham Epstein, *The Negro Migrant in Pittsburgh* (Pittsburgh: University of Pittsburgh, 1918), 46.

2. U.S. Census Bureau, *Thirteenth Census, Population* (Washington: Government Printing Office, 1913), 3:572; Epstein, *Negro Migrant in Pittsburgh*, 7.

3. Pennsylvania Department of Internal Affairs, Bureau of Statistics, and Information, *Report of the Productive Industries of the Commonwealth of Pennsylvania for 1916-1917-1918-1919* (Harrisburg, 1920), 14.

4. Ira De A. Reid, "The Negro in the Major Industries and Building Trades of Pittsburgh" (M.A. thesis, University of Pittsburgh, 1925), 8.

5. Pennsylvania Department of Public Welfare, *Negro Survey of Pennsylvania* (Harrisburg, 1928), 12-13.

6. U.S. Census Bureau, *Negroes in the United States, 1920-32* (Washington: Government Printing Office, 1935), 55.

7. Arna Bontemps and Jack Conroy, *Anyplace But Here* (New York: Hill and Wang, 1966), 287.

8. John Bodnar, Roger Simon, and Michael P. Weber, *Lives of Their*

Own: Blacks, Italians, and Poles in Pittsburgh, 1900-1960 (Urbana: University of Illinois Press, 1982), 69-72; Epstein, *Negro Migrant in Pittsburgh,* 9; Ira De A. Reid, *Social Conditions of the Negro in the Hill District of Pittsburgh* (Pittsburgh: General Committee on the Hill Survey, 1930), 21, 25-26.

9. Alonzo G. Moron, "Distribution of the Negro Population in Pittsburgh, 1910-1930" (M.A. thesis, University of Pittsburgh, 1933), Table V.

10. Helen Tucker, "The Negroes of Pittsburgh," in *Wage-Earning Pittsburgh,* The Pittsburgh Survey, ed. Paul U. Kellogg (New York: Survey Associates, 1914), 425-26.

11. Moron, "Distribution of the Negro Population," Table V.

12. Ibid.

13. Reid, *Social Conditions,* 26.

14. Duquesne *Times-Observer,* Aug. 4, 1916, 1; Epstein, *Negro Migrant in Pittsburgh,* 8; Tucker, "Negroes of Pittsburgh," 426; Emily W. Dinwiddie and F. Elisabeth Crowell, "The Housing of Pittsburgh's Workers," in *The Pittsburgh District: Civic Frontage,* The Pittsburgh Survey, ed. Paul U. Kellogg (New York: Survey Associates, 1914), 87-102; John T. Clark, "The Migrant in Pittsburgh," *Opportunity* 1 (Oct. 1923), 304.

15. Epstein, *Negro Migrant in Pittsburgh,* 12, 15; Wiley A. Hall, "Negro Housing and Rents in the Hill District of Pittsburgh" (M.A. thesis, University of Pittsburgh, 1929), 19; Pennsylvania Department of Public Welfare, *Negro Survey of Pennsylvania,* 36, 42.

16. Philip Klein, *A Social Study of Pittsburgh* (New York: Columbia University Press, 1938), 201-2, 273-75; Pennsylvania Department of Public Welfare, *Negro Survey of Pennsylvania,* 33.

17. Epstein, *Negro Migrant in Pittsburgh,* 12; Abram L. Harris, "The New Negro Worker in Pittsburgh" (M.A. thesis, University of Pittsburgh, 1924), 16.

18. Duquesne *Times-Observer,* Sept. 14, 1917, 1; W. P. Young, "The First Hundred Negro Workers," *Opportunity* 2 (Jan. 1924), 15-19; interviews: Lee C., June 9, 1976, Anthony D., June 18, 1974.

19. Interviews: Charles B., July 16, 1976, Joseph M., Nov. 16, 1973; minutes, Industrial Welfare Workers' Meeting, Mar. 30, 1918, Urban League of Pittsburgh (ULP) Records, Archives of Industrial Society, Hillman Library, University of Pittsburgh.

20. Interview: Maria S., May 13, 1976.

21. Minutes, Industrial Welfare Workers' Meeting, Mar. 30, 1918, ULP Records.

22. Epstein, *Negro Migrant in Pittsburgh,* 15; Hall, "Negro Housing," 14; Reid, "Negro in the Major Industries," 25.

23. A. M. Byers Company Personnel File, Archives of Industrial Society (hereafter Byers Company Personnel File).

24. Young, "First Hundred Negro Workers," 15–19; interview: Joseph M., Nov. 16, 1973; Moron, "Distribution of the Negro Population," 33–34.

25. Interviews: Harvey C., Dec. 2, 1973, Ed R., June 10, 1976, James S., June 7, July 14, 1974, Jean B., July 29, 1976, Charner C., Feb. 21, 1976, William H., June 17, 1976, Julia D. (pseudonym), May 3, 1976.

26. Minutes, Industrial Welfare Workers' Meeting, Mar. 23, 1918, ULP Records; interviews: Maria S., May 13, 1976, Lee C., June 9, 1976.

27. Interviews: Walter H., Oct. 25, 30, 1973, Wesley M., Apr. 2, 1976.

28. Margaret Byington, *Homestead: The Households of a Mill Town,* The Pittsburgh Survey, ed. Paul U. Kellogg (New York: Charities Publication Committee, 1910), 3.

29. Interview: Lillyan P., Nov. 9, 10, 1973, Alfred B., Apr. 21, 1976, Harvey C., Dec. 2, 1973.

30. Byington, *Homestead,* 3, 29–30.

31. Interview: Lillyan P., Nov. 9, 10, 1973.

32. Pittsburgh *Courier,* Sept. 12, 1925, 3; interviews: Charles B., July 16, 1976, Joseph M., Nov. 16, 1973, Ernest F., Apr. 19, 1976.

33. Interviews: Harrison G., Aug. 23, 1974, Queen W., Oct. 8, 1976, John T., Nov. 1, 23, 1973.

34. Epstein, *Negro Migrant in Pittsburgh,* 18; interviews: Laura L., Nov. 21, 1973, Lillyan P., Nov. 9, 10, 1973.

35. Clark, "Migrant in Pittsburgh," 304; Epstein, *Negro Migrant in Pittsburgh,* 13, 15–16.

36. Minutes, Industrial Welfare Workers' Meeting, Mar. 30, 1918, ULP Records; Hall, "Negro Housing," 31–33, 42–44; Pennsylvania Department of Public Welfare, *Negro Survey of Pennsylvania,* 36–37, 41.

37. Epstein, *Negro Migrant in Pittsburgh,* 11, 18; John T. Clark to Elsie Mountain, Nov. 2, 1920, ULP Records.

38. Reid, "Negro in the Major Industries," 24; Pennsylvania Department of Public Welfare, *Negro Survey of Pennsylvania,* 39.

39. Interviews: Harrison G., Aug. 23, 1974, Matthew J., May 28, 1976.

40. Interviews: Laura L., Nov. 21, 1973, Queen W., Oct. 8, 1976, Lillyan P., Nov. 9, 10, 1973, Olive W., July 23, 1976, Maria S., May 13, 1976.

41. Report of Women's Employment Secretary, Apr. 1919, ULP Records; John T. Clark Letters, Carter G. Woodson Collection, Library of Congress, Washington, D.C.

42. Interview: Charles B., July 16, 1976.

43. Interviews: Henry B., Aug. 2, 1974, Harvey C., Dec. 2, 1973, Matthew J., May 28, 1976, Gilbert M., Apr. 9, 1976, Charner C., Feb. 21, 1976, William H., June 17, 1976.

44. Bodnar, Simon, and Weber, *Lives of Their Own,* 56–58.

45. David Brody, *Labor in Crisis* (Philadelphia: Lippincott, 1965), 80–82; A. H. Young, "Employing Men for the Steel Mill," *Iron Age* 98 (Nov. 16, 1916), 1108–9; Robert J. Peters, "Industrial Employment of Negroes in Pennsylvania," *Labor and Industry* 13 (Jan. 1926), 25; E. C. Ramage, "The Foreman in Relation to Employment," Pennsylvania Department of Labor and Industry, *Bulletin* 7 (1920), 134.

46. Interviews: Willie S., July 15, 1974, Joseph M., Nov. 16, 1973, Charner C., Feb. 21, 1976.

47. Employment reports, July–Dec. 31, 1927, Jan. 1–Dec. 31, 1928, ULP Records.

48. Interview: John T., Nov. 1, 23, 1973.

49. Interview: Charles L., Jan. 28, 1977.

50. Interviews: Clarence M., Aug. 5, 1974, Matthew J., May 28, 1976, Harrison G., Aug. 23, 1974.

51. Interviews: Clarence M., Aug. 5, 1974, Matthew J., May 28, 1976.

52. Interview: Ben E., July 31, 1974.

53. Interview: Harrison G., Aug. 23, 1974.

54. Lawrence W. Levine, *Black Culture and Black Consciousness: Afro-American Folk Thought from Slavery to Freedom* (New York: Oxford University Press, 1977), 131–32, 383–86.

4

A Reserve Army

PITTSBURGH BLACKS saw their occupations gradually compressed during the first half of the twentieth century from a heterogeneous range of jobs into a comparatively narrow spectrum of employment. Between World War I and the Depression the demand for black labor, which drew southern migrants to western Pennsylvania, came mainly from employers of common labor in the manufacturing, construction, mining, and domestic service fields. As thousands of new male and female black workers arrived in the city to claim these positions, the occupational structure of the black work force tilted sharply toward the lower end of the urban job hierarchy. Northward migration and proletarianization of Pittsburgh blacks proceeded hand in hand.

For black workers as a group, job prospects dimmed during the migration period. The menial, unskilled jobs that employers offered to the male migrants in particular differed markedly from the semiskilled and skilled positions that black men had held in several Pittsburgh plants before World War I. Black women's economic status in the city changed less, but only because their occupations remained concentrated in the area of unskilled domestic employment. Though segregation of blacks at their work places and discrimination against blacks in wages were not widespread in the Pittsburgh area, employers refused by and large to raise blacks above the level of common labor. This, and the migrants' insecure tenure in the casual labor positions to which they were confined, shaped the contours of their work status.

Black men experienced the swiftest changes in the processes of migration and proletarianization. The roughly 8,500 male black workers in the city between 1900 and 1910 had fallen lopsidedly into two occupational fields, industry and domestic service, leaving small numbers scattered over the other areas of employment. Those in the domestic service jobs actually had composed almost two-fifths of all the city's male black workers (table 2). Black men had dominated the porters' jobs in hotels and train stations. They had also filled most of the janitors' positions in the city. Large numbers were servants, waiters, and "domestic laborers." Far fewer had entrepreneurial or self-employed jobs like barbers or restaurant keepers.[1]

Black men had long worked in Pittsburgh industry when the first waves of the World War I migration reached Pennsylvania. Between 1900 and 1915 their numbers in industry were growing, even though employers relied mainly on recent European immigrants for common labor and on white Americans or old-stock immigrants for skilled and supervisory jobs. Small numbers in 1910 had worked in the city's building trades, printing establishments, railroad yards, and machine shops. Carpenters, brick masons, and plumbers had made up over half of the black construction workers in the city before the migration. A few had kept alive older hand trades like shoemaking and blacksmithing. But even before the migration the largest and most stable group of skilled black men were iron- and steelworkers.[2]

Some black men had first entered Pittsburgh mills as strikebreakers in the 1870s and 1880s. Of these, a few won the highly paid craft positions. Other black craftsmen had migrated to Pittsburgh mills before World War I from foundries and iron mills in Maryland and Virginia, and some in this group also succeeded in plying their trades in the Pittsburgh metals industries. Black iron- and steelworkers in all skill levels, however, comprised only 3 percent of the city's total mill work force in 1910.[3]

What was most remarkable about the group of pre–World War I black mill workers was not its size but its comparatively large number of skilled men. In 1910 more than one-quarter of the black steelworkers in the city had been heaters, puddlers, founders, and rollers, the highest paid, most prestigious positions in the industry (table 3). At the gigantic Homestead mill

Table 2

Black Men's Occupational Structure in Pittsburgh, 1910–30,
Percentage and Concentration (C) in Occupational Fields

Occupational Field	1910		1920		1930	
	%	C	%	C	%	C
Manufacturing industry	31.9	462	53.4	676	45.9	499
Nonmanufacturing industry	12.8	186	8.2	104	15.0	163
Public service	2.3	33	1.9	24	2.4	26
Professional	1.6	23	1.5	19	2.2	24
Proprietors, managers, and officials	2.2	32	0.7	9	0.7	11
Clerical and sales	11.9	173	5.1	65	4.6	57
Domestic and personal service	37.4	542	29.1	368	29.1	313
Total	100.1 (N = 8,479)		99.9 (N = 15,040)		99.9 (N = 19,135)	
Percentage total male work force black	6.9		7.9		9.2	

Source: U.S. Census Bureau, *Thirteenth Census* (1913), 4:590–91; *Fourteenth Census* (1922) 4:1197–99; *Fifteenth Census* (1932), 4:1416–17.

Note: The concentration measure (C) shows blacks' proportional representation in different occupational fields. A figure of 100 means that the ratio of blacks in the occupational field to all black workers in Pittsburgh equalled the ratio of blacks to the city's total work force. Figures less than 100 indicate that blacks were proportionately underrepresented; figures over 100 indicate overrepresentation.

outside Pittsburgh, 17 percent of the black men had been skilled workers. At the Black Diamond Steel and Iron Company, blacks held all of the puddlers' jobs. Carnegie's Clark Mills placed two-thirds of its blacks in semiskilled and skilled positions and assigned several blacks to foremen's jobs. These examples do not alter the fact that the majority of black men had been unskilled mill workers, but they do suggest that before the coming of thousands of new black workers, common labor had not been the only type of job given to blacks. On the contrary, the proportion of black men in skilled, semiskilled, and unskilled mill jobs had nearly matched those of the entire industry work force, both in the city and in the surrounding mill towns.[4]

Table 3

Percentage of Male Black Iron- and Steelworkers in Pittsburgh, 1910-30

Occupation	1910	1920	1930
Furnacemen, smelters, heaters, puddlers, etc.	20.2	2.6	1.9
Iron molders, founders, casters	3.2	1.2	1.9
Rollers and roll hands	3.3	2.3	0.4
Blast furnace and steel rolling mill operatives	6.5	4.4	3.5
Operatives, other iron and steel departments	0.4	0.7	2.7
Laborers, blast furnaces and steel mills	64.5	85.0	72.6
Laborers, other iron and steel departments	1.9	3.8	17.0
Total	100.0	100.0	100.0
	(*N* = 786)	(*N* = 5,120)	(*N* = 2,853)

Source: U.S. Census Bureau, *Thirteenth Census* (1913), 4:590-91; *Fourteenth Census* (1922), 4:1197-98; *Fifteenth Census* (1932), 4:1416.

The increase in black steelworkers after 1915 came with astonishing speed and far outstripped the relative growth of the male work force as a whole. From a tiny minority before 1916, black mill hands shot upward to an industry level of about 20 percent in 1923. Figures from individual mills showed how rapidly a sizeable black work force emerged. At the Carnegie Steel Company's facility at Duquesne, the greatest number of blacks employed before 1916 was six. In 1916 there were twenty; in 1917, seventy-five; in 1918, 230. For all the Carnegie mills in the Pittsburgh area, black workers increased from 1,500 before 1916 to 4,000 in 1917. During World War I blacks entered several Pittsburgh mills where no blacks had ever worked before, including the plants of Oliver Iron and Steel, Pittsburgh Forge and Iron, A. M. Byers Company, and Lockhart Iron and Steel. In all, nearly 500 blacks were hired by these firms between 1916 and 1917.[5] The 1920 census showed that the number of black male workers in Pittsburgh had increased 52 percent since 1910, while the total growth in male employment in the city during the same period had been around 6 percent. In the city's iron and steel mills black men raised their representation between 1910 and 1920 faster than the overall increase in mill workers— 554 percent for blacks against 20 percent for the work force as a whole.[6]

The rapid addition of black workers in Pittsburgh's basic metals industry did not continue long after the end of the war. The short but severe depression of 1920-21 temporarily halted the hiring of southern black migrants and caused layoffs among many who had earlier gotten jobs. But with recovery in 1922 came a renewed influx of blacks to the mills, which peaked in the boom year of 1923. Steel producers not only needed additional workers that year to expand output but also to form new crews in blast furnace and open hearth departments for the additional shift brought about by reducing daily working hours from twelve to eight. Judge Elbert H. Gary, president of U.S. Steel, estimated that his corporation would need 60,000 additional laborers to make the eight-hour day possible. He counted on southern blacks for most of the new recruits.[7]

These wide swings in labor demand overlay an older pattern of erratic employment in the steel industry. Since the development of modern steel mills in the 1880s, steel managers had preferred to run furnaces and finishing plants at top speed when they had a backlog of orders for products. But as soon as blank spaces began to appear on their order books, they banked the furnaces, shut down rolling mill machinery, and laid off their workers until demand for steel warranted another period of production at breakneck speed. Periods of frantic activity during World War I and the early 1920s only accentuated this established alternation from hectic work to idleness. It was the lucky migrant who not only arrived in the Pittsburgh area at an employment peak but who also did not soon get thrown out of work by unpredictable fluctuations in the industry.[8]

Whatever the demand was for southern black workers in Pittsburgh at any given time during the migration, the newcomers seldom had job opportunities outside a narrow range of common labor positions. The thousands of southern blacks who became unskilled workers in mills and factories and at building sites, hotels, stores, and warehouses were the characteristic urban black workers in northern cities after 1915. The skilled black industrial and domestic workers of the pre-migration years became far less significant statistically. As more and more southern blacks came to the city, the black work force as a whole grew more dependent on wages from unskilled jobs. Relatively few black workers experienced this change as a sudden alteration in their personal fortunes. But many suffered deeply from the consequences of confinement to common labor: hard work, low wages, and frequent periods of unemployment.

The effect of black migration on the general skill level of Pittsburgh blacks was nowhere clearer than in the iron and steel mills. The proportion of black workers in city mills who were unskilled jumped from 66 to 90 percent between 1910 and 1930 (table 3). The black share of all unskilled jobs in the industry grew from 3 to 26 percent in the same period. The steel companies that rapidly increased their number of black workers during World War I funneled nearly all of the new black employees into unskilled jobs. Of the 4,000 blacks working at the Carnegie mills in 1917, 95 percent were unskilled. At the Jones and Laughlin, National Tube, and Oliver Iron and Steel mills, all of the blacks in 1917 were employed as common laborers. The A. M. Byers Company records show that its employment office placed most southern blacks in the category "laborer" between 1916 and 1930. The migrants at Byers who got different job titles also did hot, heavy work, as the names of their positions suggest: "drag-off," "pull-up," or "cinder wheeler."[9]

This tidal wave of southern black common labor swamped the skilled black workers in Pittsburgh, most of whom had gotten their jobs before the war. Black puddlers, melters, rollers, and heaters, who had been one-fourth of the black steelworkers, composed less than a tenth of the black workers by 1930, a tiny holdover from the years before the mass migration. The black building trades workers underwent a similar transformation during the migration. Though the number of black construction workers more than quadrupled between 1910 and 1930, the proportion who were skilled or apprentices fell from 56 percent to just over one-quarter, while the percentage of laborers and helpers rose over the twenty years from less than half to almost three-quarters.[10]

Of all the major fields of employment for black men in Pittsburgh, domestic work underwent the least change in numbers and relative proportions of higher and lower skill groups. Black male domestics between 1910 and 1930 grew by a comparatively modest 56 percent. The absolute number in the skilled or entrepreneurial categories like barber and lunchroom keeper rose slightly. Those in the menial domestic occupations like janitor, porter, and domestic laborer also increased but not as rapidly as did unskilled blacks in industry. Though they were losing the social prominence in the black community that they had enjoyed in the nineteenth and early twentieth centuries, male domestics maintained their representation in the better lines of work.[11]

It was entirely unremarkable that southern migrants entered Pittsburgh industry through the door of unskilled labor. Irish, German, Italian, and Slavic immigrants who preceded them enjoyed no higher initiation to the job market. Black men and women, though, could not progress in significant numbers above the common labor positions even when they had worked at a mill for several years. Their advancement in the industrial hierarchy of skill and hourly earnings was checked by the general decline of skilled work, by the intermittent unemployment that characterized the 1920s, and by employers' practices in job assignments, promotions, and wage payments.

The overall decline in the proportion of skilled workers in Pittsburgh industries affected black workers. Steel mill managers who before World War I had succeeded in trimming large numbers of skilled jobs from their payrolls continued to weed out these positions during the migration. The skilled mill workers in Pittsburgh declined from 15 to 6 percent of the industry work force between 1910 and 1930. At the city's construction sites the total number of workers increased steadily, but of this growth from 1910 to 1930, fully 90 percent were laborers and helpers. The percentages of brick masons, carpenters, station-

ary engineers, electricians, and plumbers were all lower at the
end of the migration than they were at the beginning. The fate
of skilled black workers in Pittsburgh in part reflected what was
happening to the city's skilled men generally.[12]

The slackening pace of economic growth in Pittsburgh during the 1920s stifled other possibilities for black laborers'
advancement.[13] Again, the trend showed up most clearly in the
steel industry. One study claimed that between 1923 and 1929,
more than 27,000 iron- and steelworkers in Pennsylvania were
furloughed and that by 1930, 12 percent were out of work.
There were probably no more black men at work in Pittsburgh
in 1930 than there had been in 1925, despite the arrival of
additional southern black job seekers in the interim.[14] The
unemployment rate of all unskilled workers in Pittsburgh in the
spring of 1928 was around 50 percent.[15]

Pittsburgh employers used the growing mass of black workers
in their mills, factories, and mines in a new way. They readily
put blacks to work anywhere in the flow of production where
additional labor was needed, sometimes at places where blacks
had never before been seen. But at the same time employers
ended the practice of assigning some blacks to skilled work. In
keeping with the development of the new black work force as a
reserve of unskilled, casual labor, employers spread the black
workers widely through their plants, but always in the lower
reaches of the skill and pay ranges.

Although European immigrant workers were grouped according to nationality or kinship in particular parts of some Pittsburgh factories, blacks often worked throughout their employers'
shops and yards.[16] The Byers Company assigned the first black
migrant employees of the World War I years mainly to four areas
of its iron mill—welding, finishing, bar mill, and warehouse—
but also placed them in a number of other departments. In the
1920s Byers dispersed black migrants still more widely, working them in all phases of operations from plant maintenance, to
production, to shipping. Sizeable percentages of southerners
remained in single departments at the end of the decade, but the
company's policy clearly was to assign recruits wherever common labor was required.[17] Larger industrial concerns adopted
the same general practice, the Carnegie Steel Company mills,

and Westinghouse Electric and Manufacturing Company among them.[18] Other companies limited their new black employees to one kind of job or to a few specific departments. Richard C. remembered one open hearth furnace at the Jones and Laughlin Steel mill on Pittsburgh's Southside, which had a black crew: "Down in the number 1 shop . . . they was mixed down in there. But this little furnace was the number 21 all set off by itself and most all of those [helpers] were black." The Mesta Machine Company up to 1922 hired blacks only as janitors. In addition to cases such as these, Pittsburgh firms formed gangs of common laborers composed mostly or entirely of black workers.[19]

When some Pittsburgh area industries concentrated their black labor in segregated labor gangs, they also placed black subforemen at the heads of these units. The subforemen had a narrow scope of authority; their primary responsibility was to cajole, inspire, or browbeat gangs to complete their tasks in good time.[20] According to employers' designs, these black supervisors were also to help reduce the rampant turnover among the southern black workers by forming better relationships with their gang members than white supervisors could. In any case, the black "straw bosses" or "pushers" were common in Pittsburgh industry as long as there was a steady flow of new black workers into the shops and mills. The peak number of black subforemen was reached in 1923. Thereafter, fewer were found, although in December 1925 an investigator found fifty-three in a single mill that employed 1,500 blacks.[21]

However flexible industries were in applying black labor to departments needing additional hands, most managers religiously observed the custom of barring blacks from high-skill, high-wage jobs. Funneling blacks into a lowly segment of the skill and pay range undercut the social status and earning power of skilled southern migrants and in the long run also forced hardship on those unskilled newcomers who decided to hold their northern jobs and seek advancement. Black artisans or skilled domestics who had learned their trades from an older generation of southern black craftsmen paid dearly for the chance to earn a living in Pittsburgh. They could be men like John T. or Joseph M. who gave up small businesses to work as mill and factory hands in Pittsburgh.[22] Or they could be industrial craftsmen like the two railroad firemen and the engine inspector who had to work in other industries because Pittsburgh locals of their unions would not permit them to join.[23] Or they could be skilled iron molders who came to the Pittsburgh area only to find that they were restricted to the semiskilled position of machine molders.[24]

Undoubtedly there were more black men with skills in Pittsburgh during the migration years than census figures indicated, simply because employers gave them no choice but to work in unskilled positions. Among 529 migrants questioned by Abraham Epstein concerning their work backgrounds, slightly more than 10 percent had followed a trade in the South; but of the 493 migrants who gave information on their Pittsburgh jobs, only 4 percent said they had skilled jobs. Data assembled for a 1928 study shed light on the position of southern men in Pittsburgh's domestic service and construction jobs. In surveying a group of high school students in Pittsburgh, this investigation found that over one-fourth of the students' fathers worked either as laborers or janitors. The remaining three-fourths of the fathers were scattered over many other occupations, 11.5 percent in the building trades and 7 percent in skilled domestic service jobs. But when the students gave information on what types of work their fathers had been trained to do *other* than that for which they were then employed, over one-third said that their fathers had mastered a building trade and about one-tenth a domestic service skill.[25]

The result of employers' practices in assigning work to their new black employees was the emergence of a range of "black" jobs in Pittsburgh. The particular jobs reserved for blacks varied from one mill or employer to another. At U.S. Steel Corporation mills in Pittsburgh and the nearby mill towns, black men could advance no higher than first helper in the open hearth department or catchers, chippers, and crane and dinghy operators in rolling mills. At the A. M. Byers iron mill few southern migrants ever worked at any position other than common labor. Since the Byers Company's wrought-iron pipe products depended to a considerable extent on the old ironmaking crafts of puddling, heating, and bending, it was noteworthy that only small percentages of the firm's black workers held jobs in the mill departments where such skilled work was performed.[26] In industrial work, moreover, the jobs saved for blacks usually demanded tremendous exertion. Many of these jobs had another element in common—heat.

The prevailing belief among Pittsburgh employers during the migration was that black men—especially the newcomers from the South—possessed a special capacity for hard labor in high temperatures. Such work was viewed as the migrants' forte,[27] and supervisors came to rely on black migrants for the enervating tasks of tearing down and rebuilding spent furnaces, carrying scraps of hot metal away from metal shears, or cleaning up spilled metal and slag after the molten contents of blast or open hearth furnaces had been tapped. A black employee at U.S. Steel's Duquesne mill drew a vivid picture of the difficulties of such work: "You always have to put boards down and bags around your knees and you still feel the heat on your knees. Colored and white are given this work but colored are given this type of work mostly. They put colored in the hot checkers especially on hot days."[28] Blacks' customary job assignments in the battery and powdered steel departments of coking plants similarly exposed them to intense heat, just as did handling asphalt on road building crews, stoking coal in boilers, and working over cook stoves—all labor that fell increasingly to black men and women in these years.

Employment managers in the Pittsburgh area in 1930 agreed that blacks performed best at "hot and dry operations" and at "wet and hot jobs," among others. The supervisors thought blacks were least proficient "on wet and cold jobs" or "when exposed to weather." Nonetheless, the managers of steel works denied blacks who toiled during the torrid summer months in the heat of furnaces the only benefit of such jobs—keeping warm during the winter. They transferred the black men to outdoor jobs during the winter and gave the furnace jobs to white workers.[29]

Black work in Pittsburgh was also marked by a lack of occupational advancement. The Pittsburgh Plate Glass Company used blacks as machinists, chemical mixers, and pot makers, but never as the highly skilled mirror polishers. The Standard Sanitary Manufacturing Company likewise kept its black employees

out of the highest skill positions.[30] Wesley M., the South Carolina
migrant and Homestead mill worker, was voicing a familiar
complaint when he asserted, "I worked in that mill and I have
learned those white boys [their] jobs. [They] would put them on
my job, [and I would] learn them their jobs, but still I couldn't
get the [better] job." A black mill hand at Duquesne said, "In the
labor department, the colored has a hard way to go. They leave
the white get more time than the colored. There was nothing
you could do about it." "In general," said another black steelworker in the early 1930s, "colored have been kicking about the
same level. The company just don't want them to go higher."[31]

The southern blacks working at the A. M. Byers mill found
the same managerial reluctance to upgrade men of their race.
More than half of all the migrants in a sample of Byers's southern black workers had only one job assignment before leaving
the company, but those in the sample who were reassigned or
who left the company and returned later to be hired again still
made only negligible progress in terms of hourly wages. These
migrants as a group were only slightly better paid in their
second, third, and fourth assignments than they were in their
first one. The small improvement in wages over successive jobs
(table 4) did not change the migrants' status as a pool of common labor in the Byers plant. In only a minority of cases did
shifting from one job to another actually elevate the migrants'
position in the mill. Only 30 percent of the sampled migrants at
the Byers plant were promoted to their second job; of this
favored group a mere 14 percent were again promoted to their
third assignment.

These upward shifts through the pay levels at the Byers plant
were seldom real promotions in any case. The company, like
other employers of black migrants in Pittsburgh, seldom awarded
a newcomer with a permanent assignment to a job better than
the one it initially assigned. Byers managers seemed to use
black laborers as substitutes when a regular member of a production crew failed to come to work. Such shuffling of workers
may have been recorded as "promotions" in the company's
employment records, but was more likely temporary transfers
to maintain the pace of production. The migrant laborer who
filled in for another worker got paid at a higher rate but had no

Table 4

Percentage of Migrants at Pay Levels
at the A. M. Byers Company, 1916–30

Pay Level	First Job	Second Job	Third Job	Fourth Job
Low	86	83	82	80
Medium	12	15	15	18
High	2	2	3	2
Total	100.0	100.0	100.0	100.0
	(*N* = 648)	(*N* = 294)	(*N* = 173)	(*N* = 112)

Source: A. M. Byers Personnel File, Archives of Industrial Society, Hillman Library, University of Pittsburgh.

Note: Since actual wage rates fluctuated from 1916 to 1930, pay levels cannot be described by one set of hourly rates. The differential between "low," "medium," and "high" levels was five cents per hour and remained the same throughout the fourteen-year period.

tenure in the better job, unless the absentee never returned.[32] For this reason, black migrants' movements to more remunerative jobs at the Byers plant had little lasting effect either on their general status among the company's personnel or, as we shall see later, on their transient work pattern.

The corollary to the racial boundaries that employers drew in the skill and pay hierarchies was lower earnings for black workers. The gap between blacks' and whites' wages was smallest in common labor and greatest in the most skilled jobs. Standard hourly wages for unskilled jobs in different industries prevailed in the Pittsburgh area as they did in other manufacturing centers, and employers tended to pay these rates to whomever they hired to do "bull work." When southern blacks first entered Pittsburgh mills in large numbers during World War I, they got paid around twenty-five to thirty cents per hour for unskilled work. The sharp demand for labor pushed this rate up to around fifty cents per hour by 1920, but it fell back to between forty and fifty cents per hour from 1922 until the end of the decade.[33]

Even though blacks earned the same wages for unskilled work as whites did, they were unfairly paid in two ways. First, black workers as a group received lower total earnings than whites because very few blacks ever held jobs above the unskilled

level. Second, those blacks who did gain semiskilled or skilled
jobs were the ones who found differences between their wages
and those of the white workers in similar positions. Reid reported
black core makers in Pittsburgh foundries earning a top wage of
sixty cents an hour, but white core makers earning up to ninety
cents an hour. There were similar disparities in pay between
white and black molders, polishers, chippers, and grinders
in the metals industries.[34] These racial differences in wages
paralleled differences between white and black workers in
methods of payment, union versus nonunion wage scales, and
job assignments in particular work places. Because few unions
of skilled white workers admitted qualified blacks, skilled southern migrants who got jobs in their own trades had to work at
the lower nonunion wage scales. Black building tradesmen
were most affected, making in some jobs only one-third of the
union rates. Relatively few blacks had the opportunity to work
at the jobs that were paid on a piece rate or tonnage basis.
These jobs often allowed individuals or groups to earn more
than the average hourly wage listed for the positions. Generally,
employers gave black workers jobs requiring less attention,
detail, and refined product than the jobs given white workers,
even within the same skill level. A white and a black could both
be molders, but the former would be doing intricate handwork,
while the latter would be operating a molding machine and
earning much less. Where the social prestige of occupations
determined earnings, blacks' wages also lost ground to whites'.
This was true, for example, in domestic and service trades.
During the early twentieth century foreign immigrants began to
serve the prominent, affluent white clientele who had formerly
employed black cooks, barbers, and personal servants. Black
domestics turned to customers of their own race who could
not afford to pay as well as white patrons. A similar shift
removed black porters from the best downtown Pittsburgh hotels,
restricting their work to railroad stations, Pullman cars, roominghouses, and department stores.[35]

   The net change in black men's occupational status in Pittsburgh industry from World War I until the Depression was
from a small percentage of employees limited to only a few
firms, but working at all skill levels, to a sizeable proportion of

male workers, employed by most firms but concentrated in low-skill jobs. This represented a significant change in black men's position in the labor market, but it did not insure them stable employment and decent living standards. Blacks remained mostly in manufacturing and domestic service positions, laboring at the jobs that became most expendable during the frequent drops in labor demand.

Joblessness repeatedly lashed Pittsburgh's working class as a whole during the 1920s. The brief slumps in production in 1920–21 and 1924 punctuated a gradual decline in employment in Pittsburgh—especially in the metals industry—that threatened all wage earners, young and old, married and single, white as well as black. Some observers claimed that mill managers favored blacks over whites when it came to deciding who would be laid off at a particular plant. The black welfare workers at the Carnegie Steel Company's Homestead and Duquesne mills reported that black workers had been kept on at rates equal to or greater than those for white workers in the 1920–21 depression. The Byers Company announced that it retained its black workers during the 1924 slump and rationalized that "the men upon whom they could rely the most" had been rewarded.[36]

If such claims had any credibility, they did not reflect the general practice in the Pittsburgh area in furloughing workers. As the 1920s wore on, job losses pressed with increasing and uneven force on black workers. Between 1920 and 1930 there was an overall decrease in male employment in Pittsburgh iron and steel industries of 33 percent, but a drop among black mill workers of 43 percent.[37] Employers jettisoned their black workers faster than their white employees during the intermittent economic slumps as well. Blacks working in the metals industries of Pittsburgh from 1920 to 1921 dropped 66 percent, while the white workers fell 55 percent. Again, blacks decreased in all Pittsburgh industries by 19 percent between 1924 and 1925, while white workers declined by only 0.4 percent.[38]

In 1926, when black employment in Pennsylvania reached its second highest level of the period from 1922 to 1940, the Pittsburgh Urban League noted the suffering of blacks in Pittsburgh: "during the last six months a greater number of Negroes have been under-employed than ever before. The workman counts himself fortunate who averages four (4) full days of work each week."[39] By that time the general optimism among American businessmen regarding the economy had a hollow ring for northern urban blacks. The Urban League warned black migrants away from the city in 1928 and 1929. "Of course," wrote the League's director to the wife of one job seeker in the South, "you realize how difficult it is to find work in Pittsburgh today."[40] An investigator in the Hill District during the summer of 1929 found that over one-third of the men and women he interviewed had been idle for periods varying from one week to three months in the preceding year. The winter months became a regularly recurring season of hardship in the black community: "many Negroes, out of work and penniless, ask to be sent to the Allegheny County Work House for the winter."[41] Though southern blacks continued to move to Pittsburgh and other northern cities during the late 1920s and early 1930s, they no longer came in response to opportunities for work. Between the mid-1920s and 1940 black migration to Pittsburgh better measured the hardship of southern rural life than the attractions of urban, industrial communities.

While black men grouped in ever greater concentration in heavy industry, during and after World War I black women remained in the same types of jobs they had held in 1910. The city's white female workers moved into clerical, sales, and professional jobs, leaving domestic and personal service jobs in the black women's hands. The difference between the development of the black male and black female spheres of work in Pittsburgh was thus striking: for better or worse, black men's occupational distribution changed to reflect Pittsburgh's industrial market; black women were caught in a nonindustrial job category that became with each year more exclusively their own.[42]

From 1910 to 1930 nearly 90 percent of Pittsburgh's black women jobholders were domestic workers (table 5). This was a hugely disproportionate concentration, since in the same period black women made up only between 8 and 10 percent of the city's female work force. Most of the black women not employed as domestics worked in manufacturing industry, and only very small percentages labored in other occupational fields. When southern black women came to Pittsburgh, therefore, they found

Table 5

Black Women's Occupational Structure in Pittsburgh, 1910–30,
Percentage and Concentration (C) in Occupational Fields

Occupational Field	1910		1920		1930	
	%	C	%	C	%	C
Manufacturing industry	6.1	74	6.7	74	4.4	44
Nonmanufacturing industry	0.0	—	0.1	1	0.2	2
Professional	1.4	17	2.2	24	1.9	19
Proprietors, managers, and officials	3.0	36	1.8	20	1.7	17
Clerical and sales	1.8	22	3.7	41	3.0	30
Domestic and personal service	87.7	1,057	85.5	950	88.8	897
Total	100.0 (N = 4,168)		100.0 (N = 5,195)		100.0 (N = 6,923)	
Percentage of total female work force black	8.3		9.0		9.9	

Source: U.S. Census Bureau, *Thirteenth Census* (1913), 4:591–92; *Fourteenth Census* (1922), 4:1200; *Fifteenth Census* (1932), 4:1418.

Note: The concentration measure (C) shows blacks' proportional representation in different occupational fields. A figure of 100 means that the ratio of blacks in the occupational field to all black workers in Pittsburgh equalled the ratio of blacks to the city's total work force. Figures less than 100 indicate that blacks were proportionately underrepresented; figures over 100 indicate overrepresentation.

that virtually the only work open to them was the very same that they had had before moving north.[43]

If few black women in Pittsburgh got industrial jobs, their representation in factories was not disproportionately low. Pittsburgh offered relatively few factory jobs for any women. The preponderance of heavy manufacturing jobs in the Pittsburgh area labor market barred women from most industrial positions by the employment practices of the early twentieth century. Pittsburgh ranked seventh among nine major cities in the proportion of adult women employed in 1920.[44] The textile mills that had provided wage labor for Pittsburgh women in the mid-nineteenth century were gone, leaving behind a myriad of smaller enterprises employing women: bakeries, candy factories, cigarmaking shops, industrial laundries, glass factories, and dressmaking shops. Only a handful of Pittsburgh's heavy manufacturing firms hired large numbers of white women to perform tasks such as winding coils for electric motors or threading bolts and screws. In general, women worked on the margins of Pittsburgh's largest, most technologically advanced industries.[45]

Though World War I strengthened the demand for women workers in industry, there were relatively few positions available for black women. Employers whose male workers went into the army or into better paying jobs during the war sometimes hired white women to fill their places. If the jobs that the white women had formerly held went begging, employers sometimes sought black women. The strong demand for industrial labor during the war in this way tugged even at black women, whose customary occupations were farthest removed from industry. When the war ended and demobilized soldiers returned to their old occupations, employers dismissed white women from the men's jobs. Black women in their turn got bumped out of industrial work altogether.[46]

This process and black women's lowly status in the Pittsburgh area work force came to light in the reports of the Urban League women's employment secretary. During the latter part of 1918 the secretary placed female job applicants in several positions with downtown department stores. But the New Year brought a slackening demand for black women. "A decided turn has taken place in the Industrial situation during the month of January," the secretary wrote in 1919. "At this time, we find it rather difficult to place women owing to the many men returning and other men being thrown out of work on account of plants closing down." In March 1919 the secretary reported, "Fewer opportunities for [black] women owing to readjustment." The Boggs and Buhle department store dismissed black women hired during the war and filled their jobs with white women. "They assured the Secretary the [black] girls' work was satisfactory but they are re-adjusting their employment regulations in order to make place for returning soldier employees." The secretary claimed black women who lost wartime jobs in the "readjustment" were looking for domestic positions.[47]

The reports on black women's short-lived factory employment are scattered and fragmentary. The women who filled five power machine operator jobs at the National Shirt Factory could not do the work satisfactorily. On the other hand, the treasurer of Lockhart Iron and Steel Company wrote to John T. Clark of the Urban League that the six black women hired to do exhausting jobs at the company's mill had "done their work remarkably well."[48] Black women in Pittsburgh and elsewhere were probably enthusiastic about the industrial jobs that they had during the war. Compared to working in private homes, labor in factories, warehouses, or railroad yards offered shorter hours, better pay, and less intimate contact with supervisors. Women enjoyed working together in crews undertaking group tasks that involved the coordinated effort of several individuals. Industry jobs gave young black women especially independence from their homes and chances to travel and make plans for the future.[49]

However black women in Pittsburgh responded to the challenge and difficulty of wartime industrial work, it was very unlikely given the general exclusion of women from heavy industry that they would be retained once the war ended. They might have stood better chances for holding onto positions in department stores, but here the employers' faithful observance of a racial division of labor worked against them. Only white women could wait on store customers. Black women were generally placed at tasks out of the shoppers' view as stock girls, wrappers, or sheet writers. Few black women even had the opportunity to be elevator operators in the stores. An additional obstacle to steady employment in the downtown stores was the seasonal demand for work. The large establishments hired black women for the Christmas rush but kept very few of them as permanent employees. All these encumbrances on black women's job prospects came despite their employers' reports that they were "giving the very best service."[50]

The war's most important impact on black women workers could be seen in their attitudes toward their customary work as laundresses, cooks, and cleaning women. As soon as alternative jobs in factories and stores appeared, black domestics startled placement workers by demanding much higher daily wages. "Women with large families can hardly get help at any price," gasped one official. "Fully 80% of the female applicants applying for work want days work at $3.50 or $5.00 per day. Days work used to be done by widows with children, but now young girls refuse to be strapped down to regular housework. Hundreds of jobs go begging at $15 per week."[51] Even when jobs in stores and factories began to disappear after the war, black women for a time remained selective about domestic opportunities. "We have a large number of openings for domestics which we find a little difficult to fill owing to many openings for kitchen work, which applicants readily accept because this work pays well with one whole day off," the Urban League's women's employment secretary reported.[52]

Though some black women entered jobs in Pittsburgh light industry after 1918, widespread opportunities to work outside domestic service did not reappear until World War II.[53] Between the world wars, practically the only places open to black women were white families' kitchens, commercial laundries, and the janitorial staffs of downtown stores and offices. Within their domestic service domain, black women fell mainly into the two classifications, "laundresses" and "servants." From 1910 to 1930, "servants" alone accounted for well over half of all black female domestic and service employees. When we add black laundresses to the servants, we have only around 10 percent of the females in the occupational field left to count. In domestic and personal service, as with the overall occupational structure of black women in Pittsburgh from 1910 to 1930, there was little change in the proportions at work in the different jobs (table 6).

The continuity in black women's work in Pittsburgh stood out in contrast to the rapid changes taking place in white women's occupations. The new female jobs of this period, such as telephone operators, typists, office secretaries, and receptionists, grew swiftly in number and in proportion to other fields of employment for women. Employers nearly always refused to hire black women for these jobs, even when they had succeeded in being trained for the work. Those white women who took domestic service jobs during this period seldom competed for

Table 6
Percentage of Female Blacks in Domestic Service Jobs
in Pittsburgh, 1910–30

Occupation	1910	1920	1930
Barbers, hairdressers, and manicurists	2.3	3.4	1.7
Charwomen and cleaners	3.3	1.5	2.1
Housekeepers and stewardesses	3.9	2.7	2.2
Janitors and sextons	1.0	1.7	0.9
Laundresses (not in laundry)	25.3	26.9	17.0
Laundry operatives	1.1	1.3	2.2
Nurses (not trained)	1.5	0.5	0.4
Servants	60.5	58.0	69.4
All other occupations	1.1	4.0	4.1
Total	100.0	100.0	100.0
	(N = 3,655)	(N = 4,443)	(N = 6,151)

Source: U.S. Census Bureau, *Thirteenth Census* (1913), 4:592; *Fourteenth Census* (1922), 4:1200; *Fifteenth Census* (1932), 4:1418.

the servant and laundry positions open to black women. Instead they became barbers, hairdressers, manicurists, charwomen, cleaners, housekeepers, and stewardesses. The number of women in such jobs grew during the 1910s and 1920s, but in each of them the percentage of black women declined.

Domestics' work in Pittsburgh had its advantages for southern black women, many of whom had worked as laundresses or cooks in their places of birth before moving north. The similarity between the tasks involved in southern cooking and cleaning and those in the same types of work in the North permitted the female migrants to adapt relatively smoothly and quickly to urban jobs. Except at department stores, their occupations in Pittsburgh did not depend on seasonal fluctuations in demand, either. Whether employed at a commercial laundry or as a housecleaner for a private family, black women could find themselves supporting their temporarily unemployed husbands as well as their children out of their meager earnings. Such benefits hardly compensated for the narrow choice of jobs, the menial work, and low wages, however.

Black migrants had hoped to gain jobs in Pittsburgh that would both improve their economic status in the short-term and provide them permanent access to the mainstream of advancing northern industrial labor. By the mid-1920s, if not earlier, these hopes had been dashed. Southern migration and the entry of blacks into basic manufacturing jobs had drastically changed the pre–World War I occupational position of blacks. The migrants were not enclosed by an occupational color line as they had been in the South. Still, they found themselves limited to a relatively restricted range of jobs with distinct characteristics.

Black migrants breached the walls of Pittsburgh industry only to find themselves in a casual labor market from which they could not escape. Racial discrimination often barred migrants with craft skills from working at their trades, and they reluctantly joined unskilled newcomers in the labor gangs. The unskilled southerners could enter the urban job market easily, even though they were rural migrants, because casual labor required neither training nor skill nor even literacy. Such work provided little security or stability. Wages were low, employment was intermittent, and job tenure was extremely weak. Within this category of work, wage earners seldom advanced to better jobs. Employers made no commitments to promote or train those in casual labor, preferring to keep them on the payroll only as long as work needed to be done.[54]

Casual labor as a specific type of employment grew in the latter half of the nineteenth century when American manufacturers needed a larger proportion of their labor force that could expand and contract with economic conditions. Before World War I southern and eastern Europeans, Scandinavians, Chinese, and blacks in the South all supplied muscle for such jobs.[55] Since there was seldom opportunity for immigrants or blacks to climb out of this employment into steadier work, labor unions became the only way to alter the casual labor market in favor of employees. Not only were blacks in northern industry restricted by racial discrimination to this employment field more thoroughly and consistently than other workers, but the prospects for creating unions that would include blacks glimmered momentarily between 1916 and 1922, then went out. With the failure to organize interracial trade unions, black workers lost the most promising avenue of escape from casual labor.

Though the proportional distribution of employment opportunities for blacks were as limited in other northern cities as they were in Pittsburgh, southern blacks did not become a solid mass of common laborers.[56] Here and there a college-trained migrant rose into the professions, a well-liked factory hand assumed a minor supervisory job, or a particularly capable worker moved into an autonomous, highly paid position.[57] A small percentage entered unions of skilled workers and succeeded in obtaining the full benefits of union membership: higher wages, job security, and advancement according to seniority. For the majority of male and female migrants who became urban workers, though, the chances of getting better jobs than the first ones they found after reaching the North were greatest where unions were weak or nonexistent, and where industries needed black backs, arms, and hands.

The role defined for black migrants in the northern economy imposed particularly difficult problems on southern black families looking for a northern destination where both black men and black women could hope for job advancement. Occupational structures occasionally permitted a slight elevation above the level of common labor for either unskilled men or women, but seldom for both in the same city. According to one student of blacks' jobs, the best chances for male migrants to advance above unskilled work existed in the open shop, heavy industries where large numbers of black men had entered during World War I and where no white-dominated trade unions stood in the way. Cities like Pittsburgh, Youngstown, Cleveland, and Buffalo were dominated by such industries. But since the best opportunities for black women to move beyond domestic labor lay in cities with a large number of light industries like garment-making, food-processing, or meatpacking, the advantage to black men often came at the expense of black women, and vice versa. Only a few industrial districts combined a large number of jobs where both black men and women had some hope for movement out of the mass of unskilled labor. New York, Chicago, and Philadelphia were the largest of these.[58]

For this reason Pittsburgh, the urban center of the nation's greatest coal mining, coking, and steelmaking area, became a place more attractive to southern black men than to female black wage earners. There was a chance, at least, for the male migrants in the mills who could endure the terribly bad working conditions as unskilled laborers to rise to a semiskilled job. That so few did in the type of industry relatively open to the advancement of black workers suggested the pitfalls of northern employment.

Contemporary black perspectives on the entry of southern migrants to the northern urban world of work had been sanguine before unemployment began to mount in the late 1920s.[59] To some observers, the opening of mill gates to thousands of male black workers signaled the creation of a new order in industry. No longer would employers have a sufficient number of white laborers to ignore the reservoir of black men employed in Pittsburgh's peripheral service jobs. But industrial employment became both a curse and a blessing for the southern recruits. Though they earned higher wages in mills and factories than they had in the South, black migrants' positions in heavy industry remained at the very bottom of the occupational hierarchy, where employees' tenure was always weakest. The effect of the migration on the occupational standing of Pittsburgh's black work force was consequently two-sided. On the one hand, black workers played a larger part in the manufacturing industries than they ever had before. On the other hand, their overall status as unskilled, low-paid employees in the casual labor market left them more exposed to the threat of joblessness and destitution than in the years before the migration.

NOTES

1. U.S. Census Bureau, *Thirteenth Census,* 4 (Washington: Government Printing Office, 1913), 590-92; John Bodnar, Roger Simon, and Michael P. Weber, *Lives of Their Own: Blacks, Italians, and Poles in Pittsburgh, 1900-1960* (Urbana: University of Illinois Press, 1982), 61.

2. *Thirteenth Census,* 4: 592.

3. Ibid.; Sterling D. Spero and Abram L. Harris, *The Black Worker*

(New York: Columbia University Press, 1931), 249-50; "Problem of the Negro Laborer," *Iron Trades Review* 60 (Apr. 1917), 836.

4. Margaret Byington, *Homestead: The Households of a Mill Town,* The Pittsburgh Survey, ed. Paul U. Kellogg (New York: Charities Publication Committee, 1910), 40; Richard R. Wright, Jr., *The Negro in Pennsylvania* (Philadelphia: AME Book Concern, 1912), 93; Helen Tucker, "The Negroes of Pittsburgh," in *Wage-Earning Pittsburgh,* The Pittsburgh Survey, ed. Paul U. Kellogg (New York: Survey Associates, 1914), 429.

5. U.S. Senate, Committee on Education and Labor, *Investigation of Strike in Steel Industries, Hearings,* Sept.-Oct. 1919 (Washington: Government Printing Office, 1919), Part II, 531 (66th Congress, S-145-11A); Abraham Epstein, *The Negro Migrant in Pittsburgh* (Pittsburgh: University of Pittsburgh, 1918), 31; U.S. Census Bureau, *Fourteenth Census,* 4 (Washington: Government Printing Office, 1922), 1197-98.

6. *Thirteenth Census,* 4:590-91; *Fourteenth Census,* 4:1197-98.

7. Pittsburgh *Courier,* July 14, 1923, 1.

8. U.S. Senate, *Report on Conditions of Employment in the Iron and Steel Industry,* 3, *Working Conditions and the Relations of Employers and Employees,* S. Doc. 110, Serial 6098 (Washington: Government Printing Office, 1913), 205-14; David Brody, *Steelworkers in America: The Non-Union Era* (Cambridge, Mass.: Harvard University Press, 1960), 17-18.

9. Epstein, *Negro Migrant in Pittsburgh,* 31; A. M. Byers Company Personnel File, Archives of Industrial Society, Hillman Library, University of Pittsburgh (hereafter cited as Byers Company Personnel File).

10. *Thirteenth Census,* 4:590-91; *Fourteenth Census,* 4: 1197-98; U.S. Census Bureau *Fifteenth Census,* 4 (Washington: Government Printing Office, 1932), 1416.

11. *Thirteenth Census,* 4: 590-91; *Fourteenth Census,* 4: 1197-98; *Fifteenth Census,* 4: 1416.

12. Brody, *Steelworkers in America,* 30-33; Katherine Stone, "The Origin of Job Structures in the Steel Industry," *Radical America* 7 (Nov.-Dec. 1973), 29-35.

13. William T. Hogan, *Economic History of the Iron and Steel Industry,* 3 (Lexington: D. C. Heath, 1971), 812-13; Glenn E. McLaughlin and Ralph J. Watkins, "The Economics of Maturity," in *Pittsburgh,* ed. Roy Lubove (New York: New Viewpoints, 1976), 114.

14. Horace Davis, *Labor and Steel* (New York: International Publishers, 1933), 91; Abram L. Harris, "The New Negro Worker in Pittsburgh" (M.A. thesis, University of Pittsburgh, 1924), 45-46; Ira De A. Reid, "The Negro in the Major Industries and Building Trades of Pittsburgh" (M.A. thesis, University of Pittsburgh, 1925), Table C, 10-10a.

15. Pennsylvania Department of Labor and Industry, *Labor and Industry* 15 (June 1928), 35; ibid., 15 (July 1928), 18.

16. Bodnar, Simon, and Weber, *Lives of Their Own,* 62-63.

17. Byers Company Personnel File.

18. Interview: Walter H., Oct. 25, 30, 1973; "Report on a Visit to Pittsburgh, Pa. — August 12 and 13, 1920," U.S. Department of Labor, Division of Negro Economics, Record Group 174, File "Miscellaneous," National Archives and Records Administration, Washington, D.C.

19. Interviews: Richard C., Aug. 8, 1974, Ernest F., Apr. 19, 1976; minutes of meeting, Pittsburgh Chapter of the National Association of Corporation Training, Unskilled Labor and Americanization Section, Feb. 2, 1922, National Urban League Papers, Industrial Relations File, Series 4, Box 4, Library of Congress, Washington, D.C. (hereafter cited as Corporation Training meeting); Reid, "Negro in the Major Industries," 30, 31.

20. Interviews: Ed R., June 10, 1976, Ben B., Nov. 30, 1973; Pittsburgh *Courier,* Oct. 27, 1923; John T. Clark, "The Negro in Steel," *Opportunity* 4 (Mar. 1926), 88.

21. John T. Clark, "The Negro in Steel," *Opportunity* 2 (Oct. 1924), 300; Clark, "Negro in Steel" (1926), 88; Reid, "Negro in the Major Industries," 19; typescript, "Speech in Kansas City" (1923?), 3, Urban League of Pittsburgh (ULP) Records, Archives of Industrial Society.

22. Interviews: John T., Nov. 1, 23, 1973, Joseph M., Nov. 16, 1973.

23. Guichard Parris and Lester Brooks, *Blacks in the City: A History of the National Urban League* (Boston: Little, Brown, 1971), 138.

24. Reid, "Negro in the Major Industries," 14.

25. Epstein, *Negro Migrant in Pittsburgh,* 21-22; Floyd C. Covington, "Occupational Choices in Relation to Economic Opportunities of Negro Youth in Pittsburgh" (M.A. thesis, University of Pittsburgh, 1928), 56-57.

26. Reid, "Negro in the Major Industries," 12-16; Horace R. Cayton and George S. Mitchell, *Black Workers and the New Unions* (Chapel Hill: University of North Carolina Press, 1939), 32; Byers Company Personnel File; interviews: Walter H., Oct. 25, 30, 1973, Ernest F., Apr. 19, 1976.

27. Cayton and Mitchell, *Black Workers and the New Unions,* 31.

28. Ibid., 33; Charles R. Walker, *Steel: The Diary of a Furnace Worker* (Boston: Atlantic Monthly Press, 1922), 47-48, 130-31.

29. Ira De A. Reid, *Social Conditions of the Negro in the Hill District of Pittsburgh* (Pittsburgh: General Committee on the Hill Survey, 1930), 53-54; John T. Clark, "The Migrant in Pittsburgh," *Opportunity* 1 (Oct. 1923), 305.

30. Reid, "Negro in the Major Industries," 15.

31. Interview: Wesley M., Apr. 2, 1976; Cayton and Mitchell, *Black Workers and the New Unions,* 34; Bodnar, Simon, and Weber, *Lives of Their Own,* 239.

32. Interviews: Richard C., Aug. 8, 1974, Walter H., Oct. 25, 30, 1973, Jerome G., Aug. 1, 1974.

33. Reid, "Negro in the Major Industries," 16-17; Byers Company Personnel File; Epstein, *Negro Migrant in Pittsburgh*, 31.

34. Reid, "Negro in the Major Industries," 16.

35. Ibid., 18, 36-37; Wright, *Negro in Pennsylvania*, 75-76; Tucker, "Negroes of Pittsburgh," 429, 431.

36. Minutes, Industrial Welfare Workers' meeting, Jan. 22, 1921, ULP Records; Clark, "Negro in Steel" (1926), 87; minutes, Corporation Training meeting.

37. *Fourteenth Census*, 4: 1197-98; *Fifteenth Census*, 4: 1416.

38. Pennsylvania Department of Internal Affairs, *Report on the Productive Industries . . . 1920* (Harrisburgh, 1921), 556; *Report on the Productive Industries . . . 1921* (Harrisburg, 1922), 634; *Report on the Productive Industries . . . 1924* (Harrisburg, 1925), 126; *Report on the Productive Industries . . . 1925* (Harrisburg, 1926), 534.

39. John T. Clark, "Industrial Problems in Cities. Pittsburgh," *Opportunity* 4 (Feb. 1926), 69.

40. A. C. Thayer to Mrs. Pauline Washington, Mar. 13, 1929, ULP Records.

41. Reid, *Social Conditions*, 14n, 55.

42. A shorthand measurement of the difference in occupational structure between black and white workers is the index of occupational differences: the higher the index number, the greater the difference in structures; the lower the number, the smaller the difference. The index of black women's occupational differentiation from white women's in Pittsburgh went from 46 in 1910 to 61 in 1920, then to 62 in 1930. The index for black men, on the other hand, went from 40 in 1910 to 21 in 1920 and to 29 in 1930. Data for these measurements are from: *Thirteenth Census*, 4:591-92; *Fourteenth Census*, 4:1206; *Fifteenth Census*, 5:1418. See also Jack P. Gibbs, "Occupational Differentiation of Negroes and Whites in the United States," *Social Forces* 44 (Dec. 1965), 161.

43. *Thirteenth Census*, 4: 591-92; *Fourteenth Census*, 4:1206; *Fifteenth Census*, 5:1418.

44. J. A. Hill, *Women in Gainful Occupations, 1870 to 1920*, monograph no. 9 (Washington: U.S. Census Bureau, 1929), 10-11.

45. Elizabeth Butler, *Women and the Trades*, The Pittsburgh Survey, ed. Paul U. Kellogg (New York: Charities Publication Committee, 1909), 17-20.

46. U.S. Department of Labor, Women's Bureau, *Negro Women in Industry* (Washington: Government Printing Office, 1922), 10; Maurine W. Greenwald, *Women, War, and Work: The Impact of World War I on Women Workers in the United States* (Westport: Greenwood Press, 1980), 22-27.

47. Reports of the Women's Employment Secretary, Jan., Mar. 1919, ULP Records.

48. Report of the Women's Employment Secretary, Mar. 1919; T. J. Gillespie to John T. Clark, Nov. 7, 1918, Industrial Relations File, ULP Records.

49. Greenwald, *Women, War, and Work,* 27-31.

50. Reports of the Women's Employment Secretary, Nov., Dec. 1918, Jan., Mar. 1919.

51. Typescript, "Newark Conference," in Continuation Committee file 1920, ULP Records.

52. Report of Women's Employment Secretary, Dec. 1919.

53. Harris, "New Negro Worker," 58.

54. Richard Edwards, *Contested Terrain: The Transformation of the Workplace in the Twentieth Century* (New York: Basic Books, 1979), 167-70.

55. David Montgomery, "Common Labor in America" (unpublished paper in my possession), 12, 13; James R. Green, *The World of the Worker: Labor in Twentieth Century America* (New York: Hill and Wang, 1980), 3-31.

56. Pennsylvania Temporary Commission on Conditions of the Urban Colored Population, *Report* (Harrisburg, 1943), Table XXVII, 471; Joyce S. Peterson, "Black Automobile Workers in Detroit, 1910-1930," *Journal of Negro History* 44 (Summer 1979), 179; Gilbert Osofsky, *Harlem: The Making of a Ghetto* (New York: Harper & Row, 1963), 136-37; St. Clair Drake and Horace R. Cayton, *Black Metropolis* (New York: Harcourt, Brace, 1945), 112; William V. Kelly, "Where St. Louis Negroes Work," *Opportunity* 5 (Apr. 1927), 116.

57. Clark, "The Negro in Steel" (1924), 300; Reid, "Negro in the Major Industries," 15; Harris, "New Negro Worker," 51.

58. Niles Carpenter, "Negro in Industry," in Charles S. Johnson, *The Negro in American Civilization* (New York: Holt, 1930), 391-94.

59. Walter F. White, "The Success of Negro Migration," *Crisis* 19 (Jan. 1920), 112-15; Emmett J. Scott, *Negro Migration during the War* (New York: Oxford University Press, 1920), 124-25; memorandum, Mar. 8, 1926, Karl F. Phillips to U.S. secretary of labor, U.S. Employment Service, Record Group 183, National Archives and Records Administration. For a dissent from the generally optimistic views, see Kelly Miller, "The Negro as a Workingman," *American Mercury* 6 (Nov. 1925), 310-13.

Picking cotton, circa 1921. National Archives, 83-ML-93

Negro community house, Homestead, Pennsylvania, circa 1918. Urban
League of Pittsburgh Records

Office of Negro Welfare Work, Homestead, Pennsylvania, May 1918.
Urban League of Pittsburgh Records

Negro bunkhouse, Carnegie Steel Company, Pennsylvania, circa 1918.
Urban League of Pittsburgh Records

West Carson Street construction, Pittsburgh, August 1919. Carnegie Library of Pittsburgh, P-5566

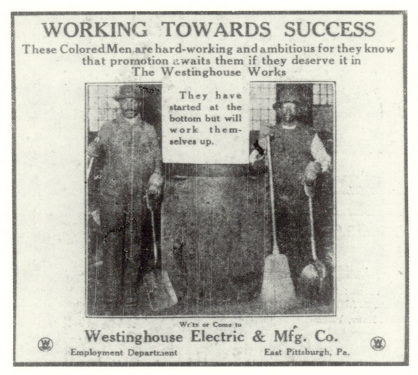

Advertisement for black workers. Pittsburgh *Courier*, June 16, 1923

Tapping a blast furnace, Pittsburgh, July 1938. Arthur Rothstein, Library of Congress, 26562-D

Annual picnic sponsored by Carnegie Steel Company, Duquesne, Pennsylvania. Urban League of Pittsburgh Records

Black women in packing room of Pittsburgh department store, circa 1918. National Board of YWCA Archives

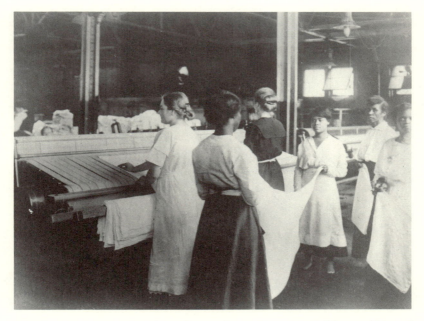

Black and white women laundry workers, circa 1918. National Board YWCA Archives

Black migrant housewives of the Lawrenceville Community Uplift
Club; the home economics worker of the Urban League of Pittsburgh
is in the front row, far left. John T. Writt, Jr., Urban League of
Pittsburgh Records

Wooden tenements in the Hill District, 1914. City Photographer
Collection, Archives of Industrial Society, University of Pittsburgh

Wylie Avenue (Hill District), looking west, April 1930. City Photographer Collection, Archives of Industrial Society, University of Pittsburgh

5

Working in the Mills

SOUTHERN MIGRATION and the transformation of Pittsburgh's black working class involved more than the simple quantitative increase in black industrial employees and more, too, than the changed status of black wage earners in the city's work force. The formation of a southern-born, unskilled majority in Pittsburgh's black proletariat was equally a process of cultural change, whose epicenter lay in the iron and steel mills that recruited most of the black migrants. Thousands of southern black men entering Pittsburgh's basic industry brought with them habits of work and job goals rooted in tenant farming, southern wage labor, and the experience of northward migration. Their customary habits and perceptions of labor were challenged by industries' well-developed policies on personnel administration, shop floor supervision, and work incentives for their employees. The migrants' employers tried to stabilize the new black workers, but as long as demand for labor was relatively strong and black mobility correspondingly high, the efforts at reform fell short of their goal. Until the late 1920s the mills and factories of the Pittsburgh area provided a fertile medium for migrants' work culture to take root and flourish.

Whether in agriculture or industry, the work pattern of rural blacks was characterized by unskilled gang labor, alternating periods of hard effort and relaxation, and geographic mobility. Though different in many respects from industrial labor in Pittsburgh, this work pattern was a surprisingly adequate preparation for the kind of jobs southern blacks got in steel mills. The work pattern in southern agriculture involved much farming knowledge but little technique or skill, except perhaps in plowing or in ancillary activities like barn-raising or black-smithing. Fieldwork in cotton growing was essentially common labor, often done by small groups in bursts of intense exertion followed by weeks of rest. Tenants who worked feverishly for six or eight weeks during harvests or during chopping and thinning season anticipated an imminent release from the pressure to insure a good crop. This short-term commitment to fieldwork was paralleled by the brief residence of many rural blacks on any one tenant farm and by their largely seasonal participation in wage labor at the work camps or industries of their locality.

Wage-paying jobs for rural blacks also provided a transition from farming to industrial labor. Among the southern industries that attracted a significant number of rural black seasonal employees, the logging and lumber industry was one of the largest. It had come to the South in the late nineteenth century to harvest the pine and hardwood forests that had remained largely untouched. In production units large and small, gangs of men toiled at felling trees, hauling them to sawmills, sawing them into boards, and shipping the finished products to wholesale customers. The small lumbering operations, called "peckerwood" or "coffee pot" mills, employed some southern blacks who later moved to Pittsburgh, initiating them to the demands of semi-industrial labor.[1] The black sawmill workers did the heavy, unskilled work in the labor gangs, moving cut tree trunks onto sawing benches, carrying off sawed lumber to be stacked, and piling brush and branches onto heaps to be burned. One Pittsburgh migrant described his sawmill work as simply revolving logs ninety degrees so that a buzz saw could remove bark from each side. Other migrants moved tree trunks to and from the saw.[2]

Though the turpentine fields of the South employed laborers year-round, rural blacks frequently sought seasonal or temporary work in them. Blacks were assigned to cut notches into the pine trees where the gum would collect. Others hauled large boxes from tree to tree, gathering the gum and then taking it to be poured into vats. The work itself was not intricate, but physically demanding. Brickyards, railroad tie-cutting camps, railroad track maintenance gangs, fertilizer factories, and the wharves of river and ocean ports also drew rural blacks seeking temporary work. Though labor routines might differ from one type of industry to another, the actual tasks in any migrant's nonfarm employment in the South — lifting, hauling, and piling — were essentially the same wherever he worked.[3]

Unskilled mill work in Pittsburgh offered the migrants substantially the same kind of tasks they had done on their nonfarm jobs in the South. In the gangs of a general labor department, southern blacks had no regular chores to perform each day. They worked wherever hands were needed, mostly on pick-and-shovel jobs, such as unloading materials for furnaces or cleaning up in various sections of the mill. Sometimes labor gangs spent much of their time outdoors, especially if they were generally responsible for maintenance and repairs. Labor gangs for a particular department of a steel mill had a slightly more specialized function. In the open hearth department, for example, the labor gang had to keep the area beneath the furnace spouts free of steel that had overflowed the ladles or ingot molds. Cleaning away spilled slag was also the work of the labor gang. Both tasks required the use of picks to loosen the hardened material and shovels to clean it off. Rebuilding a deteriorated furnace demanded the work of a labor gang in cleaning out the old refractory brick, assembling the new bricks and other construction materials, and helping in the heavier tasks of the rebuilding itself.[4]

This type of work was the mode in which a majority of the black migrants labored when first employed in the mill. Whether in the general labor department or the open hearth gangs, in blast furnaces or rolling mill crews, heavy toil and group effort characterized the working conditions. But the new black workers might also do other jobs. Just above the labor gang's level were work crews in which a finer division of labor coordinated the members' efforts. In front of the open hearth furnaces a group of workers tended to the "cooking" of steel. These men watched the metal's progress and the condition of the furnace, tested the steel, added necessary ingredients to the molten metal when called for, and relined the furnace after a "heat" had been emptied into the ladle. These tasks fell to one or another of four men: three helpers and the melter foreman.[5] Each had to know just when to perform his particular job, for if he dawdled only a moment, the furnace could be damaged or a fellow worker injured by exposure to intense heat. But the work of the helpers involved no more actual skill than could be expected from a regular labor gang member. And at any time the migrant on a pick-and-shovel job could be called to the front of the furnace to substitute for an absent helper.

Drawing on their acquaintance with gang labor in the South, migrants adapted readily to the unskilled tasks in Pittsburgh mills. Southern blacks could apply their previous experience to other aspects of industrial employment as well. The rate at which mill laborers performed their jobs recalled the rhythms of both cotton field and work camp. Unlike the even, continuous tempo of assembly-line manufacture, the creation of steel moved in pulses of tremendous human exertion, followed by spaces of exhausted inactivity. Migrants to Pittsburgh who had alternated their annual seasons of intensive fieldwork with weeks of rest recognized this labor pattern. Lines of "black" employment in the South such as stevedoring, railroad construction, and lumbering had also attuned black migrants to the intermittent bursts of energy required during a shift in the steel mills.

Many migrant mill laborers, therefore, could soon swing their tools with veteran unskilled steelworkers. They were unlikely to misjudge the demands of a ten- or twelve-hour shift as less experienced recruits sometimes did. Though they had to learn the knack of particular tasks around the furnaces and rolls, their accustomed work pace meshed well with gang work in steel production. Only the more highly skilled occupations, to which very few black men—southern migrant or Pittsburgh-born—were ever promoted, required a different set of work habits.

If southern blacks' schooling in gang labor provided them with a comparatively easy passage from rural to industrial jobs, it could not smooth out many facets of the migrants' introduction to mill work. Inseparable from their tasks in the mills were the new supervisors and gang bosses, the thousands of immigrant and native-born steelworkers, and the steel companies' standards for job performance. Most shocking to many southern blacks were the physical surroundings: the sheer size, deafening noise, and unfamiliar juxtaposition of men and machines, particularly around open hearth furnaces and in rolling mills. Though not all of the new black workers found themselves in these departments of the mills, those who entered the cavernous furnace sheds and rolling shops discovered work places different from any they had previously seen.

Southern sawmills were usually in isolated locations, their work crews small, and the labor itself carried on either outdoors or in open-sided sheds. This semirural environment was certainly different from most northern factories and mills. Even further removed from modern industrial work sites were the remote turpentine camps, small outposts of stills, bunkhouses, and tool sheds in the midst of large pine forests. A fertilizer factory or steel fabricating plant provided a work milieu more similar to that awaiting the southerners in Pittsburgh industry: large-scale machine processes; greater numbers of workers; the indoor factory world, utterly separate from the outdoors. Migrants who worked in larger manufacturing industries on their way out of the South were better prepared for the surroundings of a Pittsburgh steel mill. But nothing short of the great steel works in Birmingham, Alabama, could have adequately prepared southern blacks for the sights and sounds of Pittsburgh's open hearth departments, blast furnaces, and rolling mills.

By the time migrants joined Pittsburgh's work force, the steelmaking processes of an earlier period, based on the knowledge and skills of craftsmen and their helpers, had been revolutionized by technological and managerial changes of the late nineteenth century. Not only had the need for master mechanics been reduced greatly, but machinery had also encroached on the ranks of unskilled laborers, replacing whole armies of toiling steelworkers at points where once great numbers of men had borne along the metal from one stage to the next in its transformation.[6]

When he walked onto the floor of an open hearth department, the newly hired southern black migrant might have suspected that he was the only person in the area, alone in the midst of gigantic automatic machines:

In the semi-darkness he can see the great ladle of molten iron, tilting gradually to discharge its contents into one of the furnaces. Somewhere in the gloom above is the little box where sits the operator of the overhead crane; he controls this tilting motion. Another furnace door slowly opens; the visitor has to be shown the door-boy, on the far side of the charging-floor, who has pulled the lever to make it open. The charging machine's arm fixes itself into the end of a buggy full of scrap iron, lifts off the buggy, pokes it into the furnace, and dumps it. Inside the machine, barely visible among the flashing switches, is the worker who controls the operation.[7]

Even southern blacks who had worked at other industrial trades gawked at the forces unleashed in a steel mill. Ben E. had worked in coal mines for several years when he got a mill job. "One thing that impressed me very much was to look at the steel, the iron. All that I had seen in previous years was all finished and hard and everything. To come [to Pittsburgh] and see it running like water—it was very amazing."[8] A place in which human beings were dwarfed by mechanical processes of such vast scope and sophistication undoubtedly took some getting used to. A character in black novelist William Attaway's *Blood on the Forge* expressed thoughts that might have occurred to many southerners on their first day of work: "The magnets, traveling cranes and steam shovels that do the loading and unloading—in a week they handle piles of stuff that would keep a crew of a thousand guys busy for months. That charger . . . it fills eight furnaces quicker than it takes the crews to make back or front wall. Them hoppers moving up the side of the blast— they fill it before a guy can get the sweat off his forehead. What does that make a man?"[9]

The gargantuan scale of operations produced a din that in itself could have disoriented men accustomed to smaller industrial units. The bedlam of a rolling mill, with its harsh clamor of rolls, screaming saws cutting through solid metal, and rumble of locomotives pulling freight, assaulted the ears on every side. Before the new employee became used to the noise level and the sequence in which machinery appeared out of the mill's dust-laden atmosphere to perform Herculean labors, more experienced workers were constantly warning him of the imminent danger lurking on every side. Alarming shouts rang in the air, adding to the confusion that engulfed the black recruit.[10] "Some places look like torment, or how they say it look," a Pittsburgh migrant wrote to his pastor in the South.[11]

The mills' strangeness to black migrants was often cited in explanations of the newcomers' transiency in the city and their high rates of job turnover. A press dispatch in September 1923 reported that southern blacks generally could not adapt "to the presence of machinery overhead . . . with the result that while large numbers have been attracted to the Pittsburgh area in the last few years by the prospect of high wages, they seldom remain long in the employ of the mills." Black industrial welfare workers employed by Pittsburgh area mills made a similar observation: "It was the impression that the noise and bustle of the modern steel mills contribute much toward Negro inefficiency."[12]

Southern blacks' transiency in Pittsburgh—one of the most noticeable results of the migrants' introduction to northern industry—was far more complex than such explanations would suggest. Though it sprang from sources unique to southern blacks, it merged with spiraling rates of turnover among American workers generally, especially during World War I. High levels of employment and a rapidly expanding economy always allowed wage earners to move freely from job to job, while declining employment reduced labor turnover.[13] Those workers with the highest rates of turnover were younger, recently hired, and assigned to unskilled, disagreeable work. These characteristics neatly described many southern black employees in Pittsburgh industries, as we have seen. In addition to such general factors, blacks' transiency also stemmed from their bad housing, their temporary work plans in Pittsburgh, and employers' discriminatory personnel policies. Some employers took blacks' rapid movement in and out of the mills as irrefutable evidence of their failure to adjust to northern industry. But transiency signaled in sometimes subtle ways the migrants' resistance to the methods by which industries sought to shape the new black work force.

There was a strong relationship between blacks' transiency in Pittsburgh and their employment patterns in the South. The

meaning of regular, year-round labor was foreign to most rural
southern blacks. Acquainted with the tasks of unskilled manual
labor, many were ignorant of industrial jobs as permanent occupations. Upon arrival in the city, the migrants' intention often
was to keep the comparatively high-paying jobs in Pittsburgh
mills only briefly. They did not regard their initial work assignments as the first level in an ascending line of jobs, leading to a
future of steady, secure employment. Neither did they immediately expect the Pittsburgh jobs to anchor them in the black
communities of the city. Their home, marriage, family, and
social status did not quickly begin to revolve around the livelihood flowing from the mills. For many black workers who had
just arrived in the city, future plans were oriented either to the
South or to goals that were not yet fixed.

Their mill supervisors saw them as unambitious and footloose,
but the new black workers were simply bringing to Pittsburgh
the objectives in wage labor that they had learned in the South.
The migrants, in fact, were anything but indifferent toward
their mill jobs. As their narratives about job hunting indicated,
they were intent on the short-term goals of drawing wages and
accumulating a cash reserve. But once these had been realized,
the mill job could be "jacked" and the wages spent in Pittsburgh,
in other northern cities, or in the South. Migrants formulated
their initial plans for Pittsburgh jobs from a simple principle
that a local Urban League official explained shortly after the
end of World War I: "to obtain all the money they could in as
short a time as possible."[14]

Pittsburgh mills and factories gave southern blacks few incentives to become long-term employees and in some ways actually
underwrote the migrants' job turnover. The hot, dangerous,
dead-end work most frequently given to new black workers was
not the sort of labor most men stuck to day in and day out, from
one year to the next. Hastily improvised bunkhouses in the
most dilapidated residential sections did not satisfy many men.
Heat, fumes, dust, and racial discrimination could be briefly
tolerated by those whose first goal was to accumulate cash, but
men who sought rewards commensurate with their effort in the
furnace shops and rolling mills spurned such employment to
try their luck elsewhere.

Pittsburgh industries were also implicated in black transiency by their methods of paying new workers. Employers realized that some migrants had fallen deeply into debt before they received their first wages. Some owed money for the cost of transportation from the South to Pittsburgh and for boarding-house lodging that companies arranged for them. Since these charges were deducted from the migrants' semimonthly pay envelopes, black workers were often left with too little money for necessary or incidental expenses during their first weeks on the job. Other men simply arrived in Pittsburgh or in one of the nearby steel towns having exhausted their savings on the trip north. In order to support many of the penniless newcomers, firms instituted frequent wage disbursements and loan programs. These methods of advancing pay varied from one company to another. At the Westinghouse Electric and Manufacturing Company and the A. M. Byers Company, the pay offices loaned money to employees.[15] While the provisions of this type of program are not well documented, migrants presumably had to repay the money on a schedule set by the companies. Other firms, including the giant Carnegie Steel Company mill in Homestead, designated a day during each pay period when the migrants could draw wages earned up to that time. "Drag day" was the term southern blacks used to refer to this interim distribution of wages.[16] These liberal pay practices made it easier for black migrants to fulfill their customary short-term objectives for wage labor and escape the onerous mill jobs. Having worked in some cases for only a few days, they could quit work and leave Pittsburgh with cash in their pockets.

The Homestead mill tried to keep its drag day from increasing black job turnover and transiency. By immediately filling the position of any employee who drew all his wages before quitting, it sought to discourage the plans of cash-hungry transients. The man who quit had to take his chances of getting hired again at the mill when (and if) he returned to Homestead. On the other hand, the worker who left some of his earnings with the payroll department during an absence could return within a specified period of time and reclaim his mill job.[17] But both the penalty and the incentive were meaningless for black migrants who did not intend to work in the mills for half a year, much less the rest of their lives. "We couldn't see it," said Joe G., a South Carolina migrant to Homestead. " . . . the boss and all of them would tell us, 'Leave one pay in the mill, so when you come back you won't lose no time . . . [but] every year I would get my money and go home.'"18

Under the exigencies of temporary migration, drag day became the migrants' payday. Many southern blacks working in the mills looked forward to drawing their earnings and quitting their jobs for a while to return to southern homes or to travel about the North visiting friends and relatives or just seeing the sights. Many also used their cash to enjoy a period of rest in Pittsburgh and the mill towns, lounging with other relaxing steelworkers until they felt like returning to work. For the employers, drag day represented, first, the tenuous control they could exert over black migrants and, second, the crisis to which steel companies had contributed through their own policies. For as long as demand for unskilled labor remained buoyant, southern blacks could work when they pleased and lay off when it suited them.

The influences of frequent wage payments, heavy labor, and the migrants' short-term work goals sent turnover rates among blacks soaring. Among a sample of southern blacks who did stints at the Byers iron mill, the average total number of days migrants were on the company payroll was 318. This number included the time spent in up to four different job assignments at the mill. For the great majority of migrants at Byers who had no more than four assignments, the actual length of employment was three months or less. One-fourth of the migrants in the sample stayed at their jobs no longer than a week, while a roughly equal proportion accumulated more than one year's employment at the company (table 7). In 1918, when the Byers Company employed an average of approximately 150 southern blacks, the turnover rate among the migrants was 185 percent. In 1923 the Byers Company had to make 1,408 separate hirings of black migrants to maintain an average southern black work force of 228. In the same year the migrants working at Byers made a total of 436 separate departures from the company. The rates of hiring and separation together produced a

Table 7

Duration of Black Migrants' Employment
at the A.M. Byers Company, 1916–30

Duration	Percentage
One day to one week	25.7
One to two weeks	9.9
Two weeks to one month	11.3
One to three months	18.2
Three to six months	6.6
Six months to one year	1.2
One to two years	12.2
Two years or more	14.9
	100.0
	(N = 665)

Source: A. M. Byers Personnel File, Archives
of Industrial Society, Hillman Library, University of Pittsburgh.

turnover rate among southern blacks at Byers in 1923 of 1,068 percent.[19]

While industrial spokesmen fumed over black workers' penchant for rapidly quitting their new positions, there were few comparisons of white and black turnover to show which group was more mobile. "When times are good Negroes are not so dependable as whites. Too much pay day lay off," was the remark from the Pittsburgh Steel Company. The Standard Steel Car Company agreed: "Turnover is too high to depend on the Negro for a permanent labor force."[20] One manager who complained about blacks' interest in quickly drawing out their earnings admitted that their turnover was no higher than white workers'. Black and white transience in the work place tended to equalize where blacks were least discriminated against in company benefit programs, wages, and opportunities for job advancement. Conversely, turnover rates diverged most sharply where the two races received markedly different treatment, especially in the quality of company housing and in treatment by foremen.[21]

Employers, supervisors, and investigators of the migration in Pittsburgh more frequently compared the southern blacks to each other than to white workers, blaming the young, unmarried men for most of the transience. Abraham Epstein found that in the migrants' extremely volatile movements among Pittsburgh firms during World War I, the married men stayed longer in the city than single men.[22] References to the transient element among Pittsburgh's migrants usually contrasted this group with older, married, more ambitious men on whom employers could count for steady work.[23] While social workers and industrialists frequently berated the mobile young migrants themselves for their freebooting style, others laid the blame for black transiency on the labor agents who recruited men from the South indiscriminately, sending north large numbers of idly curious, drifting workers.[24]

Young, single migrants at the Byers mill bore out these criticisms, although older, married migrants in the mill looked steady only by comparison to their junior counterparts. Southern blacks at Byers tended to work longer the older they were when hired. But single men left Byers before married men of the same age group. And married men with children had the longest tenure at the company among all southern blacks. Those between the ages of sixteen and twenty-five had an average length of employment of approximately nine months. The heads of families in that age group worked for an average closer to eleven months.[25]

Supervisors' opinions on how to handle the young, unattached migrants varied from providing off-hours recreation opportunities to weeding them out of their personnel altogether. A widespread notion was that careful selection of black migrants in the employment process could separate the floaters from the earnest family men and allow for the development of a less transient black work force from the ground up. Careful screening of new employees was impossible in the boom periods when mills and factories competed fiercely with each other for black workers. But some employers claimed that they took advantage of depressions and migrants' intermittent vacations to examine individual work records and rehire only the men who had already performed well on their jobs.[26]

Conscious selection of "good" workers and reviews of blacks' job performances were only two steps within a general campaign among industrial firms to reform their black migrant employees. A trade journal pointed to the need for such a campaign in 1923: "The negro is going through a process of 'industrial assimilation.' He could not be expected to make a first-class factory hand within a few weeks of his removal from the cotton fields of the South."27 The migrants' transiency and job turnover reached levels that employers could not countenance, though they probably would have been content with a certain amount of turnover among casual, unskilled laborers. But the volatility of blacks' movements in and out of the mills threatened the steelmakers' supply of common labor, and they began long before 1923 to try to keep a larger proportion of southern blacks from moving so freely.

The industrialists' efforts to reform southern black mill workers focused on the migrants' leisure rather than their work. Blacks' previous experience with gang labor and with pick-and-shovel tasks made them ideal recruits for the mill jobs to which they were assigned. Employers knew that job conditions contributed to blacks' turnover, but they saw the crux of the problem outside the mill gates. Here mill managers believed that black workers loafed when they should have been working, spent their earnings rather than saved them, and indulged tastes for fast living that were inimical to good work habits.

Pittsburgh and the outlying industrial towns offered migrants a rich variety of entertainments, occasions for informal socializing, and opportunities to spend their earnings as they pleased. Passing their free time in pool halls, boardinghouses, black-owned barbershops, or on street corners was a favorite leisure ritual. Others preferred attending dances, professional or amateur baseball games and boxing matches, movies, or musical shows. But even more objectionable to the employers were the haunts of many other young men: brothels, taverns, card and dice games, race tracks, and similar outposts of the "sporting life." These places attracted large numbers of migrants each payday. Mill managers fretted over the wages squandered, the fist and knife fights, and the nourishing of "vicious habits."28

To compete with the southern black workers' informal organization of their free time, many of the largest steel works in the Pittsburgh area created networks of company-sponsored social and recreational groups. Bands, glee clubs, athletic teams, and community centers were established between 1917 and 1921 under the direction of the mills' personnel departments. These groups were segregated and in most cases directed by a black "welfare" worker employed by the sponsoring company. Open to the members of the black communities generally, the organizations' primary purpose was to draw in the young black man working in the mills, detach him from the informal social life of the boardinghouse and street corner, and begin to anchor him in the city or the mill community.[29]

The black welfare workers were key figures in the company schemes for migrants' free time. Some served in a general capacity as interpreters of the employers' policies to the migrants, but most of them directed the organizations for black workers, did social work in the communities adjacent to the mills and factories, or helped to recruit black labor for their employers. Steel mills in Clairton and Braddock as well as the Pittsburgh Plate Glass factory at Ford City each had a black personnel officer directing community houses for black workers. The Carnegie Steel Company hired assistants to help their chief welfare workers at the Duquesne and Homestead mills. These men supervised community centers, health programs, reading rooms, bands, and athletic teams.[30]

The steel companies themselves seemed to depend on the welfare agents only as long as they were hiring large numbers of new black workers. Generally only the largest steel mills hired black personnel assistants during World War I. From four in May 1919, the number of black welfare workers increased to more than twelve at the peak of southern black migration in 1923. As of 1925, there were nine companies with blacks working in their personnel, safety, or welfare departments.[31]

The welfare worker's role in the campaign to reform migrants became pivotal whenever southern blacks suddenly massed at industrial plants and in adjacent neighborhoods where few blacks had ever been before. When Lockhart Iron and Steel Company expanded its black work force from ten to 160 during World War I and then to between 200 and 300 in 1923, it called on Lincoln University graduate W. P. Young to unravel the severe problems that resulted. Lockhart's mill was in the industrial suburb of McKees Rocks, whose native-born and immigrant townspeople recoiled from the sight of the black community that developed next to the mill between 1916 and 1925. Lockhart provided only crude bunkhouses for single male migrants and cramped apartments for black families. The company made no provisions for the new southern blacks' free time, letting them stand alone against the hostility meted out by local citizens, shopowners, and civic organizations. The black migrants responded to the inadequate arrangements at Lockhart by quickly quitting their jobs and moving away from McKees Rocks, seeking amusement in Pittsburgh, miles away, laying off frequently, and setting up card and dice games on paydays, which often led to arguments, violence, and injury.[32]

Young, whom Lockhart hired in 1918, had to attack the conditions along a wide front. He viewed the housing problem as the root of many other "disorders." "We are all agreed," Young wrote in 1924, "that the man long content with bunkhouse fare will only, in rare instances, prove the most desirable type of workman." Though he could not do away with Lockhart's bunkhouses, Young improved accommodations for single men by increasing privacy and upgrading washing facilities and maintenance. The bunkhouse gambling ended after a payday altercation led to a shooting death of one of the migrants. Additional apartments for families were built that offered more space than the original ones. With these changes providing a new foundation for southern migrants' employment at the company, Lockhart's black workers became, in Young's view, "a progressive little community," with a free laundry, store, recreation center, and church. Of the black population of approximately 400 in 1923, there were 101 children, nearly half of whom had been born in the apartments that Lockhart had built for the migrants.[33]

A crusading welfare worker like Young had to go beyond the little migrant settlement near his company's plant to deal with problems that arose in the larger community. Banks in McKees Rocks at first turned away blacks, alleging that the temporary workers withdrew money soon after depositing their earnings.

Police in the town bullied and harassed newcomers. Local magistrates treated them unfairly when they were brought into court.[34] In situations like these, the black welfare worker represented both his employer's interest in insuring basic services for black workers as well as the migrants' interest in obtaining fair treatment and a decent standard of living.

The black agents at other Pittsburgh firms carried out the more narrowly conceived task of bringing southern blacks' after-hours behavior into line with the employers' model of clean living. J. W. Knapp, the personnel director at Bethlehem Steel's Duquesne Works, spoke bluntly about the accomplishments made in this connection by the use of a black worker: "One of the many successful efforts has been the investigating of our men off duty, through the Welfare Worker. By this means we are able to catch up the loafer, thus ridding the community of undesirables. . . . Through our Welfare Worker, we were able also to trace out disorderly houses and close them up promptly."[35]

At Knapp's mill the company also hired a "very efficient" nurse, part of whose duties apparently was to visit the southern blacks' homes. The nurse found "several cases" of black men and women cohabiting. "Upon being notified of these discoveries we succeeded in rectifying these cases by insisting that the parties be legally married."[36] Other employers may not have chosen to enforce their own notions of morality in the black neighborhoods around their mills. But Bethlehem's policies revealed the close connections in managerial thought among work, leisure, family life, and the moral standards for a model employee.

Many factors were at play in the impact that employers' reform campaigns had on the migrants. Part of the employers' rationale in launching extensive programs for the black migrants was to retain precisely those black men who would otherwise have quit their jobs out of dissatisfaction with inadequate arrangements for their leisure time. The community centers, clubs, and athletic organizations were called into existence by the total lack of facilities for the incoming black workers and by the exclusion of newcomers from the services and programs for whites in Pittsburgh and the surrounding mill towns. We may assume that some of these migrants responded positively to the companies' efforts on their behalf.

Pittsburgh industrialists as well as the black social workers whom they employed appraised the results of these programs more often on the basis of changes in the migrants' turnover rates. At Lockhart Iron and Steel, Young claimed that his campaign for better housing and a higher moral tone cut job turnover from an average of 25 percent per month in 1918–19 to an average of around 8 percent per month in 1922–23. In the mid- to late 1920s similar reductions in turnover at several firms came about through the enrollment of black workers in company savings plans, stock option purchases, group insurance, and pension and relief funds. Ira Reid reported, "In plants where bonuses are paid, and pensions or insurance plans, and forms of stock purchase participation provided the turnover tends to be reduced and a stable class of workers provided. This is true among Negroes only when they have been made to realize the value of the pay received in other forms than wages. In the Standard plant [Standard Sanitary Manufacturing Company] it took two years for the plan of stock participation to 'get over' to the Negroes. In 1925 the employment office is using great precaution to keep the Negro workers from over subscribing." A dramatic drop in black turnover at the Westinghouse Electric and Manufacturing plant between 1923 and 1925 was ascribed to blacks' growing interest in that company's insurance plan. But none of these claims took into account other factors that might have reduced turnover, especially the drop in demand for black labor after 1923.[37]

Whatever influence employers' reform campaigns had among Pittsburgh's black migrants, they probably fell short of molding the new southern workers into steady, ambitious, thrifty industrial workers. In the first place, steel companies only instituted their reform programs when they were rapidly enlarging the number of migrant employees. The high demand for black labor was the very condition that made it possible for migrants to shift from job to job, drag on their pay, leave town, return later to Pittsburgh, and quickly get rehired. Steel companies also limited the authority of their black welfare workers and consequently curtailed their credibility and effectiveness among the migrants.[38] Finally, some black industrial workers simply

preferred leisure pursuits that surrounded them in the company of their own kind. Especially for the young, single men,
bunkhouse card games, dance hall recreation, poolroom banter,
and occasional binges were their chosen ways to release tensions and recover from hot, back-breaking work.

The migrant mill laborers' turnover rates, short work stints,
and leisure pursuits may have functioned in part as a form of
resistance to the employers' reform campaign. Such a possibility did not occur to supervisors, welfare agents, or social workers.
Though there is no direct evidence that this was the case, it is
highly likely that southern blacks rejected the attempt to mold
them into an elastic body of common labor that would expand
and contract quickly with industries' needs. Some did this
simply by persisting in their short-term approach to labor and
others by openly challenging the personnel policies and work
conditions in Pittsburgh firms. Most mill managers would have
described these men as incorrigible floaters or malcontents,
contrasting them with the steady, hard-working southern blacks
who settled quickly in the Pittsburgh area.[39] But such a dichot-
omy left no room for interpreting the migrants who rebelled
against their treatment at the hands of foremen and supervisors
and who rejected the mills' working conditions as well as the
efforts to eradicate their southern work culture.

Part of blacks' rebelliousness against industry personnel policies had as much to do with their experiences before arriving
in Pittsburgh as it did with their jobs in the North. From their
dealings with landlords, store owners, foremen, and public officials in the South, they expected exploitation at the hands of
northern employers. But they also came to Pittsburgh with a
heightened sense of their own rights and capabilities as free
workers. Referring to the migration during World War I, George
E. Haynes, an authority on black labor, said, "There was created
in the mind of Negro rural peasants and urban wage-earners a
new consciousness of the fact that they have the liberty and the
opportunity to move freely from place to place. The migration
. . . gave the rank and file the belief that they could move to
another part of the country and succeed in gaining a foothold in
its industrial life and activity."[40] If northward migration stimulated this collective frame of mind, it was further strengthened

by the wartime refrain of liberty, democracy, and individual
rights that affected the whole realm of labor-management
relations.[41] Black workers no less than white workers read into
these phrases a particular meaning for their own experiences
and race history.

Black migrants did not quietly accept discrimination in Pittsburgh mills and factories. In many cases industries' policies of
holding black workers within the unskilled ranks produced
confrontations between migrants and supervisors. When his
foreman selected another worker for a better job for which
John B. was the more qualified, John B. left his work station to
complain to a department supervisor. He succeeded in getting
the better job, but remained convinced years later that "they
would have twisted it around somehow if I hadn't acted up."[42]
At the Duquesne mill of the Bethlehem Steel Company, the
personnel director described a whole category of intransigent
black workers. "Our problem is with . . . [t]he one who can't get
along with his foreman. A shift to another foreman sometimes
satisfies him, or to another kind of work; then again it takes a
shift to another department to do it."[43]

Such skirmishing between migrants and supervisors over
matters of job assignment, pay, promotion, and working conditions probably went on constantly in the mills and factories of
the Pittsburgh area. Though few of the migrants who worked at
the A. M. Byers mill were fired, nearly half of those who were
discharged lost their positions through insubordination. Byers's
foremen recorded cryptic explanations for these firings. "Dis-
obeying foreman" was listed more frequently than any other
single reason for sacking a black migrant, but "refused to work,"
"discipline," and "friction with foreman" also spelled the end of
several migrants' jobs. The company discharged one migrant,
accusing him of the unforgivable sin—"wants to be foreman."[44]

The southern blacks who were fired from the Byers mill,
however, were only a small part of a larger group there that
rebelled. Many quit their jobs, refusing to work under conditions that they considered undesirable. Their objections to
their work described concisely the type of labor most often
assigned to black workers in Pittsburgh: "too heavy"; "too hot";
"too hard"; "not steady." Among the southern blacks voluntarily

leaving the Byers plant after their initial job assignment and giving specific reasons for their departures, 37 percent complained about their supervisors, working conditions, or other workers. Though their wages at Byers were likely much higher than those they had earned at industrial jobs in the South, some migrants even complained that they were too poorly paid for their work. Other migrants' discontent with their jobs was implied rather than stated when they claimed to be quitting the Byers mill for the sake of a "better job."[45]

It is this sort of evidence that suggests that southern blacks who were fired from Byers and from other mills and factories in Pittsburgh were not simply delinquent. The migrants' behavior at Byers also indicated that black transiency and job turnover involved more than their customary work pattern and their unfamiliarity with Pittsburgh jobs. Blacks' transiency also expressed for southern migrants what it did for many white workers as well: a refusal to accept certain jobs or to submit to employers' authority over those jobs.[46]

Reports from welfare workers at steel mills around the Pittsburgh area tended to substantiate the link between quitting jobs and rebellion. A welfare workers' discussion of blacks' anger at their treatment by white foremen recalled the insubordinate migrants who were fired by the Byers Company. "Negroes refuse to obey orders. This was interpreted to mean that the Negro understands English and when sworn at knows what the boss says . . . the Negro refuses to be yelled at."[47] Turnover among black mill workers often stemmed as much from their treatment at their jobs as from their disappointment with housing and recreation in Pittsburgh. "The strawbosses . . . are *responsible for much of the dissatisfaction and trouble with* Negro workmen. They are usually foreign and understand nothing but the work to be accomplished."[48] The Jones and Laughlin Steel Company's by-products plant tried an experiment in hiring southern whites as foremen over its black workers. The new foremen caused "a bad situation" in the plant by arbitrarily firing some of the 300 blacks working there and replacing them with white workers.[49]

The Jones and Laughlin Company may have miscalculated in its efforts to find proficient foremen for black migrants, but many other Pittsburgh employers failed to perceive the ways in which race relations in the South informed southern blacks' view of the treatment accorded them in steel mills. The black welfare workers asserted that "the Negroes are often sullen and sore at any rough action on the part of their white foremen because of their treatment for years in the South and their feeling of revenge has been pent up."[50] What was true of the relationships between employers and blacks generally was even more true of any question concerning the black workers' earnings. "In matters of wage agreements," wrote Dwight Farnham, the Chicago personnel manager, "it is particularly essential to avoid misunderstanding, as long and bitter experience has made the negro suspicious of the white man in financial matters. This is particularly true of the Southern negro."[51]

Whether because of their experience with white abuse and fraud in the South, or because they were determined to collect their earnings in cash as soon as they could, Pittsburgh migrants demonstrated an acute sensitivity to any hint of employer manipulation of their pay. Gilbert M. got his first Pittsburgh job in a wire mill. Unlike most Pittsburgh migrants, he worked at a piece-rate wage, operating a small machine. On his first day at work, clerks kept looking over his shoulder to record the amount he produced. "Everybody coming by me said: 'What does this job pay?' Timekeeper came by, he'd take my time. He said, 'How much does this job pay?' The foreman came by, he'd take my time. He said, 'How much does this job pay?' At three o'clock when we quit I came out and I said, 'Damn! I'm not gonna work at no job where I don't know how much I'm making. I've got a *little* bit of brains." He went straight to another steel works. Here he earned an hourly wage amounting to only half as much money per day as he might have made on the piece-rate job.[52]

Piece rates were advantageous for other migrants with temporary work goals, but these migrants could also react viscerally to any sign of their company changing the terms of their pay schemes. John T. had difficulty drawing his wages after he got a job at the Westinghouse plant in East Pittsburgh in 1924. He had earned far more than the average pay by putting in many hours of overtime, but the paymaster did not believe a new employee, let alone a black recruit, could have made so much. "One pay [day] I had $118.50. That was money then. They held it up; I had to go to the employment office to get my money. The next pay, the paymaster held it up again." John T. stormed down to the employment office and upbraided the paymaster. "I have stood here from seven in the morning to nine, ten at night! You were in bed sleepin'. I'm working for my money! Don't you play with my money or, man, you've done the wrong thing!"[53]

While not typical, vocal protests against discrimination by the articulate and aggressive migrant mill hands almost certainly expressed resentments that most of the southern blacks felt. Wesley M., who did not object when white workers were promoted in preference to him time and again, was perhaps closer to the average migrant employee. "There was nothing I could do!" he claimed, but he felt frustrated and angry.[54] Whether rebellious or resigned, southern blacks in Pittsburgh industry believed their treatment frequently unfair and harshly exploitative.

Collective, organized protest among black industrial workers in Pittsburgh cropped up less frequently than did individual defiance of authority. One instance of group protest concerned mistreatment of black workers within a single plant. C. A. Atkins, a steam pipefitter and graduate of Hampton Institute in Virginia, was among a group of black men who got jobs in 1918 at the Westinghouse Electric and Manufacturing Company. The employment office assigned them to the die casting department. But when the new employees showed up to work, the white workers confronted them with a petition signed by ten men. The petition stated that "if any Colored men were put regularly on the machines that the whole department would strike."[55] The foreman of the department persuaded Atkins and the other black workers to take temporary positions in the brass foundry, but instead of going to work there, the men went to the Urban League office in downtown Pittsburgh to register a complaint.[56] More ambitious was the meeting in August 1923 of black steel furnace workers. The men drew up a petition to the steel companies, asking them to discontinue the practice of putting blacks on the "hot" jobs during the summer, then replacing the black men with white workers when cooler weather came.[57]

These glimmerings of collective protest among black workers are too faint even to suggest more widespread group resistance that might have gone unrecorded. They show only that objections to discrimination and mistreatment by black workers assumed forms other than the resistance of individual employees. The occurrence of collective protest also challenged employers' beliefs in black migrants' preference for quitting jobs individually rather than organizing protest groups to amplify their complaints.

Viewed from another perspective, the kinds of confrontation we have described sprang from the process by which rural people entered American industry. Since the early nineteenth century, European and American-born men and women had left their traditional agricultural and handicraft pursuits to make livings in manufacturing towns and cities in the United States. Each wave of migration to the factories involved what historian Herbert G. Gutman has described as a transformation of the migrants' customary habits and rhythms of work. American businessmen imposed on successive groups of industrial recruits a new regimen of labor, the hallmarks of which were punctuality, sobriety, steadiness at work, and obedience to employers. The newcomers to industry often resisted these new codes of behavior and the subordination to authority that went with them.[58]

Southern blacks' movement into northern industry produced a variation on this pattern. On one side, black migrants faced a less severe challenge to their premigration way of life than did either artisans or immigrant laborers. Blacks were English-speaking Protestants whose familiarity with seasonal gang work and other forms of common labor ushered them with comparative ease into the labor force. On the other side, Pittsburgh migrants encountered both the hardships of unskilled mill labor and the efforts by employers to place strict and arbitrary limits on their job advancement. Unlike other newcomers to American industry, southern blacks could expect neither rising incomes, better jobs, nor greater respect from fellow workers in exchange for meeting the mills' standards.

If European immigrants and American artisans sometimes valued industrial work that allowed them skilled workers' prestige or preserved traditional family patterns, black migrants in Pittsburgh either had to fight against their occupational status in Pittsburgh or resign themselves to permanent poverty and insecurity. Northward migration strengthened blacks' historical resolve for equality, dignity, and prosperity. Thus, their response to their new industrial work experience was to demand to be hired at employment offices, to protest against discrimination in pay and promotion, and to grasp work opportunities wherever they could, including those provided by strikes of organized workers. But many migrants also shielded themselves from the demoralizing impact of low-paying, exhausting work by refusing to stay on their jobs for more than a short time. Pittsburgh migrants' temporary work pattern resembled both their own customary orientation to labor and many European immigrants' strategies to return to native villages with American cash after a brief stint in industry.[59]

The entry of preindustrial peoples to American factories involved the process of matching work aptitudes to the labor needs of particular industries, and here southern blacks' transiency may have been more than the perpetuation of old patterns of employment, protection against northern working conditions, or flouting of supervisors' reform programs. Just as European immigrants gravitated to localities whose industries required the proficiencies and skills they could offer, so southern rural blacks inclined toward certain lines of employment to which their accustomed work style was best suited.[60] In his contribution to Alain Locke's *The New Negro,* Charles S. Johnson wrote that Detroit, Chicago, and Pittsburgh each "draw different types of workers whose industrial habits are interlaced with correspondingly different cultural backgrounds. . . . The technical intricacy of the automobile industry . . . sifts out the heavy-handed worker who fits admirably into the economy of the steel industries, where 80 percent of the operations are unskilled. A temperamental equipment easily adapted to the knife-play and stench of killing and preserving cattle is not readily interchangeable either with the elaborated technique of the factory or the sheer muscle play and endurance required by the mill."[61] Where many Pittsburgh employers, journalists, and social workers perceived in blacks' transience only the abrasion between agricultural and industrial modes of labor, there may actually have been a degree of occupational selectivity.

Though we cannot test this formulation with evidence from only a single city and one type of industry, southern blacks' transiency in Pittsburgh was clearly a way of seeking certain jobs in preference to others. The southerner who first tried work in a Detroit foundry and tired of the rapid pace and dust might apply for an open hearth job in a Pittsburgh steel mill. Black coal miners in the same fashion could exchange their pit tools for the wheelbarrows and shovels of a Pittsburgh factory yard gang. The heat and fumes of forges, furnaces, and rolling mills could also propel other migrants to try cleaner and quieter domestic service jobs.[62] The significance of this experience with northern jobs was that it made the shaping of a black industrial working class a process that the migrants as well as the mill managers could manipulate. Like the Slavic, Italian, and Jewish immigrants to Pennsylvania from 1880 to 1920, southern blacks had at least a narrow range of occupations and migration destinations from which they could choose.[63] The migrants could not frequently ascend the steps of the skill and pay levels of heavy industry, but they could shift from one type of job or work environment to another within the common labor field. They could exert some control over their own adaptation to the northern urban jobs to the same degree that they could maneuver within this occupational niche.

It warps our understanding of southern blacks' experience to overestimate their ability to control their industrial destinies. But ignoring altogether Pittsburgh migrants' efforts to make mill work amenable to their culture produces an even more distorted view. Though southern blacks were the most exploited and oppressed working-class group in northern cities during the migration years, they possessed an approach to wage labor that reflected their experiences and objectives. These customs and attitudes allowed them to apply their own standards to their work experience. The black man in Chicago whom Farnham quoted spoke for thousands of southern industrial recruits when he told his disapproving supervisor: "If you doan' like de way a' wukhs, boss, you can jes' give me mah time!"[64]

NOTES

---

1. Nollie Hickman, *Mississippi Harvest: Lumbering in the Longleaf Pine Belt, 1840-1915* (University: University of Mississippi Press, 1962), 241-45; Vernon H. Jensen, *Lumber and Labor* (New York: Farrar and Rinehart, 1945), 77-78; T. J. Woofter, Jr., "Migration of Negroes from Georgia, 1916-1917," in U.S. Department of Labor, Division of Negro Economics, *Negro Migration in 1916-17* (Washington: Government Printing Office, 1919), 85; interviews: Wesley M., Apr. 2, 1976, Charner C., Feb. 21, 1976, Joseph G., Nov. 26, 1973, Ed R., June 10, 1976, Clarence M., Aug. 5, 1974, Caleb B., Apr. 9, 1976, Leroy M., July 9, 1974, Ben E., July 31, 1974, Walter H., Oct. 25, 30, 1973, Jean B., July 29, 1976.

2. Interviews: Charner C., Feb. 21, 1976, Walter H., Oct. 25, 30, 1973, Joseph G., Nov. 26, 1973.

3. Pete Daniel, *The Shadow of Slavery: Peonage in the South, 1901-1969* (Urbana: University of Illinois Press, 1972), 36-37; interviews: James S., June 7, 14, 1974, Richard C., Aug. 8, 1976, Gilbert M., Apr. 9, 1976, Lee T., May 26, 1976, Harvey C., Dec. 2, 1973, Jasper A., July 12, 1976, Lee C., June 9, 1976.

4. Charles R. Walker, *Steel: The Diary of a Furnace Worker* (Boston: Atlantic Monthly Press, 1922), 19-22, 47-48.

5. Ibid., 32-37, 65-68, 75; Whiting Williams, *What's on the Worker's Mind, by One Who Put on Overalls to Find Out* (New York: Charles Scribner's Sons, 1920), 34-35; J. M. Camp and C. B. Francis, *The Making, Shaping, and Treating of Steel* (Pittsburgh: Carnegie Steel, 1919), 314-32.

6. David Brody, *Steelworkers in America: The Non-Union Era* (Cambridge, Mass.: Harvard University Press, 1960), 9-17, 32; John A. Fitch, *The Steel Workers*, The Pittsburgh Survey, ed. Paul U. Kellogg (New York: Charities Publication Committee, 1910), 28-31, 40-43, 47-56; Katherine Stone, "The Origin of Job Structures in the Steel Industry," *Radical America* 7 (Nov.-Dec. 1973), 29-35.

7. Horace B. Davis, *Labor and Steel* (New York: International Publishers, 1933), 19.

8. Interview: Ben E., July 31, 1974.

9. William Attaway, *Blood on the Forge* (Garden City: Doubleday, Doran, 1941), 66.

10. Walker, *Steel*, 50-51.

11. Emmett Scott, comp., "Additional Letters of Negro Migrants, 1917-19," *Journal of Negro History* 4 (Oct. 1919), 460.

12. Associated Press dispatch, Sept. 13, 1923, quoted in Ira De A. Reid, "The Negro in the Major Industries and Building Trades of Pittsburgh" (M.A. thesis, University of Pittsburgh, 1925), 29; minutes, Industrial Welfare Workers' meeting, June 27 (1918?), Urban League

of Pittsburgh (ULP) Records, Archives of Industrial Society, Hillman Library, University of Pittsburgh.

13. Sumner H. Slichter, *The Turnover of Factory Labor* (New York: D. Appleton, 1921), 29–33, 43–84; Paul F. Brissenden and Emil Frankel, *Labor Turnover in Industry* (New York: Macmillan, 1922), 51–54.

14. Typescript, "Newark Conference," ULP Records.

15. Interview: Matthew J., May 28, 1976; A. M. Byers Company Personnel File, Archives of Industrial Society (hereafter cited as Byers Company Personnel File).

16. Interviews: Matthew J., May 28, 1976, Ernest F., Apr. 19, 1976; minutes of meeting, Pittsburgh Chapter of the National Association of Corporation Training, Unskilled Labor and Americanization Section, Feb. 2, 1922, National Urban League Records, Industrial Relations File, Series 4, Box 4, Library of Congress, Washington, D.C. (hereafter cited as Corporation Training meeting).

17. Interview: Gilbert M., Apr. 9, 1976.

18. Interview: Joseph G., Nov. 26, 1973; J. W. Knapp, "An Experiment with Negro Labor," *Opportunity* 1 (Feb. 1923), 20; Edward S. McClelland, "Negro Labor in the Westinghouse Electric and Manufacturing Corporation," ibid., 1 (Jan. 1923), 23.

19. Byers Company Personnel File.

20. Reid, "Negro in the Major Industries," 30–31.

21. Abram L. Harris, "The New Negro Worker in Pittsburgh" (M.A. thesis, University of Pittsburgh, 1924), 50–52; Reid, "Negro in the Major Industries," 21.

22. Abraham Epstein, *The Negro Migrant in Pittsburgh* (Pittsburgh: University of Pittsburgh, 1918), 10, 21.

23. "The Value and Trend of Welfare Work among Negroes in Industry," A. H. Wyman, National Urban League Papers, Industrial Relations File, Series 4, Library of Congress (hereafter cited as "Welfare Work among Negroes"); conference of Negro Industrial and Personnel Workers, Feb. 19–20 (1920?), ULP Records; John T. Clark, "The Negro in Steel," *Opportunity* 4 (Mar. 1926), 88.

24. Corporation Training meeting; Epstein, *Negro Migrant in Pittsburgh,* 21.

25. Byers Company Personnel File.

26. Reid, "Negro in the Major Industries," 23; Harris, "New Negro Worker," 50–52; L. W. Moffett, "Careful Selection of Negroes Urged," *Iron Age* 112 (Oct. 4, 1923), 892–93.

27. A. J. Hain, "Our Immigrant, the Negro," *Iron Trade Review* 73 (Sept. 1923), 731.

28. Knapp, "An Experiment," 20; Rob Ruck, "Black Sandlot Baseball: The Pittsburgh Crawfords," *Western Pennsylvania Historical Magazine* 66 (Jan. 1983), 59, 61–62; interviews: Joe G., Nov. 26, 1973, Wesley M., Apr. 2, 1976, Joseph M., Nov. 16, 1973.

29. Reid, "Negro in the Major Industries," 23–24; John T. Clark,

"The Negro in Steel," *Opportunity* 2 (Oct. 1924), 300–301; interviews: Charles B., July 16, 1976, Harvey C., Dec. 2, 1973.

30. Ruth Stevenson, "The Pittsburgh Urban League" (M.A. thesis, University of Pittsburgh, 1936), 56, 58–59.

31. Reid, "Negro in the Major Industries," 23; John T. Clark, "The Migrant in Pittsburgh," *Opportunity* 1 (Oct. 1923), 305.

32. W. P. Young, "The First Hundred Negro Workers," *Opportunity* 2 (Jan. 1924), 15–19. For additional biographical information on Young, see below, 195.

33. Ibid., 16.

34. Ibid., 18.

35. Knapp, "An Experiment," 19.

36. Ibid.

37. Young, "First Hundred Negro Workers," 17; Reid, "Negro in the Major Industries," 22–23; Clark, "Negro in Steel" (1924), 301.

38. See 192–93 herein.

39. Knapp, "An Experiment," 20; Clark, "Negro in Steel" (1926), 88; Corporation Training meeting; "Welfare Work among Negroes."

40. George E. Haynes, "Effect of War Conditions on Negro Labor," Academy of Political Science, *Proceedings* 8 (1918), 171.

41. Brody, *Steelworkers in America,* 187–98, 220–24, 234–36; Stanley Shapiro, "The Great War and Reform: Liberals and Labor, 1917–1919," *Labor History* 12 (Summer 1971), 333–35.

42. Interview: John B., Mar. 10, 1976.

43. Knapp, "An Experiment," 20.

44. Byers Company Personnel File.

45. Ibid.

46. David Montgomery, *Workers' Control in America* (New York: Cambridge University Press, 1979), 102–8.

47. Minutes, Industrial Welfare Workers' meeting, June 27 (1918?), ULP Records.

48. Minutes, Industrial Welfare Workers' meeting, May 23 (1918?), ULP Records.

49. Reid, "Negro in the Major Industries," 26, 28.

50. Minutes, Industrial Welfare Workers' meeting, June 27 (1918?), ULP Records.

51. Dwight Farnham, "Negroes a Source of Industrial Labor," *Industrial Management* 56 (Aug. 1918), 125.

52. Interview: Gilbert M., Apr. 9, 1976.

53. Interview: John T., Nov. 1, 23, 1973.

54. Interview: Wesley M., Apr. 2, 1976.

55. J. T. Clark to Mr. Wilson, May 10, 1918, ULP Records.

56. John C. Bowers to John T. Clark, May 14, 1918, ULP Records.

57. Clark, "Migrant in Pittsburgh," 305.

58. Herbert G. Gutman, *Work, Culture, and Society in Industrializ-*

ing America: Essays in American Working Class and Social History (New York: Knopf, 1976), 13-15, and *passim*.

59. John Bodnar, Roger Simon, and Michael P. Weber, *Lives of Their Own: Blacks, Italians and Poles in Pittsburgh, 1900-1960* (Urbana: University of Illinois Press, 1982), 122-24.

60. Frank Thistlethwaite, "Migration from Europe Overseas in the Nineteenth and Twentieth Centuries," in *Population Movements in Modern European History,* ed. Herbert Moller (New York: Macmillan, 1964), 73-92.

61. Charles S. Johnson, "The New Frontage on American Life," in *The New Negro,* ed. Alain Locke (New York: Albert and Charles Boni, 1925), 288.

62. Interviews: Ben E., July 31, 1974, Jasper A., July 12, 1976, Gilbert M., Apr. 9, 1976, Charner C., Feb. 21, 1976.

63. Caroline Golab, *Immigrant Destinations* (Philadelphia: Temple University Press, 1977), 30-34, 107-10.

64. Farnham, "Negroes a Source," 124.

6

Black Migrants and the Crisis of the Labor Movement

EVEN BEFORE the influx of southern migrants began during World War I, Pittsburgh trade unions and black workers had an antagonistic relationship. Most unions excluded blacks from membership on the basis of race and lack of skills, then attacked them for crossing union picket lines during strikes. But the migration from 1916 to 1930 broadened the conflict. On the one hand, unions trying to organize nonunion industries encountered thousands of southern blacks who had never before been involved in the labor movement. On the other hand, skilled blacks from the South in greater numbers than ever before sought to join racially exclusive craft unions in Pittsburgh. In earlier periods white and black workers had joined forces only sporadically in the South and hardly at all in the North.[1] The migration brought unorganized migrants onto the terrain that organized employees hoped to conquer.

More than the historical enmity between black and white workers, however, the timing of southern migrants' entry to Pittsburgh mills and mines made their industrial status an explosive issue. Titanic battles between organized workers and antiunion employers shook American society just as the new black workers were taking their places in the northern labor market. The American Federation of Labor (AFL), propelled by an increasingly discontented northern working class, assaulted the bastions of open shop industry in the early twentieth century and asserted new prerogatives in job control over trades that had already been unionized.[2] Struggles for supremacy between employers and unions in meatpacking plants, steel

146

mills, coal mines, machine shops, foundries, and on railroads drew the new black workers into the fray. Pittsburgh became the storm center in two major clashes: the 1919 steel strike and the 1925–28 coal strike. Mirroring developments in the nation at large, employers defeated organized labor in both strikes with the aid of black strikebreakers.

These episodes in Pittsburgh reinforced the existing attitudes of both white union members and employers toward southern blacks. Unionized employees came to regard migrants as almost congenitally antiunion, while employers embraced a racial stereotype that rendered southern blacks inherently more loyal to bosses than to other employees. Both views distorted the part blacks took in the major strikes, and neither reflected the migrants' actual motivations and values. Southern blacks sought new fields of industrial employment where they could earn livings and feared that unions of white workers would exclude them from northern jobs. But in most cases they also refused to strike a bargain of faithful obedience to industrialists in return for work opportunities. The migrants defined their advancement in opposition to both racially antagonistic union members and to paternalist, discriminatory corporations.

Skilled southern migrants faced a choice when they reached Pittsburgh: take nonunion jobs in their own trades or find a different line of work. Black building tradesmen were probably the largest group of migrants who could qualify for union membership. But with a few exceptions, most of the construction unions in the city formally or informally barred them from joining. The skilled black iron- and steelworkers, who had gotten their positions before the migration, were usually nonunion men, as were most of the black teamsters in Pittsburgh. Ironically, the racial exclusion of skilled blacks from the predominant craft unions left unskilled blacks in the construction industry as the largest bloc of black union members in the city.

Pittsburgh craft unions prevented blacks from joining their organizations through a variety of formal and informal means. Though few unions had constitutional provisions for excluding blacks, they could bar them by wording their initiation pledges to obligate new members not to work with blacks. Some craft organizations resorted to technicalities, such as scrutinizing a black applicant's admission test to find a minute flaw by which to reject the candidate. Others discouraged young blacks from seeking the apprenticeships that were necessary for union membership.[3] Ultimately, however, local unions of skilled whites counted on the firm resolve of their own members not to work with blacks as the best safeguard for racial exclusivity. The Bricklayers Union, for example, actually enrolled some black men, but then jeopardized their livelihoods. Antipathy toward black members and frequent refusals by white masons to work with blacks accomplished practically the same thing as an outright denial of admission would have. When the black union members were snubbed by white members at a work site, it was the black workers who were forced to quit the job.[4]

Decentralized authority within the AFL abetted the recalcitrance of member unions at the national, state, and local levels. The AFL itself prohibited the color bar in membership but could not enforce the policy on largely autonomous constituent unions. By the same token, national organizations, whether interested in enrolling black members or not, deferred to the sentiments of local branches. When thirty black plasterers in Pittsburgh applied for a separate local union charter to the Operative Plasterers' Association, the national officers explained that the existing (white) plasterers' local would have to approve the blacks' application first. This approval could not be obtained, despite a meeting between the white local's secretary and the group of black plasterers. The secretary later told an investigator that members of his local would "never consent to have colored people among them." The fear that blacks would work for lower, nonunion wages was an additional reason for not granting a charter for a black local. Asked why unionized black plasterers would accept nonunion pay, the secretary explained that no employer would hire a black plasterer if a white man were available at the same rates.[5]

Employers sometimes cynically used the racism of craft unions to exonerate themselves from charges of discrimination. In other cases, especially where highly skilled workers virtually controlled the production on a shop floor, adamant objections to the company hiring blacks left employers with no choice but to concede to the white men's demands or close down the plant. And if a manager still insisted on bringing blacks into a factory (in most cases for lack of any other labor supply), the white workers could employ other means of keeping the newcomers out. At a Pittsburgh glass plant in the winter of 1916-17, "the company attempted to use Negro labor . . . but the white workers 'ran them out' by swearing at them, calling them 'Nigger' and making conditions so unpleasant for them that they were forced to quit."[6]

The wartime federal policies favoring de facto recognition of AFL unions brought little benefit to black workers in Pittsburgh. Not a single black electrician belonged to the union of that trade in 1918. When black structural ironworkers got jobs building the Pennsylvania Chocolate Factory during World War I, the white ironworkers threatened to strike unless the black men left their jobs. The construction superintendent requested that the blacks be admitted to the union and allowed to stay. "They [union members] positively refused to consider these men. The heads of the local would not be prevailed upon to let these Negroes join the Union under any circumstance." The superintendent solved the problem by lowering one of the blacks to a position as common laborer and promoting the other to a foreman's job. Both of the black craftsmen continued doing the type of work they had before the white unionists' protest.[7]

Knowing that they would seldom get work at union rates even if they were admitted to a union, many black men finally gave up trying. They sacrificed dearly in terms of wages. A union electrician in Pittsburgh in 1925, for example, made $1.375 per hour, while nonunion electricians earned from $.50 to $1.25 per hour. Nonunion black latherers, plumbers, painters, and plasterers made even smaller wages relative to the union scales.[8] Two black painters from Georgia were denied admission to the Brotherhood of Painters in 1916. One found painting work at one-half the union scale, while the other had to take a laborer's job in a steel mill for $2.70 per ten-hour day, less than half the painters' union rate for eight hours.[9]

The arrival of some skilled southern blacks in Pittsburgh hardly altered most of the building trades' traditional opposition to black membership. Only the Carpenters Union felt compelled to ask the Pennsylvania Federation of Labor for a black organizer to help enroll some of the black carpenters coming into the city. Not only was their petition ignored, but also the Pittsburgh local itself did nothing to sign up some of the new black carpenters on its own. Other unions, such as the Bricklayers, Plumbers, Structural Iron Workers, and Electric Workers, effectively barred blacks by one means or another.[10]

Blacks in the building trades did have a home in the Pittsburgh labor movement if they were lathers, cement finishers, hoisting engineers, or hod carriers. The Lathers local 33 in Pittsburgh admitted blacks on the same basis as whites and accepted black apprentices as well, so long as the apprentices were related to union members. The Cement Finishers often accepted black members but during World War I denied admission to several, perhaps because two large construction firms in the Pittsburgh area refused to employ blacks on their projects. In the mid-1920s, however, one observer said of the Cement Finishers, "More harmony [between white and black members] seems to prevail here than in any other union."[11] The Hoisting Engineers Union accepted black members under the threat of a successful black organization in the same trade. From around 1900 to 1908 the black engineers had had their own organization, the National Association of Afro-American Steam and Gas Engineers and Skilled Laborers in America. It competed for jobs so actively with the white union that at last the black engineers were invited to join the white local. Few new blacks were admitted after 1908, however. Black hod carriers and unskilled construction workers also had united with their white counterparts in Pittsburgh to found the Hod Carriers, Building, and Common Laborers Union. In 1916 the union took in more than 150 southern blacks. By the mid-1920s it had about 350 black members and successfully withstood an attempt by the Pittsburgh Building Trades Employers' Association to cut the union's wage scale.[12]

The Hod Carriers stood apart in another sense from other building trades unions that accepted blacks. Originally formed to protect American workers from "cheaper" immigrant employees in the construction industry, the native-born members—black and white—formed separate locals from foreign members. In other organizations the currents of ethnic and racial identities more often grouped blacks together with European newcomers and preserved a separate branch for white Americans. The Cement Finishers was an organization comprised mostly of blacks and immigrants. On the other hand, the Plumbers Union local in Pittsburgh discriminated against foreigners and blacks with fine impartiality. Black and white hoisting engineers, united from 1908 through the World War I period, split again in the postwar years when about thirty white members, "victims of the racial propaganda of the period," seceded to form their own local.[13]

The barriers to black membership in nearly all of the unions in Pittsburgh served to reinforce blacks' belief in individual merit as the only just basis for employment. Southern blacks who had long tenure as members of building trades and railroad unions had faced growing hostility from white union members. In the early twentieth-century South whites stiffened their demand that employers dismiss the black workers and create more preserves for skilled whites. Southern migrants to Pittsburgh who had been thus deprived of lifelong occupations were naturally wary of organized labor in the North. Black workers who had been drawn into the interracial unions of the South around the turn of the century — the United Mine Workers, Brotherhood of Timber Workers, or New Orleans dock workers — sometimes had more favorable attitudes toward unions. But with the exception of coal miners few men from the southern regions or industries once controlled by interracial unions came to Pittsburgh.[14]

Black migrants in Pittsburgh who had no previous involvement with unions formed their opinions from the events that surrounded them in the North. They could only conclude that black progress and white unions did not mix. In 1912 an investigator found a general hostility to unions among Pittsburgh blacks, who blamed white organizations for keeping them out of highly paid crafts.[15] Racist sentiment among some Pittsburgh whites frustrated blacks' employment opportunities even when unions were not strong enough to do so. Blacks were hired as waiters during World War I when the Waiters' Union struck a Pittsburgh establishment. The black waiters lost their jobs when white diners refused to be served by blacks. Similarly, blacks who took the places of Kaufman Department Store drivers in 1916 found themselves the objects of white shoppers' anger. The white drivers had organized a union and demanded improvements in their work but had been locked out. Although at least half of the new black employees had performed well at their duties, the store manager yielded to a union campaign among Kaufman patrons and fired the recruits.[16]

The price that both black migrants and the labor movement in Pittsburgh had to pay for the failure to unite all workers showed up more clearly in the unions' campaigns involving unskilled black migrants. In the steel and coal strikes the migrants had a ready answer to union organizers who urged them to join organizations composed largely of white workers. Another side to the impediment for the labor movement represented by the unions' historical ban on black membership was the stifling of a black labor leadership in Pittsburgh. Such a cadre might have influenced unskilled black migrants during the great strikes. The few building trades unions that encouraged black participation were too clearly exceptions to the prevailing practice in the labor movement to provide either organizational models or a group of seasoned, active black leaders. Lacking any constructive models for participation in unions, the southern blacks in the steel mills and coal fields around Pittsburgh were exposed both to the blandishments of staunchly antiunion employers and to the bitter hostility of white unionists.

Southern blacks' rapid entry to Pittsburgh industries from 1916 to 1918 and the tensions between black and white union members in the crafts organizations set the stage for the post–World War I strikes in western Pennsylvania. Racial antagonism in the steel industry, in fact, went back as far as the industry's labor organizations themselves. When three craft unions combined in 1876 to form the Amalgamated Association of Iron, Steel, and Tin Workers, they carried into the new organization established policies excluding black workers. From 1876 to 1881 the Amalgamated Association refused to invite blacks to join, partly because very few blacks worked in iron and steel plants in the North at that time. But northern steelmakers who wished to combat the Amalgamated Association noted the substantial number of blacks employed in southern mills, and from the late 1870s until the mid-1880s Pittsburgh employers capitalized on the craft and racial exclusiveness of the union by hiring southern black puddlers and rollers to take the places of white strikers. Though the black craftsmen did not always consent to break strikes in Pittsburgh, they frequently came to work when organized men had walked out, battering down union organizations.[17]

Not even the Amalgamated Association's decision in 1881 to admit black members reduced tensions between black and white steelworkers in Pittsburgh. The Garfield Lodge, a separate union local for black workers, was founded in 1887 but did not share the robust growth in numbers and power that the Amalgamated Association as a whole enjoyed in the 1880s and early 1890s. The black steelworkers seemed doubtful of white workers' sincerity in asking them to participate in the union.[18] Although some blacks crossed the Amalgamated Association's picket lines in the 1892 Homestead strike, their role in this signal defeat for the union paled in comparison to the Carnegie Company's use of detectives, U.S. troops, and transfers of work from the Homestead mill to neighboring plants that were not on strike.

A much more damaging blow to interracial unionism in the Pittsburgh steel industry came nine years later. Several black union members at the Butler Street mill of the Carnegie Steel Company came out on strike in 1901 in answer to the Amalgamated Association's strike call. Seeking work to sustain them during the walkout, three of these black unionists went to a neighboring town, accompanied by a white officer of the Butler Street mill's lodge, to get jobs at a unionized plant that was not involved in the strike. The white union men at this plant refused to work with the black men, despite the fact that they were all members of the same union. In disgust, the three black strikers went back to work at the Butler Street mill, becoming scabs for the duration of the strike and attracting back to the same mill other black employees who had joined the strike in sympathy with the union.[19] This dramatic breach of fundamental union teaching and practice remained foremost in black steelworkers' collective memory for many years, a reminder of white unionists' perfidy.

After 1901 the Amalgamated Association quickly lost its hold on the large, modernized steel mills of the Pittsburgh area. Its vacillating policies toward black steelworkers made little difference in its fortunes from then until 1918. Mill owners in and around the city became trail blazers in American industry's open shop drive of the early twentieth century. Using European immigrants for their common labor and native-born workers — white as well as a small number of blacks — for their skilled labor requirements, Pittsburgh employers no longer called for more southern blacks. Though prominent in the personnel of particular mills, black steelworkers in the Pittsburgh area in the first decade and a half of the twentieth century were not vital to the mills' policies of barring unions, providing company benefits to skilled workers, and stabilizing the shifting mass of unskilled foreigners.[20]

The same factors in the World War I period that attracted southern blacks to Pittsburgh also challenged the steel industry's domination of its workers. Spiraling labor demand and cessation of foreign immigration to the United States turned employers back to the South in search of a new source of labor. Urgent need for war supplies was transmitted to steelworkers in the form of orders for harder labor over longer hours. To internalize the demand for more work, steel companies used the same patriotic war spirit that employers in many other industries fostered. Steelworkers heard the message that the war for democracy depended most of all on their efforts. Their bosses urged them to subscribe to war bond drives, contribute to the Red Cross, and do everything they could to support the American war effort. Though they faced unremitting pressure in the mills for increased exertion and saw their real wages losing ground to rapid inflation, steelworkers generally responded positively to the new demands that the war placed on them.[21]

The war in Europe implied a new and different part in the steel industry for workers. The immigrant steelworkers took an especially deep draught of the prowar propaganda that justified their sacrifices in the name of defending democracy. When employers pointed out that the steelworkers' round-the-clock toil protected democratic rights for Europe's oppressed nations, the foreigners quickly accepted the idea but transformed its meaning to address their own situation. Once content to accept jobs on the steel companies' terms, the immigrant workers in Pittsburgh became increasingly restless. As the war drew to a close, they began to demand changes in their industrial status that would bring the democracy for which they had labored to their work places and redeem the economic sacrifices they had made. When a coalition of twenty-four trade unions launched a joint organizing drive in the fall of 1918 under a representative National Committee for Organizing Iron and Steel Workers, the foreign-born, unskilled mill workers quickly formed the backbone of the campaign.[22]

Though steelworkers of all nationalities and races in Johnstown, Pennsylvania, Wheeling, West Virginia, and Cleveland, Ohio, supported the National Committee, neither black nor white American steelworkers in Pittsburgh took much interest. The native-born white workers in Pittsburgh were uneasy at the sight of militant immigrant workers. Since the early years of the twentieth century, steel corporations had carefully nurtured a small group of skilled workers by granting them benefits not extended to lower ranks of workers. The employers' attempts to discredit the National Committee by accusing its leaders of radicalism—an effort loudly joined by the Pittsburgh newspapers and by antilabor citizens' and veterans' organizations—spoke to these skilled workers' fears of an uprising among the common laborers that would overturn their privileged status in the industry's work force.[23]

The black steelworkers in the Pittsburgh area were also immune to the unions' appeals. William Z. Foster, who assumed the position of head organizer for the National Committee, reported that generally the workers joined the organizing drive "from the bottom upward; that is, in response to the general appeals made to the men in the great mass meetings, ordinarily the first to join the unions were the unskilled, who are the workers with the least to lose, the most to gain, and consequently those most likely to take a chance."[24] But the black laborers in Pittsburgh mills were among the exceptions to this rule. They relied on the steel companies for jobs that paid well not only by the standards of their previous southern jobs, but also by comparison with other common labor positions in northern industry. The steel industry had brought some of them to the Pittsburgh area from the South and had readily hired thousands of others who reached the city on their own. Many of these newcomers depended on the mill jobs to fulfill temporary work goals. Such men, like thousands of young immigrants who came to Pittsburgh before them, did not want to become permanent steelworkers. Contrary to Foster's view, these unskilled workers had little reason to jeopardize their work goals in a strike for demands that would mostly benefit settled mill hands.[25]

Whether Pittsburgh residents or southern migrants, the black workers knew the troubled history of blacks in organized labor. The National Committee did too little to convince Pittsburgh's black steelworkers that the union campaign would depart significantly from the historic pattern. The Amalgamated Association, the most important union participating in the movement, persisted in its traditional insensitivity toward blacks in the steel industry. A union member from an Ohio lodge warned his brothers that employers would use black strikebreakers to combat the organized workers when they walked out of the mills. "Even now the tramp, tramp of the black man is heard as the exodus nears the turbulent clime of the North. A few short years ago the tramp, tramp was South by the white for the liberation of the slave. Now, the hordes of the blacks are on their way North for the enslavement of the whites. Ugh, this stinks, let's quit."[26] While Foster thought that black organizers should be used in the Pittsburgh area, Amalgamated Association representatives were lukewarm to the idea, and no blacks were ever hired on the union's staff. It was not until the strike was faltering that the National Committee formed a delegation to ask Samuel Gompers, president of the AFL, to discuss Negro "scabbery" with race leaders.[27]

Though the National Committee had not enrolled nearly enough steelworkers to form a strong organization when the strike began on September 22, 1919, the rank and file left the mills in numbers that surprised the organizers and shocked the employers. More than 300,000 struck on the first two days, and at the beginning of the walkout's second week, closer to 400,000 men had left their jobs.[28] More than one-quarter of the strikers were in the Pittsburgh area. Yet the strike began with uneven support in this heartland of the industry. U.S. Steel put up a stiff fight to maintain some of its operations in late September and October. The workers at Jones and Laughlin Steel Company, having lost a strike during World War I, joined the walkout reluctantly.[29] In Clairton, Monessen, and Donora — Monongahela Valley mill towns surrounded by coal fields and strong miner support for the steelworkers' movement — the strike began especially strongly.[30]

The steel companies pressured the strikers in every imaginable way, from outright physical harassment to subtler threats against their livelihoods. Deputized antistrike citizens thronged the Pittsburgh area, patrolling mill districts and keeping a sharp watch on the immigrants who, the newspapers warned, were ready at a moment's notice to begin a bloody insurrection. The Pennsylvania State Police as well as the employers' Coal and Iron Police also occupied the mill towns around the city. Wherever these mounted officers showed up to enforce the peace, they soon began arbitrarily arresting strikers and suspected strikers, breaking up union meetings, and driving organizers out of the area. Because the strike did not completely shut down the mills in and around Pittsburgh, the steel companies could shift work from crippled plants to other mills where nonstrikers kept furnaces and rolls running. The employers also attempted to assemble skeleton crews composed of supervisors and loyal workers who could, on an appointed day, enter closed mills to start up machinery as though the plant were resuming production. False reports fed to newspapers told strikers that their fellow unionists had given up and returned to their jobs, that the walkout had failed.[31]

The steel companies' tactics played on the divisions among the workers. The relatively few skilled white workers who joined the strike at its inception fell prey to the employers' bluffs and went back to work before other strikers.[32] Their desertion likely damaged the union, because skilled men's expertise in operating machines and controlling work flow only allowed Pittsburgh mills to make a better show of starting up operations in the teeth of the strike. In terms of absolute numbers, however, black steelworkers in Pittsburgh hurt the unions' chances for success even more than the skilled men did. Nearly all of the blacks already employed when the strike began remained at their jobs. New black workers entered the mills during the walkout, too. One observer estimated that 6,000 blacks poured into Pittsburgh area plants, some having been transported from the South, others arriving at the struck mills on their own. Another individual familiar with employers' strategy knew of 365 blacks recruited from Alabama, Kentucky, and Tennessee to work in Pittsburgh during the strike. Other black strike-breakers were hired off the streets of Pittsburgh, Baltimore, and other cities.[33]

Among the black migrants in Pittsburgh were two different types of strikebreakers. One resembled in age, family status, and work attitudes the younger immigrant steelworkers who also refused to support the strike. Strictly temporary employees, without conjugal families, eager for nearly any kind of work, this sort remained furthest from the organizing drive. The added income they could earn during the strike loomed much larger in their eyes than the possible gains union membership might eventually yield. Harvey C., a single man in his early twenties when he came to Homestead from Alabama, explained his actions during the strike in words that expressed the out-look of the entire group: "All we knew, we was gettin' a job. . . . I wanted to work; I didn't know what the strike was all about."[34]

Another type of black strikebreaker did not fit this mold. He tended to have several years' work and residence in the city behind him by 1919, a wife and children living with him, and a greater inclination to stay on a job than the temporary southern black workers. The black migrants at the A. M. Byers mill who worked during the strike represented this kind of strikebreaker. Most of them had come to the city in 1916 or 1917 and had been hired at the Byers mill before the strike began. They also put in more time with the company during their employment than did Byers's black migrants as a group. Like Joseph M. in Homestead, who had come to the Pittsburgh area in 1916 and had become a regular mill hand before the strike began, such men had shed at least some of the transiency characteristic of the earliest period of migrants' residence in Pittsburgh. They had learned mill work and skills of urban survival and had established some relationship with their white co-workers. Unlike the greenhorn migrants, they were not completely blind to the long-term advantages of unionism. Yet they refused to go out with their co-workers who joined the strike.[35]

Black strikebreakers benefited at most temporarily by working during the walkout. The black migrant strikebreakers at the Byers mill generally did get promoted by the company during or shortly after the strike. For example, one southerner who began his employment at Byers in 1918 rose during the strike from his job as a test helper to the position of a tester in the finishing department. The new job paid sixteen cents more per hour than his former job. This man stayed on at Byers for more than a decade. Another black strikebreaker got a promotion during the strike from an end dresser in the bending department to a bender's job. His hourly wage nearly doubled.[36] At other mills some blacks assumed semiskilled and even skilled positions formerly withheld from them. Carnegie Steel plants at Braddock, Homestead, and Monessen moved the strikebreakers to more skilled, better paid jobs to maintain production.[37]

With a few exceptions, the improvements that blacks realized through strikebreaking were both modest and short-term. These benefits may have been very attractive to workers who planned to stay in the mills only temporarily in any case, but they did not represent secure economic foundations for migrants who wanted to remain at their jobs indefinitely. Many strikebreakers quickly lost the preferred jobs after the strike. Some firms reassigned them to common labor and gave the semiskilled and skilled work to returning strikers.[38] The severe economic slump in 1920–21, which came on the heels of the steel strike, cut short the employment of other black strikebreakers. Though black men as a group may have strengthened their position in the work force by their actions during the strike, many of them got furloughed soon after the National Committee was defeated and did not regain Pittsburgh jobs until labor demand increased in 1922.[39] Their role as strikebreakers did less to guarantee their place in the industry's work force than did the postwar decline of European immigration.

The black workers who stayed in the mills during the 1919 strike paid a price for even the temporary economic gains they realized. Fearful of reprisals from striking workers, some took refuge within mill gates. Mills in Homestead, Braddock, and Monessen turned some of their facilities into sleeping quarters for the strikebreakers. In Homestead the men who remained at work could get a meal after their shift if they brought a plate and eating utensils to their jobs.[40] At Clairton the Carnegie Company fed strikebreakers by selling food at half price from a grocery and butcher shop in the mill.[41] Other blacks who crossed picket lines did not have a choice of where to eat or sleep. One black worker recruited in Baltimore was shipped to Monessen by rail without any information about the strike or the job awaiting him. When this young black arrived and found himself virtually locked in a mill that was surrounded by striking workers, he decided to quit. The company refused to let him leave, and he tried to escape several times before he finally succeeded.[42] While some of the men who kept working during the strike may have wanted to live as well as labor in the mills from fear of the strikers outside, the companies themselves probably wished to isolate nonstrikers from union supporters to prevent the union from trying to win converts among the strikebreakers.

Though the steel companies devised a way to seal some scabs from the union pickets, violence rippled across the Pittsburgh area during the strike. Local and state police clamped tight lids on the neighborhoods around the mills, scattering the smallest gatherings of men on streets and sidewalks, attacking union meetings, and even cracking the heads of strike sympathizers.[43] The strong support for the steel companies among blacks in the Pittsburgh area generally made them natural candidates for positions as sheriff's deputies—antiunionists who were enrolled by the local law enforcement agencies, then detailed to particular mills. The armed black deputies who guarded mill property clashed with strikers on more than one occasion. In Monessen white strikers complained that black deputies searched, punched, and knocked them down.[44] In Donora an argument between two strikers and four blacks quickly led to violence. One of the black men allegedly drew a gun and began shooting at the fleeing strikers, shouting, "Come on, boys, I'll kill every one of the white folks in Donora." The black assailants remained at large after this incident, and one report claimed that they were even deputized.[45] Confrontations between strikers and mill guards were not the only altercations during the strike. Fights between whites and blacks flared even inside the mills, where some of the strikebreakers stayed in close confinement for many days.[46]

The steel companies slowly gained ground against the striking workers. By appealing for public support against what they termed an attack by unpatriotic radicals, by keeping some mills running with both black and white American workers, and by ruthlessly suppressing civil rights in the mill towns and factory districts, the companies effectively broke the strike by mid-November 1919. In some steelmaking centers the strikers' ranks held until December, though in Pittsburgh, where the unions had failed to unite all workers in their campaign, the fight was over sooner. The National Committee did not concede defeat until January 1920, but knew the outcome weeks before.[47]

The repercussions of the steel strike on black workers were as important as the events of the organizing drive and the walkout themselves. Mill supervisors, who incessantly criticized southern migrants' work habits from 1916 to 1918, discovered during 1919 that black workers' indifference to unions made them assets to steel companies. The managers' new appraisal was often expressed in terms of the foreign-born steelworkers' rebellion as well as in terms of black mill hands' desirable qualities. Employers found the southern and eastern Europeans on whom they had relied for their source of unskilled labor before 1916 increasingly restless, ever more insistent on rewards for their wartime labor. The revolt of the unskilled, associated in managerial thinking with the revolutionary aspirations of industrial workers in postwar Europe, bred a distrust of immigrant laborers among American employers.

As the industrialists' regard for foreign-born workers sank, their opinion of black migrants rose. Employers grew more appreciative of the fact that southern blacks were native-born Americans who could speak English and understand the orders shouted at them on the furnace platforms, shop floors, and in the mines. Hoping to see behavior during World War I that would confirm their belief in southern blacks' innate faithfulness to employers, the steel companies seized on migrant strikebreaking as the long-awaited validation. Black "loyalty" assumed broader significance in the patriotic fervor of the postwar years and served to set them apart even more from the "un-American" immigrant strikers.

Between the steel strike and the mid-1920s, testimonies to blacks' value as essentially conservative, nonunion workers poured from company offices in Pittsburgh and in other industrial centers. In the early 1920s Abram Harris found one Pittsburgh employer who welcomed the restriction of foreign immigration. "This employer . . . held that his industry could get along very well without foreign labor in as much as it has learned to use the Negro who shows little susceptibility to radical doctrines and who because of his southern tutelage, is more amenable to discipline than the foreigner."[48] Said an official of the Pittsburgh Urban League in February 1922 about jobless blacks in the Hill District, "Although in desperate circumstances they are not given to radical or Bolshevistic attitudes, accepting their lot with an admirable fortitude."[49] Some Pittsburgh company spokesmen in the early 1920s tempered their criticism of blacks' transiency in view of the role they had played during the strike. A representative of the Pressed Steel Car Company in McKees Rocks said, "The Negro is more peaceful. He quits the job by himself which is not the case with the immigrants." The opinion of a supervisor at the Jones and Laughlin Steel Company's Soho plant was similar: "Negroes do more work and will quit the job orderly."[50]

While businessmen briefly smiled on the southern blacks, many white mill hands reviled them as company pawns. The immigrants probably agreed with the mill managers who said flatly, "The niggers did it" in explaining the companies' victory.[51] In Homestead relations between white and black steelworkers remained tense after the collapse of the strike. According to one migrant, whether at work or in the community "whites kept religiously away from blacks and blacks [kept] to themselves."[52]

Yet there was no explosion of racial violence in Pittsburgh during or after the strike. This was a remarkable contrast to the pitched battles between black and white workers that followed strikes in East St. Louis in 1917 and in Chicago in 1919. In both cities tensions surrounding union-organizing campaigns fed into competition between whites and blacks over housing and local politics. Southern black migrants remained aloof from the organizing drives that enrolled most of the whites. When the migrants undercut the unions by breaking strikes, whites vented their frustration on the local black communities in riots that continued for days. Both in East St. Louis and in Chicago blacks defended themselves against gangs of marauding whites, and bloody clashes resulted.[53]

One reason why large-scale racial violence did not follow the steel strike in Pittsburgh was the gulf between foreign-born strikers and native-born white strikebreakers. The immigrants faced hostility from American steelworkers, white as well as black. This ethnic division in the industry's work force prevented the emergence of a consolidated white community angrily facing a consolidated black community. Once the strike began, police and local officials with close ties to steel companies prevented union organizers from rallying the strikers behind the union cause. The immigrants had to use their nationality fraternal and benefit lodges as agencies of strike support and communication. But this was a turning inward to the protection of their own countrymen, a defensive reflex far different from the bristling reactions to the strikebreaking that assumed a perverted form in the Chicago and East St. Louis race riots.[54]

The proximity of black workers' living quarters to steel plants also reduced the likelihood of widespread racial violence. Each mill town spawned its own slum housing district close to the plant gates, though none was thoroughly segregated. In Chicago's meatpacking strike of 1919, black strikebreakers from the city's South Side ghetto lived some distance from the stockyards and had to walk to work through neighborhoods inhabited by striking white unionists. The social ecology of the area around the packing plants could not have been more conducive to black/white confrontation. Fought out in dozens of mill towns and factory districts, the steel strike in Pittsburgh was decentralized. Massive police intervention provided a buffer between strikebreakers and union supporters by keeping the approaches to the mills clear of picketing strikers.

Divisions of race and ethnicity among Pittsburgh mill workers did not originate in 1918–19, but the strike did much to strengthen them. Thus the most significant impact on blacks of the organizing drive and the walkout was the increased separation among the various groups that composed the work force. For more than a dozen years after steelworkers lost the strike, southern black migrants to Pittsburgh grappled with the hardships of northern industrial labor without any class organization to aid them. They sought to tread a path of advancement between white steelworkers and their employers. But the absence of an interracial union only served to stymie blacks' progress and prolong the primacy of the steel companies.

Unlike black workers in the steel industry, black coal miners in the Pittsburgh area in the 1920s had a long history of union membership and loyalty. Yet when coal operators in western Pennsylvania broke relations with the United Mine Workers (UMW) and tried to continue production with nonunion labor, some black union members joined southern migrants who fought with UMW pickets for the jobs that the strike opened to them. Though other black miners undoubtedly stuck to the union cause during the bitter dispute from 1925 to 1928, and though large numbers of white workers also crossed the picket lines, the black strikebreakers received more notoriety in the press and in investigations of strike conditions.

Ironically, the UMW, unlike other AFL organizations during the late nineteenth century, had organized black coal miners and supported them during strikes against coal operators. While craft unions in the AFL sought ways to restrict black membership, the UMW appointed black organizers. Union miners chose blacks to serve on their highest elected councils in the late nineteenth century. The UMW was one of the few unions after the decline of the Knights of Labor in the 1890s that carried on the Knights' policy of universal labor unity and solidarity.[55]

The UMW's commitment to the brotherhood of all mine workers was hardly consistent, however. White miners at times effectively barred blacks from employment at particular mines simply by refusing to work with them, a tactic widely practiced by racist craft workers. The union did little to erase the racial division of labor in coal mining, in which black miners most often got less skilled positions, while white miners jealously guarded their higher-paid jobs. A slowly progressing

mechanization of coal mining in the twentieth century widened
the racially split job hierarchy. White miners took most of the
machine operators' jobs, leaving lower-paid manual tasks to
black workers.[56]

The UMW faced black strikebreakers as well. In Illinois,
Ohio, and western Pennsylvania it battled antiunion mine operators and black scabs on many occasions between 1890 and
1898. In 1892 and again in 1895 Henry Clay Frick, the coal
operator and Carnegie business partner, bested the union in
western Pennsylvania's Connellsville coal field, partly with the
use of black strikebreakers. These conflicts ushered the first
significant numbers of black miners into the coal industry of
the area. Though the Frick Coal Company and the Hillman Coal
Company hired sizeable numbers of blacks at their mines,
other firms relied almost exclusively on white workers until the
mid-1920s.[57]

Black strikebreaking at western Pennsylvania mines continued into the twentieth century,[58] but attempts to undermine
the union declined with the formation in 1898 of a joint union-
coal operator board for negotiating wages and working conditions in the Central Competitive Field: western Pennsylvania,
Ohio, Indiana, and Illinois.[59] At about the same time black
miners began to join the UMW in Pennsylvania. There were
roughly 1,775 black miners in Pennsylvania in 1910 and 2,900
in 1920. The union's estimate of 3,000 black members in 1925
for the Pittsburgh area was probably about right. That figure
would have represented between 50 and 60 percent of all the
black miners working in western Pennsylvania when the strike
began.[60]

After the turn of the century, the union's long-term success
depended on the organization of the growing number of nonunion miners in the southern Appalachian region, many of whom
were black.[61] But the UMW failed to bring a significant proportion of southern coal under contract, though it tried continuously
from 1902 through World War I. Despite the threat of increasing competition from the cheaper, nonunion southern coal,
most northern operators in the early 1920s agreed to maintain
union wages at the high levels reached in the postwar years,
ratifying this policy in the Jacksonville Agreement of 1924.[62]

Disgruntled coal companies soon after the signing of this Jacksonville Agreement began to abrogate the new contract and seek ways to produce nonunion coal. The Pittsburgh Coal Company followed the lead of the neighboring West Virginia operators and shut down late in 1924. This company, the largest coal producer in the United States, had supported the collective bargaining system in the Central Competitive Field since its inception and had been a key party to the Jacksonville Agreement. But it abruptly turned about-face and decided to run its mines nonunion, whatever the inevitable confrontation with the union might cost.[63] In August 1925 the company resumed production without a union contract and with nonunion miners.

The demise of collective bargaining in the coal industry around Pittsburgh led to a dramatic growth in the number of black miners in the area. The largest number of blacks in western Pennsylvania mines before the strike was around 7,200 in 1922. But by 1927 there were around 10,000. The Pittsburgh Coal Company, with only 7 percent of its work force composed of blacks before the strike, used them for nearly 50 percent of its labor at eighteen mines during the walkout.[64] The increase in black coal miners after 1925 included both former UMW members who broke ranks with the union as well as black men from nonunion backgrounds. It is not certain in what proportions these two groups combined on the crews of strikebreakers, nor how many black union men stuck to the UMW's cause, stayed off their jobs for the duration of the strike, and tried to persuade black strikebreakers to join them.[65]

Though the Pittsburgh Coal Company accepted many white as well as black men to work nonunion from 1925 to 1927, the UMW called the public's attention primarily to the importation of black scabs. The UMW singled out especially the blacks who came to the Pittsburgh area mines from rural areas of the South. These strikebreakers, the union charged, were frequently criminals and drifters. They made clumsy and inefficient workers, far worse than the union coal diggers whose jobs they took in the Pittsburgh Coal Company mines.[66] The UMW blamed the Pittsburgh Coal Company both for using the black migrants to crush the union and for permitting them to live riotously in the mining communities where they were lodged. Yet the union also appealed to public opinion by using familiar racist language in referring to the black miners. Philip Murray, UMW vice-president, told U.S. Senators in 1928 that "the Pittsburgh Coal Co., in pursuance of its program to degrade wages, lower living standards, destroy the miners' union . . . maintain[s] within its camps bawdyhouses, where prostitutes of every known kind and description are brought in to supply the beastly appetite of the strike breakers." Murray sent an open letter to the Pittsburgh Council of the Churches of Christ in 1927, which recited the black strikebreakers' outrages against moral standards.

> White men and women and Negro men and women mix and mingle together. There are cases where white men live with Negro women and Negro men live with white women. . . . Men and women bootleggers carry liquor into the camps in suitcases and hatboxes. Dope peddlers do a thriving business among the Negroes. . . . At Essen mine, on Wednesday, March 16, a young colored woman, badly intoxicated, was seen on the highway openly soliciting boys of 15 and 16 years. . . . Many of [the] . . . imported men are of the type that would quit work if they were denied their liquor, their dope and their women.[67]

The union tried to thwart the Pittsburgh Coal Company's open shop policy through public relations tactics, by picketing, and by enrolling strikebreakers who had been hired by the company. Whether through persuasion or through threats of violence, UMW pickets turned away some blacks seeking work at the Banning No. 1 and 2 mines in 1925. When local magistrates in western Pennsylvania prohibited mass picketing, small numbers of striking miners tried to control the trolley car stops on the interurban lines. Here strikebreakers could be confronted before they reached mining companies' property and police outposts.[68] The union won new members among disillusioned scabs in 1926 and 1927. Black recruits signed union cards and swore to uphold union standards.[69]

The winning of some nonunion blacks to the union did not turn defeat into victory for the UMW, however. The Pittsburgh Coal Company raised wages for the miners in its nonunion operations to a level nearly equal that of the former union scale,

but there it drew a line. In February 1927 it issued a circular to
all the men working in its mines: "Don't believe any story that
this company is going to sign up with the union on April 1st or
any other time. . . . We will never sign a scale with any union
again. . . . The Pittsburgh Coal Company has now operated on
the open shop basis for over 18 months and will always operate
that way."[70] The company underlined its resolve by refusing to
participate in the half-hearted attempts by other coal operators
to renew the Central Competitive Field agreement with the
UMW in 1927.

When negotiations in 1927 failed to produce a new agreement,
many Pittsburgh area operators took their cue from the Pittsburgh Coal Company and simply closed their mines for a period
of time, then reopened as nonunion businesses. The UMW
went on strike on April 1 against these former union employers.
Though few operators had the resources of the Pittsburgh Coal
Company with which to attract strikebreakers and resume full
operations, some slowly took up the antiunion tactics first
tested in West Virginia and then carried to western Pennsylvania.
At first, the Pittsburgh Terminal Coal Company, with seven
mines running, had only a negligible proportion of blacks in its
work force. Within months, however, the same company had
nearly a thousand blacks employed at four of its mines, compos-
ing 42 percent of the employees. Other companies at the beginning of the strike kept their mines closed to await developments
and to watch how strongly the union could oppose the spread of
the open shop.[71]

The coal operators in western Pennsylvania tried to drown
the strike in the brimming pools of unemployed labor. Through
agencies in Pittsburgh and other cities, they easily found laid
off black workers to entice to their mines. James Smith, a black
steelworker who had worked in Homestead's steel mills, was
walking the streets of Pittsburgh looking for a job. "We was
passing by on Fourth Avenue in Pittsburgh . . . and we saw a
bunch standing in the office of the Wabash Building and we
stopped at the door. They wanted to know if we wanted work.
We said we did. They said for us to come and sign up. And we
said for what. And they said to go out to a coal mine." Like other
blacks recruited by coal operators to break the strike, Smith

never heard about the strike, the barracks, or the conditions in the mines until he reached the mining camp. Will Green came to Pittsburgh area mines from a steel mill job in Johnstown, Pennsylvania. "They said everything was in good shape; in good condition, no trouble was going on at all. The report that was told to me was that everything would be just as smooth and as easy and that we could get along. But when I got here . . . I found things a whole lot different from what I had heard." Smith and Green were two of the many black recruits who quickly left the strike region, contributing to astronomic turnover rates among the open shop work crews.[72]

Of the 173 strikebreaking black miners questioned in a local survey, none claimed to be experienced coal miners. Twenty-three called themselves "steelworkers," and forty-two others gave the names of steel mill positions in response to the question about their previous employment. Though the majority of the men interviewed originated in southern states, half of them came to the coal mines from Pittsburgh and West Virginia, indicating that the coal strike was not drawing exclusively on southern agricultural labor, but on southern-born blacks who already resided in northern states. Other strikebreakers, both black and white, came from Alabama and from Michigan, where the Ford Motor Company had swollen the list of jobless by laying off 60,000 employees during re-tooling for production of the Model A car.[73]

The coal operators' open shop regime degraded both striking miners and strikebreakers, especially black workers. In one mining camp, where the employer called the Coal and Iron Police to guard the property, the officers bribed black strikebreakers to fire guns into a school attended by the children of union miners.[74] The operators' hastily improvised housing for black miners made even the steel companies' 1919 lodgings inside their mills look luxurious. Poorly constructed, overcrowded, dark, and filthy, these segregated barracks clearly were intended for low-paid, untrained, temporary workers. The operators winked at gambling, prostitution, and moonshining in the blacks' quarters, but complained to one investigator that too much police protection for the strikebreakers was making their employment unprofitable.[75]

Blacks working in some mines confirmed the union's claim that inexperienced strikebreakers slowed coal production. Black recruits told an investigator that they were given no instruction by the coal companies. Managers, bookkeepers, firemen, and baggagemen got drunk and neglected their duties. The mine supervisors made strikebreakers perform more and more work without pay. As the "dead work" increased, the company checkweighman credited ever smaller tonnage to the black miners. In some mines coal could not be dug because the supplies of blasting powder, tools, and mine cars were unreliable. Equipment breakdowns led to additional reductions in production when spare parts could not be found. The Pittsburgh Coal Company's report that its total production had decreased since the beginning of its open shop regime could not have surprised either the striking union men or the strikebreakers.[76]

Black strikebreakers had more to contend with than mere disorganization underground. They fared poorly at the hands of both the union and the employers. Foremen at the Pittsburgh Coal Company responded slowly to black miners' requests to get track laid to their rooms and to clear blocked track. This foot-dragging reduced black miners' tonnage and, consequently, their pay. In November 1925 blacks complained that "white miners now are gradually being given the best rooms in the mines and any excuse they can find is sufficient to get Negroes out of the best places in the mines." New black miners took positions as "snappers" on the motorized cars that hauled coal to the surface. Though snappers customarily had the opportunity to move up to the highly paid motorman position, black snappers did not get this promotion during the strike. The tension between white strikers and black strikebreakers broke out in deadly encounters. Several black miners died after being beaten or shot as they went to and from the mines.[77]

Black strikebreakers got no better treatment from the police who patrolled the mining district. Orsie Thomas, a black miner at Moon Run, was caught by Coal and Iron Police on January 27, 1927, at the company store. The miner had not gone to work because he felt sick that day. The police at the company store demanded to know why he was not in the mines, then hit him after he had explained. Thomas wrestled away a gun being drawn by one of the policemen, but gave it back only to be blackjacked and thrown into jail on a charge of threatening a policeman.[78] The operators built high wooden fences around the mining camps and kept nonunion miners under guard.[79] At some places the miners could not leave the camps without a pass or without telling the captain of the Coal and Iron Police where they intended to go, what they planned to do, and when they would return. Even then, the strikebreakers were tracked by police and occasionally beaten up on the highways and thrown in jail.[80]

As the strike weakened in the summer of 1928, union miners slowly returned to the mines and crews of strikebreakers dwindled. Blacks composed around one-fourth of Allegheny County coal mines in 1927, but only about one-sixth in 1928. Of 900 blacks working in four mines of one Pittsburgh area company during the height of the strike, 750 were still at their jobs when the strike died out. A year after the walkout ended, the Pittsburgh Coal Company employed 2,500 blacks. This represented a 30 percent decrease from the maximum of 3,570 employed during the strike, yet many times more than the number working prior to 1925. When Ira Reid surveyed Pittsburgh's Hill District in 1929, he found 200 black miners living there. One coal company was still sending a bus to this black ghetto every day to transport black miners to and from its mines.[81]

Whether craftsmen or common laborers, most Pittsburgh migrants rejected labor unions during union organizing drives, large-scale strikes, and periods of labor peace. Observers discerned various attitudes among black workers during the mass strikes of 1919 and 1925–28. One stance, based on ignorance of union principles, was an indifference to the labor movement. Blacks needed employment to support themselves and had little information about other workers' grievances.[82] Another attitude among the migrants reflected hostility and suspicion toward the motivations of the unions that called strikes and asked blacks to support them. At its mildest, this response came from men who tried to join unions during organizing drives. Rejected for membership, they stayed on their jobs during strikes for lack of any alternative.[83] A more virulent hostility was found

among race-conscious black workers who broke strikes to take
jobs that unions normally denied them and to weaken labor
organizations at the same time.[84]

Elite blacks were often blamed for stoking black workers'
resentment of labor unions. Black professionals and businessmen, whose patronage and political status often depended upon
support from wealthy whites, feared that blacks' participation
in the labor movement would antagonize their white friends.
The negative effects of this alienation would be twofold: black
workers might lose what chances for employment or job advancement they had already won; and the leading position of the
black professionals and businessmen would be undermined. In
any case, argued the well-to-do blacks, labor unions would prove
fickle friends of black workers, seeking their support during
strikes, but monopolizing the gains for white workers and
spurning blacks later on.[85]

Not all elite blacks in Pittsburgh were hostile to the labor
movement, however. Neither the black professionals of the
Urban League nor the editor of the largest black newspaper
encouraged black strikebreaking in the steel and coal strikes. In
1919 the Urban League organized a meeting at which both
William Z. Foster and an antiunion black spoke to a large
audience in a Hill District church. The League wanted black
workers to have as much information as possible about the
issues separating unions from steel companies. Though it offi-
cially maintained a neutral stance, the Pittsburgh League
adopted a policy of not encouraging the transportation of blacks
to Pittsburgh mills during the strike and urged the Amalgamated Association of Iron and Steel Workers to appoint black
organizers during the union campaign in 1918–19. And from
1925 to 1928 the League refused to send job applicants to the
mines where union miners were on strike.[86]

The Pittsburgh *Courier* weighed in on the side of the UMW
during the coal strike with a barrage of news stories and
editorials. The newspaper's editor, Robert Lee Vann, decried
Pittsburgh Coal Company's hiring inexperienced black migrants
from the South and elsewhere to work underground. Vann
supported the union's traditional position that only trained and
experienced miners could work safely in the pits. Not only were

the black newcomers endangering themselves and others by accepting nonunion jobs, Vann said, but they were also being used to undercut wages that the union had won for both black and white miners.[87]

Directing his remarks to southern black migrants in the Pittsburgh coal fields, Vann urged the newly arrived men to settle down in the mining towns and enlist in the union. While admitting that unions had not often befriended black workers, Vann saw no reason why this should discourage blacks from trying to join. He asked rhetorically, "The church of our Lord and Savior Jesus Christ discriminates against the Negro. Does he refuse to join a church because the white church shuts its door in his face?" Instead of following the logic of this comparison and urging the creation of a separate black miners' organization, Vann called on black strikebreakers to join striking white miners in an interracial union.[88]

Thus, if migrant strikebreakers took cues from black leaders, it was not from these influential figures. Other prominent blacks undoubtedly advised southern migrants to stay clear of unions. Black ministers whose churches had been built with contributions from Pittsburgh companies were likely to have provided an antiunion influence.[89] The black industrial welfare workers in Pittsburgh area steel mills also tended to view the 1919 strike as an opportunity for black workers to prove themselves to their employers. In January 1919 the welfare workers at one of their group meetings agreed to steer a middle course between the unions' organizing in the mills and the steel companies: "It was the general opinion that Negro labor should organize but not as yet in the Labor Union." When steelworkers walked out of the mills, however, individual welfare workers indicated their approval of black strikebreaking. Paul Prayer at Carnegie Steel Company's Duquesne mill reported that a black crane operator stayed at his job. "When the strike was ordered he manned the crane and operated it for 60 hours and thus prevented the mill from closing down. This act of extraordinary loyalty [*sic*] elicited assurance from the employer that his position as craneman is secure."[90] H. W. Thomas wrote during the strike from the Pittsburgh Steel Company in Monessen that "the door is open without obstacles being put in the way . . . no race has had a better opportunity than ours is now getting."[91]

Whatever the influence of these groups on the migrants may have been, southern blacks' thought and action during the major strikes in the Pittsburgh area reflected not so much the acceptance of other blacks' views, much less the ignorance of rural-urban migrants. On the one hand, young, single black men lacked the incentives of family responsibilities and permanent residence that made unionism attractive to other workers. On the other hand, the most adamant and articulate black strikebreakers were those with plenty of industrial work experience as well as knowledge of unions' racial biases. In the coal strike some of the blacks who came to western Pennsylvania to work in nonunion mines were ex-union men themselves.[92] One of them, Frank Wilson, wrote to the *National Labor Tribune* to dispute Vann's editorials. He had previously been a UMW member but took a job at one of the nonunion mines after 1925. Wilson portrayed the miners' union as a racist organization run for the benefit of the elected officials and salaried staff. Black miners realized little gain as union members, according to Wilson. "About all we ever get in the average union mine is loading coal. All the best jobs go to our white brother [sic] or their sons. The president of the local union and the committeemen always work in the mines at some good company job . . . They are satisfied, and will pass the buck on every subject that the coal-loader brings up in the meetings."[93] Other black miners entering Pittsburgh area mines had clashed with rank-and-file white miners. Those from West Virginia coal fields knew of the "Ku Klux" mines in which white union men collaborated with mine managers to prohibit the hiring of black union members. As they crossed picket lines in western Pennsylvania, they waved their union membership cards toward the strikers, shouting, "You would not work with me before the strike. Now I have your job and I am going to keep it."[94]

Similarly, black strikebreakers in the 1919 steel strike felt justified in staying on their jobs because of earlier disappointments with unions. "The Negro employees said they could gain nothing by tying up with labor," a black welfare workers' meeting reported, "for they had tried for years past to become part and parcel of the labor organizations and had been met with rebuff and refusal of admission." The black craneman at Duquesene who kept the mill running during the first days of the strike had been turned down by a union when he applied for membership prior to the walkout.[95] The black strikebreakers at the A. M. Byers mill probably had not belonged to a union before 1919. But they generally had worked long enough in Pittsburgh to have an understanding of black-white relationships on the shop floor.

Southern blacks' outlook on the labor movement in Pittsburgh reflected largely their own experience. Their resistance to unions stemmed from the labor movement's exclusion of blacks and from fears that organized white workers would contract with white employers to prohibit the employment of blacks. They may have needed lessons in union principles, but this education would not have changed their opinions. Most had worked long enough with resentful whites to doubt that the principles of the labor movement could be directly translated into practice. A report on black labor and the unions in Pittsburgh in the late 1920s summarized: "Negro working men are not kindly disposed to the unions—not because they do not believe in unionism but because they feel that one of their greatest enemies is the white union man."[96]

Black migrants did not allow suspicions about labor organizations to drive them into the outstretched arms of Pittsburgh employers, however. They maintained a healthy skepticism regarding the companies' intentions and refused to bind themselves to a particular firm. They saw advantages *to themselves* in breaking strikes, but loyalty to an employer was seldom an important motivation. As the welfare workers put it in 1919, "They have not heeded the call of the strikers believing that their best fortune lies in being loyal to the employer *in the present crisis.*" What even this limited loyalty could mean was discovered in 1923 by George S. Schuyler, the prominent black journalist, who spoke with a group of black strikebreakers. "Nearly all of them were dissatisfied and were only staying long enough to 'make a stake' . . . I learned that many Negroes had left as soon as they discovered what sort of job it was."[97]

As coal mine owners found out from 1925 to 1928, it was hardly uncommon for blacks to desert their employers during strikes. Southern blacks recruited to break a coal miners' strike in the Allegheny Valley near Pittsburgh in 1917 had also left their jobs when they found out that the local miners were trying to close the mines.[98] Abandoning an employer under such circumstances may have been more an effort to steer clear of trouble than a gesture of solidarity with strikers. But black strikebreakers at the Pittsburgh Coal Company's Banning mines unmistakably demonstrated their independence by refusing to participate in a company union. The company deducted forty cents from each miner's pay envelope to support the organization. "Every man talked to objected to this," reported a social worker, "and were of the opinion that it was a bit of petty graft for somebody. Meetings of these company locals were held but I did not find one out of 20 Negro miners at Banning mines I talked with who attended a meeting."[99]

Black migrants' refusal to become minions of Pittsburgh employers was a blow to corporate personnel planning between World War I and the 1930s. Following triumphs over unions between 1919 and 1922, large manufacturers unfurled banners proclaiming an American Plan for industry. Resting squarely on the open shop, this plan was designed to wean employees away from working-class organizations by instituting company-sponsored welfare plans, social and recreational programs, employee representation schemes, and incentive pay arrangements.[100] Pittsburgh firms clearly hoped that southern blacks entering their mills and factories would become a compliant, loyal segment of the work force.[101] The migrants disappointed these hopes. They frequently ignored the model of work behavior held up to them by supervisors and resisted discrimination in hiring, promotion, and job placement.

Black workers had no choice but to stake out a middle ground between battling employers and labor unions in Pittsburgh, but this posture did not insure them material benefits. Migrants saw an advantage in remaining independent from both open shop policies and organizations of wage earners and hoped to capitalize on the demand for their labor by taking jobs previously closed to them. But the dynamics of the labor market upset this calculation. Shortages of labor during the war years, the early 1920s, and the coal and steel strikes gave way to surpluses of labor when industrial depressions struck the Pittsburgh region. The degrading effects of surplus manpower on the casual labor market undid many of the temporary gains southern blacks realized by arriving in Pittsburgh during a boom period or by filling the jobs of striking workers. A more lasting improvement of blacks' economic status in industry required an interracial, all-ranks organization of labor. Such an entity was impossible in the 1920s, but black and white steelworkers and coal miners built just these kinds of labor unions only fourteen years after the 1919 debacle, though under drastically changed circumstances.

In the intervening period, the migrant laborers struggled mostly as individuals against powerful corporations and hostile workers. A few labor union officials and black leaders urged the newcomers to join organized Pittsburgh workers and to lift their sights from the mere obtaining of jobs to the improvement of working conditions. Among the changes in the migrants' outlook and relationship with fellow wage earners on which such a perspective had to wait was southern blacks' commitment to Pittsburgh as more than a place to make cash wages, but also as a place to make their homes.

NOTES

1. William H. Harris, *The Harder We Run: Black Workers since the Civil War* (New York: Oxford University Press, 1982), 25-28, 40-50; Philip S. Foner, *Organized Labor and the Black Worker, 1619-1973* (New York: International Publishers, 1974), 82-102.

2. David Montgomery, *Workers' Control in America* (New York: Cambridge University Press, 1979), 91-108.

3. Abraham Epstein, *The Negro Migrant in Pittsburgh* (Pittsburgh: University of Pittsburgh, 1918), 37, 39; Ira De A. Reid, "The Negro in the Major Industries and Building Trades of Pittsburgh" (M.A. thesis, University of Pittsburgh, 1925), 40.

4. Reid, "Negro in the Major Industries," 40-41.

5. Foner, *Organized Labor,* 166-67; Epstein, *Negro Migrant in Pittsburgh,* 40-41; Typescript report, "Meeting of Mechanics," Feb. 5, 1918, Urban League of Pittsburgh (ULP) Records, Archives of Industrial Society, Hillman Library, University of Pittsburgh.

6. Epstein, *Negro Migrant in Pittsburgh,* 32.

7. Guichard Parris and Lester Brooks, *Blacks in the City: A History of the National Urban League* (Boston: Little, Brown, 1971), 138.

8. Reid, "Negro in the Major Industries," 36–37.

9. Epstein, *Negro Migrant in Pittsburgh,* 42.

10. Reid, "Negro in the Major Industries," 41–42.

11. Ibid., 40; "Meeting of Mechanics," ULP Records.

12. Richard R. Wright, Jr., *The Negro in Pennsylvania* (Philadelphia: AME Book Concern, 1912), 95; Epstein, *Negro Migrant in Pittsburgh,* 36–37; Reid, "Negro in the Major Industries," 38; "Meeting of Mechanics," ULP Records.

13. Reid, "Negro in the Major Industries," 40–42.

14. George S. Mitchell, "The Negro in Southern Trade Unionism," *Southern Economic Journal* 2 (Jan. 1936), 27–28; James R. Green, "The Brotherhood of Timber Workers, 1910–1913: A Radical Response to Industrial Capitalism in the Southern U.S.A.," *Past and Present* no. 60 (Aug. 1973), 161–200; Paul B. Worthman, "Black Workers and Labor Unions in Birmingham, Alabama, 1897–1904," *Labor History* 10 (Summer 1969), 375–407; Foner, *Organized Labor,* 66–69.

15. Wright, *Negro in Pennsylvania,* 98–100.

16. Epstein, *Negro Migrant in Pittsburgh,* 36, 43; Andrew Buni, *Robert L. Vann of the Pittsburgh Courier: Politics and Black Journalism* (Pittsburgh: University of Pittsburgh Press, 1974), 70–71.

17. Sterling D. Spero and Abram L. Harris, *The Black Worker* (New York: Columbia University Press, 1931), 249–51.

18. Ibid., 250–51.

19. Ibid., 251–52.

20. David Brody, *Steelworkers in America: The Non-Union Era* (Cambridge, Mass.: Harvard University Press, 1960), 96–124

21. Brody, *Steelworkers in America,* 180–98; Ray S. Baker, *The New Industrial Unrest* (Garden City: Doubleday, Page, 1920), 51–53; Stefan Lorant, *Pittsburgh: The Story of an American City* (Lenox: Authors Edition, 1964), 320.

22. William Z. Foster, *The Great Steel Strike and Its Lessons* (New York: B. W. Huebsch, 1920), 77; Interchurch World Movement, *Report on the Steel Strike of 1919* (New York: Harcourt, Brace and Howe, 1920), 147–53.

23. Interchurch World Movement, *Public Opinion and the Steel Strike* (New York: Harcourt, Brace, 1921), 101–10; for attitudes of native white steelworkers to organizing drive in Pittsburgh, see *National Labor Journal,* Oct. 3–Nov. 28, 1919.

24. Foster, *Great Steel Strike,* 179.

25. David Saposs, "The Mind of the Immigrant Communities," in *Public Opinion and the Steel Strike,* 227, 235; Foster, *Great Steel Strike,* 205–7.

26. U.S. Senate, Committee on Education and Labor, *Investigation of*

Strike in Steel Industries, Hearings, Sept.–Oct. 1919 (Washington: Government Printing Office, 1919), Part II, 672 (66th Congress, S-145-11A).

27. Spero and Harris, *Black Worker,* 258; David Saposs, "Organizing the Steel Workers," 136–37, Saposs Papers, Wisconsin State Historical Society, Madison (microfilm copy at Historical Collections and Labor Archives, Pattee Library, Pennsylvania State University, University Park).

28. Foster, *Great Steel Strike,* 100–101; Saposs, "Organizing the Steel Workers," 127.

29. Foster, *Great Steel Strike,* 103; *National Labor Tribune,* Sept. 27, 1917, 1, 7, Oct. 4, 1917, 1, Oct. 11, 1917, 1.

30. Foster, *Great Steel Strike,* 52–53, 103; Saposs, "Organizing the Steel Workers," 133.

31. Foster, *Great Steel Strike,* 110–39, 165–68; Interchurch World Movement, *Public Opinion,* 96–110; David Brody, *Labor in Crisis* (Philadelphia: Lippincott, 1965), 160–61; Duquesne *Times-Observer,* June 26, 1919, 1, 12, Oct. 3, 1919, 11, Oct. 10, 1919, 1, 14.

32. Brody, *Labor in Crisis,* 163.

33. Foster, *Great Steel Strike,* 206–8; Saposs, "Organizing the Steel Workers," 136; Herbert J. Seligman, "The Negro in Industry," *Socialist Review* 8 (Feb. 1920), 171; "Synopsis of Interview on November 20, 1919 with Mr. K., official of the Urban League of Pittsburgh, Pa.," 1, Heber Blankenhorn Collection, Archives of Labor History and Industrial Affairs, Wayne State University, Detroit (hereafter cited as "Synopsis of Interview," Blankenhorn Collection). The Urban League of Pittsburgh's estimate of 6,000 blacks hired at steel mills during the strike agreed with that of other investigators. Ibid., 4.

34. Interview: Harvey C., Dec. 2, 1973.

35. A. M. Byers Company Personnel File, Archives of Industrial Society, Hillman Library, University of Pittsburgh (hereafter cited as Byers Company Personnel File); interview: Joseph M., Nov. 16, 1973.

36. Byers Company Personnel File.

37. Dennis C. Dickerson, "Black Steelworkers in Western Pennsylvania, 1915–1950" (Ph.D. thesis, Washington University, 1978), 60.

38. Reid, "Negro in the Major Industries," 28.

39. Dickerson, "Black Steelworkers," 66; Reid, "Negro in the Major Industries," 11–12.

40. Dickerson, "Black Steelworkers," 60.

41. Saposs, "Organizing the Steel Workers," 135.

42. Foster, *Great Steel Strike,* 207–8.

43. S. Adele Shaw, "Closed Towns," *Survey* 43 (Nov. 8, 1919), 50–64, 87; Foster, *Great Steel Strike,* 118–32.

44. Dickerson, "Black Steelworkers," 62–63.

45. Interchurch World Movement, *Public Opinion,* 128; Mary H. Vorse, *Men and Steel* (London: Labour Publishing, 1922), 83–84.

46. Foster, *Great Steel Strike,* 208; Spero and Harris, *Black Worker,* 262.

47. Brody, *Steelworkers in America,* 262; Foster, *Great Steel Strike,* 168, 172-73, 177-78, 190-93.

48. Abram L. Harris, "The New Negro Worker in Pittsburgh" (M.A. thesis, University of Pittsburgh, 1924), 49.

49. Minutes of meeting, Pittsburgh Chapter of the National Association of Corporation Training, Unskilled Labor and Americanization Section, Feb. 2, 1922, National Urban League Records, Industrial Relations File, Series 4, Box 4, Library of Congress, Washington, D.C. (hereafter cited as Corporation Training meeting).

50. Reid, "Negro in the Major Industries," 30.

51. Interchurch World Movement, *Report on the Steel Strike,* 177-78.

52. Interviews: Silas B., Oct. 29, 1973, Walter H., Oct. 25, 30, 1973.

53. William M. Tuttle, Jr., *Race Riot: Chicago in the Red Summer of 1919* (New York: Atheneum, 1970), 32-66, 141-56; Elliott M. Rudwick, *Race Riot at East St. Louis, July 2, 1917* (Carbondale: Southern Illinois University Press, 1964), 16-57; Chicago Commission on Race Relations, *The Negro in Chicago* (Chicago: University of Chicago Press, 1922), 6-7.

54. Vorse, *Men and Steel,* 95, 110-12.

55. Gerald N. Grob, *Workers and Utopia* (Evanston: Northwestern University Press, 1961), 34-59; John H. M. Laslett, *Labor and the Left: A Study of Socialist and Radical Influences in the American Labor Movement, 1881-1924* (New York: Basic Books, 1970), 197; Herbert G. Gutman, "The Negro and the United Mine Workers of America: The Career and Letters of Richard L. Davis and Something of Their Meaning," in Gutman, *Work, Culture and Society in Industrializing America: Essays in American Working Class and Social History* (New York: Knopf, 1976), 121-208.

56. Spero and Harris, *Black Worker,* 374.

57. Gerald E. Allen, "The Negro Coal Miner in the Pittsburgh District" (M.A. thesis, University of Pittsburgh, 1927), 15, 17; Spero and Harris, *Black Worker,* 210, 228.

58. *National Labor Journal,* Mar. 2, 1917, 4; Carl I. Meyerhuber, Jr., "The Alle-Kiski Coal Wars, 1913-1919," *Western Pennsylvania Historical Magazine* 63 (July 1980), 204.

59. Arthur E. Suffern, *Conciliation and Arbitration in the Coal Industry of America* (Boston: Houghton Mifflin, 1915), 44-50; Spero and Harris, *Black Worker,* 210.

60. Allen, "Negro Coal Miner," 34; Pennsylvania Department of Internal Affairs, Bureau of Statistics and Information, *Report on the Productive Industries . . . 1925* (Harrisburg, 1926), 452, 474, 476, 500. Abram L. Harris estimated that there were 8,000 black UMW members in western Pennsylvania in 1924. Harris, "New Negro Worker," 62.

61. Darold T. Barnum, *The Negro in the Bituminous Coal Mining Industry* (Philadelphia: Industrial Research Unit, Department of Industry, Wharton School of Finance and Commerce, University of Pennsylvania, 1970), Table 7, 18.

62. Irving Bernstein, *The Lean Years: A History of the American Worker, 1920-33* (Baltimore: Penguin, 1960), 128.

63. Ibid., 129-31; *United Mine Workers Journal,* Oct. 1, 1925, 7.

64. Allen, "Negro Coal Miner," 16; Pennsylvania Department of Internal Affairs, *Report on the Productive Industries ... 1922-23* (Harrisburg, 1924), 212, 232, 234, 256; *Report on the Productive Industries ... 1927* (Harrisburg, 1928), 199, 221, 223, 251, 252.

65. Pittsburgh *Courier,* Nov. 20, 1926, 2; *UMW Journal,* Jan. 15, 1927, 3.

66. U.S. Senate, Committee on Interstate Commerce, *Conditions in the Coal Fields of Pennsylvania, West Virginia, and Ohio, Hearings,* Feb.-Mar. 1928 (Washington: Government Printing Office, 1928), Part I, 19 (70th Congress, S475); hereafter cited as U.S. Senate, *Conditions.* Philip Murray to the Council of Churches in Christ in Pittsburgh, Mar. 23, 1927, reprinted in Allen, "Negro Coal Miner," 78-79; see also *UMW Journal,* Apr. 1, 1927, 5; ibid., Mar. 15, 1927, 5.

67. Quotation reprinted in Allen, "Negro Coal Miner, 79; U.S. Senate, *Conditions,* 20.

68. "Investigation of Pittsburgh Coal Company Mines at Midland No. 1, Banning No. 2 at Whitsett and Banning No. 1 at Jacob's Creek. November 2 and 7th, 1925," National Urban League Records, Industrial Relations File, Series 4 (hereafter cited as "Investigation of Pittsburgh Coal Company Mines").

69. Pittsburgh *Courier,* Nov. 20, 1926, 2.

70. Allen, "Negro Coal Miner," 30.

71. Bernstein, *Lean Years,* 131-32; McAlister Coleman, *Men and Coal* (New York: Farrar and Rinehart, 1943), 129-30; Spero and Harris, *Black Worker,* 229.

72. U.S. Senate, *Conditions,* 84-85; Spero and Harris, *Black Worker,* 238-39; *UMW Journal,* June 15, 1927, 3, July 1, 1927, 5.

73. Spero and Harris, *Black Worker,* 231; Keith Sward, *The Legend of Henry Ford* (New York: Rinehart, 1948), 201.

74. U.S. Senate, *Conditions,* 346-47.

75. Ibid., 346, 352; "Investigation of Pittsburgh Coal Company Mines."

76. "Investigation of Pittsburgh Coal Company Mines."

77. Spero and Harris, *Black Worker,* 233-35.

78. Pittsburgh *Courier,* Mar. 5, 1927, 8.

79. Ibid., Dec. 25, 1926, 4.

80. U.S. Senate, *Conditions,* 17.

81. Pennsylvania Department of Internal Affairs, *Report on the Productive Industries, 1927,* 199; *Report on the Productive Industries ... 1928* (Harrisburg, 1929), 199; Spero and Harris, *Black Worker,*

243; Ira De A. Reid, *Social Conditions of the Negro in the Hill District of Pittsburgh* (Pittsburgh: General Committee on the Hill Survey, 1930), 55; T. A. Hill to Horace F. Baker, May 21, 1928, National Urban League Records, Industrial Relations Department, Local Affiliates File, Series 4.

82. Spero and Harris, *Black Worker,* 129–30.

83. Interview: Joseph M., Nov. 16, 1973; minutes of Industrial Welfare Workers' meeting, Sept. 26, 1919, ULP Records.

84. Interview: Ernest F., Apr. 19, 1976.

85. Spero and Harris, *Black Worker,* 462–65; Foster, *Great Steel Strike,* 210–11.

86. Spero and Harris, *Black Worker,* 258–59; A. C. Thayer to T. A. Hill, Feb. 29, 1928, National Urban League Records, Industrial Relations Department, Local Affiliates File, Series 4; "Synopsis of Interview," Blankenhorn Collection, 1.

87. Pittsburgh *Courier,* Nov. 27, 1926, 8.

88. Ibid., Jan. 1, 1927, 4.

89. Ibid., Sept. 15, 1928, 4.

90. Minutes of Industrial Welfare Workers' Meeting, Jan. 9, Sept. 26, 1919, ULP Records.

91. H. W. Thomas to John T. Clark, Nov. 6, 1919, ULP Records.

92. "Investigation of Pittsburgh Coal Company Mines."

93. *National Labor Tribune,* Dec. 16, 1926, reprinted in Allen, "Negro Coal Miner," 73–74.

94. Spero and Harris, *Black Worker,* 375.

95. Minutes of Industrial Welfare Workers' Meeting, Sept. 26, 1919, ULP Records.

96. "Pittsburgh, Pennsylvania—A Summary of Industrial Conditions, Organized Labor and Negro Labor," National Urban League Records, Research Department File, Series 4.

97. Minutes of Industrial Welfare Workers' Meeting, Sept. 26, 1919, ULP Records (emphasis added); George S. Schuyler, "From Job to Job," *World Tomorrow* 6 (May 1923), 147–48.

98. *National Labor Journal,* Mar. 2, 1917, 4, Mar. 16, 1917, 8.

99. "Investigation of Pittsburgh Coal Company Mines."

100. David Brody, "The Rise and Decline of Welfare Capitalism," in Brody, *Workers in Industrial America: Essays on the Twentieth Century Struggle* (New York: Oxford University Press, 1980), 48–81.

101. Corporation Training meeting.

7

Making Homes

IMMENSE OBSTACLES stood in the way of southern blacks' settlement in Pittsburgh. Lacking economic power as individual workers or as a group of employees, their livelihoods were constantly buffeted by market forces and corporate personnel policies. The difficulty of securing good housing disheartened many homeseekers. Pittsburgh blacks often disdained contact with southern newcomers or, still worse, demanded that they quickly exchange their habits and customs for northern urban ways of living. The life they had known in the South seemed to them hardly better, yet southern blacks often strived to maintain contacts with kin, friends, and former workmates, both those who were in Pittsburgh and those who remained in the South. The bonds with their southern homes made it difficult for some migrants to commit themselves to permanent northern homes. There were migrants who tried to make homes in Pittsburgh and failed and others who came to the city never intending to stay. Though the relative proportions of sojourners and settlers in the total migrant population cannot be measured precisely, the former likely outnumbered the latter, given the difficulties of settling down and the high rates of transiency during World War I and the early 1920s.

Settlement meant adopting long-term plans for work, households, and community life in Pittsburgh. For many migrants, this involved staying on a job instead of quitting to look for another. For others, it entailed marriage and the beginning of conjugal families. All migrant settlers had to fit into the social and institutional framework of the black community where mutually supportive relationships could strengthen the foundations of their Pittsburgh homes. This last aspect of settlement involved the gatekeepers: individuals, groups, and organizations that could translate southern blacks' needs to the black community and the community's standards to southern blacks. For reasons that the sociologist George E. Haynes explained in 1920, most gatekeepers were black: "Those who best understand conditions that affect their daily lives, or drawbacks which the average Negro wage-earner has . . . must share with them the life of the Negro world."[1] But even within their own race, there were distinct social, economic, and cultural groups. Gatekeepers from these groups stood before different thresholds to the city, offering help in crossing the division between southern rural and northern urban life, but also demanding a price before letting the newcomers enter.

This chapter discusses how southern blacks met obstacles to settlement and the ways some migrants surmounted them to establish homes in the city and its environs. It begins by describing the main socioeconomic groups in the black community on the eve of the migration and where the newcomers fit into the social structure. The tensions between the migrants and resident blacks are taken up next. Then the chapter looks at two institutions that attempted to fill gatekeeping roles in the migrants' settlement: the Urban League of Pittsburgh and black churches. Finally, the migrants' involvement with their native southern communities and its impact on the settlement process is described.

Pittsburgh's black community and its social groups were as old as the city itself. Some of the black servants who helped raise British stockades at the forks of the Ohio River had remained to work at the frontier settlement, which quickly became a trading center and a gateway to the Ohio Valley territory. In the streets and alleys that were laid out on the triangle of land formed by the merging Monongahela and Allegheny rivers were the businesses of some of Pittsburgh's earliest black residents. The city harbored runaway slaves from the South before the Civil War and had attracted freedmen in growing numbers after the 1860s, most of whom came from the Upper South. In addition, there were fugitives from slavery who had reached Canada before the Civil War and who later returned to the United States to settle in Pittsburgh.[2]

At the beginning of the World War I migration, there were three major socioeconomic groups within Pittsburgh's black population whose members were determined by family, length of residence in the city, education, occupation, and income. An elite group included mostly old Pittsburgh families headed by well-educated professionals and businessmen. These men had assumed the prominent positions that had been held in earlier years by black shopowners and prestigious domestic servants. The barbers, butlers, caterers, and other servants who formerly had enjoyed the highest rank in the black community continued among the city's leading blacks but were no longer its representative figures.[3]

The black elite in Pittsburgh enjoyed a social and organizational life largely separate from that of other blacks in the community. Its members gathered in exclusive groups like the Loendi Club, "a center of friendly intercourse among men of some intellectual aspiration." The Loendi clubhouse in the Hill District, constructed before World War I, cost $15,000. Here the members could dine, play billiards, and discuss current topics. There were also many social organizations supported by Pittsburgh's black elite, among them Greek letter societies, women's clubs, and men's groups like the Frogs, a "good-time" organization whose membership was restricted to socially prominent young men, generally the sons of black social leaders. Well-to-do Pittsburgh blacks from various social organizations came together at exclusive gatherings to raise funds for charities. The annual Armistice Day dinner had "gleaming tables, flowers and banners, music and sociability. Churches, clubs, and sororities took tables at which they furnished their own service, and thousands of dollars were raised for charitable work."[4]

Beneath the professional and business group were two other major strata of the black community whose members seldom belonged to Old Pittsburgh families. They were generally migrants from the Upper South who had come to the city from the late nineteenth to the early twentieth centuries. The first of these groups included both prosperous skilled black workers as well as poorer but economically stable wage earners. Among the few skilled black workers were iron- and steelworkers, building craftsmen, Pullman porters, or small contractors such as the teamsters, whose ownership of a horse and wagon allowed them to hire out for city construction jobs. The small numbers of skilled black iron- and steelworkers lived distinctly better than most unskilled millhands, black or foreign-born. A reporter described a group of these black craftsmen coming to collect their pay at the mill where they were employed. "None came in their working clothes; most had polished their shoes, which were different from the ones worn at work; all were well, even stylishly dressed, and bore nothing about them to indicate their calling."[5] The homes of these men also bespoke their prosperous working-class status, with pianos or organs and drawings and landscape chromos hung on the walls.[6]

This middle group in the black community included many poorer unskilled men and women who struggled to keep above the lower class of destitute blacks and to equal the comparative security and stability of skilled blacks. These were the menial domestics such as janitors, cooks, cleaning women, laundresses, and the unskilled industrial and commercial workers. Their employment was sometimes seasonal and intermittent, forcing them to move from job to job to maintain their families. Unless they worked for wealthy white families or prestigious downtown businesses, they seldom enjoyed high status among Pittsburgh blacks, but managed through severe sacrifices to keep together households and to raise and educate their children.[7]

Some descriptions of the black lower class in Pittsburgh before World War I portrayed isolated ravine-dwellers seldom noticed by any but the investigators of the poorest in the city. Here were the highly transient casual day laborers, river boat hands, indigents, drifters, and the physically or emotionally handicapped. Those who could work at all did so infrequently. Some had no roots in the city, but others maintained homes in neglected alleys and side streets. Helen Tucker found a little colony of about seventy-five blacks occupying Jake's Run, "a narrow deep ravine leading down to the Ohio River." The black families, mostly from rural Virginia and North Carolina, selected this location for its cheap rents, an attraction for poor whites, who also lived there. Though Jake's Run blacks were employed as domestics and common laborers, their living conditions struck Tucker as much inferior to those of other working-class blacks in the city: "The standards of civilization are sucked down by immorality and neglect, for the run is practically isolated from the rest of the world."[8]

The influx of migrants after 1915 changed the structure of the black community. On the basis of income and occupation, most of the newcomers fell into the middle or lower socioeconomic groups, swelling this part of the population enormously. While their jobs aligned them with the black unskilled industrial and domestic service workers, the migrants' social status was not the same as any group of northern blacks. Southern blacks' recent arrival in the city, lack of education, and rural background set them apart from skilled and unskilled wage earners as well as from the elite. Though some southerners came from cultured urban or landowning rural families, the shortage of housing forced them to live among the unstable black lower class, where Pittsburgh blacks easily lost sight of these migrants' backgrounds and aspirations.

The rapid growth of the migrant population between World War I and the Depression produced tensions in the black community. Ignoring differences among the newcomers, many black residents of Pittsburgh lumped all the incoming migrants into one mass of crude and unkempt undesirables. Old residents who remained in the sections where migrants settled held themselves apart from the southerners. "We find that the new comer lives in neighborhoods with the old residents of the city," reported a community worker in 1919, "but there has been very little neighborliness . . . shown the new comer. He is grouped by himself."[9] Referring to the "old Pennsylvanian" group among Pittsburgh blacks, the *Negro Survey of Pennsylvania* observed in the late 1920s, "This group have [*sic*] always considered themselves somewhat superior to the 'outlander.' "[10]

The Pittsburgh *Courier* expressed an ambivalence toward the mass of arriving southern blacks felt by many older residents and native Pennsylvania blacks. While calling on black residents to tolerate the rural blacks, a 1923 editorial titled "Give Them a Chance" adopted a patronizing, unflattering tone. "We can not expect strangers in our midst to know our

customs, our habits, our various social ordinances, without
some instructions. . . . We have little reason to point to their
faults, their awkwardness, their crude customs, their revolvers
and their lack of decorum, until we are sure they have been
taught by us in all the nicer things known to our community
life."[11] The *Courier*'s attitude toward the migrants hardened in
the depression year of 1924. A February editorial claimed that
"there is little or no migration problem" in the city, but implied
that migrants were shunning wage labor in favor of criminal
pursuits. "Any man who wants work, and wants to live by
working and earning real money, can find room in the City of
Pittsburgh. The man who does not want to work, but who
prefers to live by his wits or by tricks unknown to honest toil,
had better find some other town."[12]

The rankings in the black community and the reception
accorded migrants by some old residents made the newcomers
sensitive to the differences that separated them from other
blacks. For some migrants, steel mill jobs provided a particularly concrete reference to their distinct identity in the black
population. "The people I met here," declared Harrison G., a
Georgia migrant who worked in the Jones and Laughlin steel
mills, "they weren't concerned with nothin' but a soft job. To
get a job downtown or someplace like that, that's all they wanted."
If resident Pittsburgh blacks regarded mill laborers as rough
and uncouth, the migrants took pride in their ability to perform
the most physically demanding tasks in the steel industry. John
B. got little education in rural North Carolina before he moved
to Pittsburgh, but his job at Carnegie Steel's Homestead plant
gave him another measure of personal worth. "They gave me a
job that nobody hardly wanted. . . . You had to handle the hot
steel that the shears would cut off the . . . plate, and you had to
handle it in your arms. . . . Some of the boys they put on that job
would walk off after they had been on it so long they couldn't
stand it . . . and I stuck there. I stuck with it."[13]

Southern men also confronted Pittsburgh blacks' coolness in
their relationships with the opposite sex. The migrants faced
great difficulties in finding partners in Pittsburgh, since the surplus of black men over women made eligible females very much
in demand. What was worse, the male migrants could not hope

to woo some of the black women in the city. While their earnings could buy them the company of any prostitute in the Pittsburgh area, they were seldom rich in the currency of manners and
etiquette that some northern black women expected in a suitor.
Their lack of education, strange speech and dress, and rough
work made them unappealing to northern-born black women.[14]

For their part, some male migrants found northern women
lacking in the qualities of a good helpmate. In their opinion a
woman from the North was not as steady or supporting of her
husband as a southern woman could be. Her aspirations for a
standard of living, which his employment could not support,
were more likely to burden than help the working man. "I've
met plenty of girls [in Pittsburgh]," Harrison G. remembered of
his early residence in the city. "They couldn't talk my language
at all. All they'd want is a big time." Whether or not this was
merely a defensive reaction to northern black women's aloofness,
many southern men preferred to marry southern women. Often
sweethearts from the migrants' homes exchanged letters with
the migrants for several years after the men had come to
Pittsburgh. Correspondence and brief visits to the South sus-
tained these long-distance courtships until, with a few days'
leave from their jobs, the migrants sped home by train, got
married, celebrated with their families and old friends, then
returned north with their wives. Men who had left no girl
friend behind when they came to Pittsburgh also found reasons
for seeking a southern-born mate. One migrant felt that a Pittsburgh woman would not accompany him when he went back to
South Carolina to visit his family.[15]

The migrants' self-image inverted Pittsburgh blacks' opinion of
them. Southern blacks believed themselves superior to northern-
born men in physique, ambition, and accomplishments. The
rural Virginian Ed R. felt that country-raised southern men
were bigger and stronger than northern blacks. Other migrants
insisted that the newcomers showed more drive and initiative.
In John T.'s eyes, Pittsburgh blacks "never amounted to a dime"
and therefore could not validly belittle southern migrants. He
also claimed that the southerners made the best church members and supporters, a quality that northerners were eventually
forced to recognize.[16]

The ambivalence of the city's elite blacks toward the southerners may have influenced the reactions of other Pittsburgh
blacks toward the migrants. The leading black clergymen, professional social workers, and businessmen tried to help newcomers adjust to urban life and assume stable, productive family
lives. But well-to-do blacks at the same time felt threatened by
the growing presence of southerners. The migrants' values and
customs seemed alien to the elite, who also realized that the
migrants felt little allegiance to their leadership in the community.
The conflicting impulses to welcome and to guard against the
migrants—exemplified in the social welfare program of the
Urban League of Pittsburgh—curtailed elite blacks' gatekeeping
role in southern blacks' settlement.

Alone among the Pittsburgh civic and social welfare agencies,
the local Urban League addressed its work directly to newly
arrived black migrants.[17] Founded in 1918 at the height of the
wartime migration, the Urban League approached southern
blacks coming to Pittsburgh as uprooted rural families rather
than simply as new charity cases. The League clearly formulated
a gatekeeping role in the migration in its earliest publications.
Its purposes were: "To become a clearing house for Negro
labor. To aid the new-comer in getting decently adjusted. To
safeguard health. To increase facilities for wholesome recreation.
To attack the problem of better housing for Negroes." In 1923
the League's director described the organization to a prospective migrant in Jacksonville, Florida, as "a social welfare organization which is interested in the proper adjustment of a number
of Negroes now found in our northern cities. This work is
devoted to improving the health, housing, and recreational
conditions of our people; as well as finding employment for
them." In the mid-1920s the League continued its emphasis on
adjusting blacks from southern agriculture to urban conditions.
"We consider this work the most important approach to our
numerous problems," stated the annual report for 1924. "It
attempts to reestablish and stabilize the home life and lessen
the social ravages of such a mass movement of our rural southern families."[18]

The Urban League's efforts on behalf of southern migrants
were roughly divided between family and employment programs.

The League saw these two basic parts of its work as complementary. Jobs in its view were the foundation of the migrants' future in the city, and only steady work would lead to substantial progress in adjusting southerners to urban life. But southern blacks' home and family life could help to stabilize newly hired breadwinners. Therefore the League tried just as hard to improve migrants' housekeeping, child care, and recreation as it did to better their work records.[19]

The home economics worker was the key to the Urban League's community programs. This person surveyed migrant households, organized neighborhood groups among southern black housewives, and instructed newly arrived women in the art of urban housekeeping. In a 1925 report the home economics worker described the lessons she gave to southern migrant women: "The wives are instructed in the use of gas, electricity, marketing of foods, how to purchase and prepare cheap cuts of meat, and to make over old clothing. . . . They are warned against salesmen from credit houses, fake insurance and stock concerns."[20] The worker's goals for these neighborhood groups were to instill pride in well-kept homes, a spirit of neighborly cooperation, and the goal of economic advancement.[21] The Lawrenceville Community Uplift Club became a model for these organizations of migrant women, sponsoring infant care demonstrations, flower box competitions, and fostering a "general progressive spirit."[22] It was perhaps the Lawrenceville women whom the home economics worker had in mind when she reported: "Through groups of women . . . using churches, social centers, or any other available meeting places . . . acquaintances and neighborhood contacts have been established. These women have become much more contented, and have helped to steady and make their husbands more satisfied on their jobs."[23]

A welfare caseworker from the Urban League joined the city Morals Court staff soon after the League began its work. The court handled cases of individuals swept through its doors on charges of indecent behavior, disturbing the peace, or disorderly conduct. Instead of imposing sentences on southern newcomers to Pittsburgh, the court sometimes turned over cases to the League's worker for investigation and aid.[24] There were so many adolescent black women brought before the Morals Court that the caseworker organized community clubs where girls could pursue hobbies and recreational activities. The caseworker founded twelve clubs from 1921 to 1923 with a total membership of 320. Each club had a social leader who dealt with problems in the individual member's home.[25] Since many of the young southern blacks appearing in the court had difficulty in their schools, the caseworker's responsibilities overlapped with those of the League's home and school visitor. This League staff member became a surrogate educational officer whose gatekeeping function was explicitly defined—"a connecting link between the home and the school as an interpreter in the absence of Negro teachers in the Public School System."[26]

The Urban League's employment programs included both job placement and job adjustment efforts. Financial support from the Carnegie Steel Company in 1918 paid the salary of a men's job placement secretary on the League's staff. While the placement secretary dispatched many migrants to the mills, he also referred job applicants to smaller firms in a variety of businesses: retail, construction work, domestic service. The Urban League also had a women's job placement worker in 1918. Since the large manufacturing concerns developed their own labor recruitment schemes, the League's placement program might have been relatively more important both for migrants seeking nonmanufacturing positions and for employers—such as the city's big department stores—who at times needed black workers as badly as did the steel mills.[27]

Like the efforts of Pittsburgh industries to reform migrant employees, the League's job adjustment program aimed primarily to encourage southern blacks to stay on their jobs. For that part of its work, the League relied on the black industrial welfare workers. These agents in turn were employed by manufacturing firms in and around the city. Though the League may have been instrumental in getting some Pittsburgh companies to place black welfare workers on their staffs, it had little if any say over these workers' responsibilities and duties. While the League wanted to provide migrant common laborers with some guidance in adapting to full-time, continuous industrial labor, Pittsburgh firms had their welfare workers concentrate almost wholly on providing recreational outlets for the blacks on their payrolls, on housing arrangements, and on general personnel relations.[28] The League's representatives successfully met the migrant families in their homes and neighborhoods, but they remained several steps removed from the shop floors where the formative industrial work experience took place.

The industrial welfare workers found themselves in the difficult position of representing employers' interests to black wage earners, the wage earners' grievances to employers, and the Urban League's programs to both the migrants and their bosses. As the representatives of industries to black employees, their authority in black neighborhoods around the mills was second to none. Migrants came to them with any problem they believed their employer could solve. But the welfare workers had no power at all inside the mill gates. Migrants' difficulties with other employees, straw bosses, or foremen lay strictly outside their scope of operations. Management alone decided all questions concerning the migrants' work status. In its devolution of authority to the black welfare workers, Pittsburgh employers ceded power in their migrants' spare time, but retained absolute control during work time.

Particularly in corporation-dominated mill towns, this artificial separation of workplace and community authority undermined the welfare workers' leadership among southern blacks. If they tried to intercede with the mill's management on behalf of a migrant with a job problem, they overstepped the line separating their domain from that of the mill supervisors. To infringe too often on their employers' prerogatives would expose them to the company's wrath and endanger their position. But if they hewed to the boundaries of their delegated authority, refusing to speak for black employees when they needed support against an unfair foreman, they lost standing with the people whose welfare was their professional concern.[29] It did not help the welfare workers' predicament when some industrial managers countenanced payday crap games and alcoholic beverages in company bunkhouses.[30]

For their part, League staff members showed little inclination to indulge the migrants in such diversions. They did not focus criticism of the black workers mainly on irregular work habits, as industrial supervisors did, but on the wage earners' leisure pursuits and their impact on the black community. Shortly after the armistice ending World War I, the League warned that foreign immigration to the United States was resuming, threatening the places in Pittsburgh industry claimed by blacks during the labor shortage of the war. "Already the vanguard is reaching Ellis Island at the rate of about 3,000 per day . . . this threatened influx of foreigners is significant." But the competition for jobs, the League claimed, "means nothing to the 'saphead' Negro to whom money means just so much more 'Jakey' and 'Craps.' "[31]

In unison with Pittsburgh's industrial supervisors, the Urban League staff decried the young black men from the South whose conduct seemed to worsen social problems in the city's black community. An Urban League study of conditions in one section of Pittsburgh concluded that unattached men with money to spare caused prostitution to flourish.[32] John T. Clark, the League's executive director, campaigned publicly in 1924 for a city ordinance to ban the display and sale of guns and knives in the pawnshops of the black community. Clark's argument in favor of the proposed regulation revealed again the concern over young southern workers' spending habits: "[The ordinance] . . . would protect a large number of Negroes who have been coming into our city in the last few years and working in the mills, and have not yet established family connections in the city. These men are of the more irresponsible type, making more money than they ever have in their life, and having no cultural wants for which to spend their money."[33] Replying to a correspondent in Jacksonville, Florida, Clark indicted some black migrants with the charge that they had increased problems for southern blacks as a group in northern cities. "It would be a very serious matter if all the Negroes who want to would leave the South as it would create many serious questions in the North. As it is the rough element of the South have eliminated many of the opportunities up North by not knowing how to take advantage of the many facilities which have been offered them."[34]

Such statements echoed phrases used by other Urban League branches in their "comb and toothbrush" campaigns against southern blacks' habits and behavior. Like the Pittsburgh League staff, the black social workers in Chicago and Detroit feared that the "rough element" among the migrants would invite a backlash from old residents of the city that would impede progress for all blacks. They urged the migrants to clean and groom themselves, dress well, and conduct themselves quietly in public places. While part of this effort fell within the general drive to ease dislocations brought about by massive southern migration, much of it reflected well-to-do blacks' dismay at being associated with newcomers from the rural South.[35]

Urban League criticisms of Pittsburgh migrants also harmonized with the disparaging remarks of other elite blacks in the city. The similarity between each group's reaction to southern blacks reflected an identity of social backgrounds and status. John T. Clark and Alonzo Thayer, the executive directors from 1918 to 1930, were college-educated social workers. Clark, who held the League's top position from 1918 to 1926, earned a B.A. degree from Ohio State University in 1906. Before coming to Pittsburgh, he taught high school in his hometown of Louisville, Kentucky, and then served as housing secretary at the National Urban League's headquarters in New York City. Thayer, executive director from 1927 to 1930, graduated from Avery Normal Institute in Charleston, South Carolina, in 1900 and from Fisk University in 1904. He was on the staff of the Chicago Commission on Race Relations and headed the Atlanta Urban League before taking over the Pittsburgh branch.[36]

The black industrial welfare workers could match the educational attainments of the League's directors. Macon Lennon at Bethlehem's Duquesne plant, William P. Young at Lockhart Iron and Steel in McKees Rocks, Robert E. Johnson at Carnegie Steel's Edgar Thompson Works in Braddock, and Cyrus Green at Westinghouse Electric all had college degrees. Young held a M.A. degree from Lincoln University and had taught English, German, and Argumentation there.[37] Green came to the Westinghouse factory in East Pittsburgh from an educational secretary's position in the U.S. Army.[38] Grover Nelson at the Homestead Steel Works was pastor of a black congregation in Broughton, Pennsylvania. The League's home economics worker, job placement officers, Morals Court representative, and home and school visitor shared these high levels of training, professional expe-

rience, and commitment to progressive reform.[39] The League
and its parent organization, the National Urban League, stressed
high qualifications for the black men and women who carried
out its programs.

That a very small proportion of blacks in the United States
had such qualifications, however, also created considerable distance between the professionals of the Urban League and southern rural blacks. Neither the League's social workers, the
emerging black professional and business group in Pittsburgh,
the college-trained ministers, nor the leaders of black social
clubs could fully empathize with the migrants. Though some of
the upper-class blacks themselves had recently come from the
South, probably few shared rural southern blacks' low levels of
education and literacy, their folk culture, or their life-long experience in tenant farming and industrial common labor. Aspirations for business and professional careers, belief in competitive
individualism, and the values associated with the work ethic
tended to set the black elite still further apart from the mass of
migrants.

The sharp differences between the League's black professionals and the southern migrants determined many facets of
the social work programs designed to help stabilize the black
newcomers. The job placement office, the organizations for
female migrants, and the welfare workers' supervision of black
workers' housing and recreation in mill towns provided vital
services not available from any other single source. Yet the goal
of acculturating rural blacks to the League's notion of "efficient"
urban life led to attacks on the migrants' own culture. The black
professionals insisted that manners and habits of living learned
in the South must be dropped before the migrants could become
permanent urban dwellers. The League's campaign to reform
southern blacks served to protect and maintain the status of
Pittsburgh's leading blacks.

None of this meant that elite blacks in the city failed to play a
gatekeeper's role in southern migration to Pittsburgh. But the
way they performed their role strongly reflected attitudes of
a socially established group confronting new and uncertain
conditions. And that both upper-class blacks and southern
migrants belonged to the same oppressed minority in Pitts-

burgh did not always cushion the jarring collision between their disparate values and ways of life. Through the Urban League's women's and girls' clubs, the black YMCA on Centre Avenue in the Hill District, or some of the city's black churches, migrants enjoyed friendly, supportive contacts with "old Pittsburgher" blacks. But the general approach of elite blacks to the southerners also provoked resentment among the migrants. A cryptic report in the *Courier* afforded a glimpse at the standoff between distinct social groups within the black community. The "strategy board," a black political action group of nonprofessional men and women, complained of being snubbed by female social workers. The newspaper report quoted from resolutions adopted at the board's meeting: "Be it Resolved, that college graduates accepted hereafter for welfare work in the Third Ward, be required to successfully complete a course in simple etiquette, in order that they may have an unassumed regard for the rights and feelings of others. . . . Be it Further Resolved, that we withdraw our support from those persons or institutions who insist on thrusting this 'cold shoulder' into our faces, simply because they have enjoyed advantages denied to us."[40]

The social divisions and conflicting outlooks within the black community also affected the migrants' affiliation with black churches. Churches were important in the settlement of many blacks, because they were key institutions in the black community — the foci of social, political, and cultural as well as spiritual activities. Through participation in churches, migrants could meet gatekeepers from their own level of the black community and join numerous voluntary organizations: missionary circles, choirs, and Sunday schools. Churches also offered ambitious migrants the possibility of gaining status in such offices as clerk, trustee, or deacon. In Pittsburgh the newcomers found many denominations and classes of black churches, each with its characteristic social composition, lay and clerical leadership, and style of worship.

Elite blacks in Pittsburgh as in other northern cities attended the Congregational, Episcopalian, or Presbyterian churches. They increasingly preferred congregations in which they did not mingle with large numbers of lower-class newcomers. Ligh-

ter skin tone also distinguished the members of some upper-
class congregations from those of other black churches. But
well-to-do Pittsburgh blacks also commonly belonged to the
oldest churches of their race, whether "blue vein" or not. The
Bethel African Methodist Episcopal Church was the first black
congregation to organize in Pittsburgh. From its founding in
1808 to the migration period it attracted some of the leading
black families in the city. When Joel Spingarn, the executive
board chairman of the National Association for the Advancement of Colored People (NAACP), visited Pittsburgh in 1915 to
help organize a local chapter, he spoke at Bethel to overflow
crowds. Bethel became a symbol of black Pittsburgh's racial
pride and progress in the twentieth century, erecting a new
$50,000 building in the Hill District in 1909 with the labor of
skilled black building tradesmen.[41] Ebeneezer Baptist Church,
though not the oldest church of its denomination in the city,
boasted a large and comparatively affluent congregation.[42]

Baptist and Methodist churches were the most numerous
both in Pittsburgh and in the outlying industrial towns. These
denominations as well as the Pentecostal sects grew the fastest
in the migration years. The African Methodist Episcopal, the
African Methodist Episcopal Zion, and Colored Methodist Episcopal members in Pittsburgh increased by a total of nearly
1,000 between 1916 and 1926. Black Baptist churches in the
city numbered thirty-two in 1916 and forty-four ten years later,
with an increase in members of roughly one-third to compare
with a national membership growth of less than one-tenth for
the same period.[43] Much of the increase in congregations during these ten years was represented by "storefront" churches
with comparatively few worshippers, no permanent meeting
place, and poorly educated pastors. They stood in sharp contrast to the older, well-established black churches in Pittsburgh.[44]

The distinctions of social class, social status, and culture
among black churches could also be found among congregations of the same denomination. The arrival of thousands of
southern newcomers and the founding of many new congregations sharpened some of these intradenominational differences.
The histories of two black Baptist churches in Homestead illus-
trate this process and the larger social differences that southern

migration fostered within the black community. Clark Memorial Church was organized in the 1890s. By the time southern migrants began to flood into Homestead's steel mills and other industries, it had become the leading black congregation in the town. The old residents in the mill town looked on Clark Memorial as their church; the prominent black Baptist families belonged. The ministers of Clark Memorial held degrees from colleges or theological seminaries. Located in the Hilltop section, the church built a new edifice and a community house annex in the 1920s, with financial aid from the Carnegie Steel Company.[45]

In addition to its religious services, Clark Memorial maintained many auxiliaries, clubs, and educational programs as well as a foreign mission. In its Sunday school classes students watched movies portraying blacks' material and spiritual advancement. The church officers administered Clark Memorial's facilities and programs tightly. "Perhaps in no place in Western Pennsylvania . . . will there be found a more solid sense of business transactions . . . than in Clarke Memorial," reported the *Courier*. "The business statements of the church read like bank statements. The annual business meeting of the church covers two nights. At this time the pastor outlines the year's program, and emphasizes the policy of the church."[46]

The Second Baptist Church began as a mission among the black residents in the lower-class Ward neighborhood of Homestead. In 1905 a group of men decided that they needed a place of worship in their own section of town. But Second Baptist struggled for years to root itself in the lives of the Ward's blacks. The congregation shifted its meeting place often, at one time gathering in a room over a blacksmith's shop, at another time occupying a store front. For many years the church had a hall on Sixth Avenue, among the bars, brothels, and steelworkers' boardinghouses.[47] Pastors came and went almost as frequently as Second Baptist changed its address. Six different ministers led the church between 1905 and 1914. At last the deacons called a mill worker, the Reverend J. D. Morton, to pastor the church. Tall and gaunt, he tackled both heavy mill tasks and the Lord's work with equal energy. His followers knew him as a stern moral teacher, but an upright, honorable, and lovable man as well. Many were devoted to him. When Morton quit his mill job to

become pastor of Second Baptist, his income dropped sharply
to the $40 per month salary that the church could pay. Mem-
bers of the congregation supported Morton and his large family
with gifts of cash or necessities, though the preacher never
asked for them.[48]

From its beginnings in the lofts and storefronts of the Ward,
Second Baptist was identified with the town's poorer, less educated blacks. Though the charter members did not split off
from Clark Memorial, they founded their church to fill a spiritual vacuum created by the development of two social spheres
among Homestead blacks.[49] Second Baptist had fewer church
clubs and auxiliaries than Clark Memorial and no community
recreation center. Whether for lack of funds or from a different
idea of its worldly responsibilities, Second Baptist Church seemed
to keep closer to the duties of orthodox religious instruction
and Christian fellowship than did its Hilltop neighbor.

The difference in intellectual atmosphere between Second
Baptist and Clark Memorial appeared in the sermons their
pastors preached on Sundays. This difference is suggested by
the titles of several sermons delivered in 1923. At Clark Memorial Dr. Marshall A. Talley preached on "The Facts about Easter,"
"Things Temporal and Things Eternal," "Selfishness," and "God's
Idea of Segregation." At approximately the same time the Reverend Morton at Second Baptist chose as his topics, "The Church,
a Blessing in the World," "A New Heart," "The Divine Order,"
and "The Character of the Holy Spirit."[50] Although such evidence only hints at differences between the two churches, it
suggests other disparities. Dr. Talley's sermons seemed to carry
a relatively secular tone and a concern for social and even
political issues affecting blacks. On the other hand, the Reverend Morton's preachings might have communicated a more
other-worldly, religious message to his flock. Dr. Talley addressed
Sunday audiences almost as a lecturer, discussing the application of Christian precepts in the modern world. In the Ward
church the Reverend Morton taught inspirational lessons from
the Bible, instructing communicants on modes of personal
conduct prescribed in the Scriptures.[51]

How and why southern blacks joined one Pittsburgh congregation among the many in the city helps us understand the way

the churches affected their settlement and how the migrants changed the churches. In the rural South, where small black communities supported few churches, where one worshipped might have been only a matter of denomination. In many places the community and church embraced each other, and each Sunday's gathering brought together the God-fearing families of the entire neighborhood. In northern cities, where migrants often visited churches of the same as well as different denominations, even after they became members of a congregation, many perhaps lost the sense of belonging that they had felt toward their southern congregation. Indeed, Ira Reid found that the majority of Pittsburgh blacks in the Hill District of the late 1920s did not attend church at all.[52] But those migrants who became loyal members of a Pittsburgh church did so not simply because their religious feelings were particularly strong. Rather, they found in an urban congregation bonds with a pastor and with members whose status in the community and style of worship they could fully share.

Unfamiliar with Pittsburgh churches, many newly arrived migrants first went to the church closest to their lodgings. In North Braddock Maria B. joined First Baptist as the nearest black church to her first northern residence. Similarly, many migrants in Homestead's Ward section went to Second Baptist when they began looking for a church to attend. Another Second Baptist church, the one in the black workers' compound built by Lockhart Iron and Steel, drew most of its congregants from the company's housing.[53] In smaller towns around Pittsburgh migrants did not have two or more churches from which to choose. When these towns were too far from the city for an easy Sunday trip to church, the southerners attended the sole black church in their vicinity, or none at all.[54]

In addition to the convenience of proximity, migrants went to a particular church because of a pastor's preaching and leadership. Black preachers were important gatekeepers for southern blacks in helping them find jobs, providing food and shelter in church buildings during emergencies, and organizing social or recreational programs.[55] But they played their most vital gatekeeping role in drawing migrants into the black churches. In this respect, the poorer, less educated preachers were con-

spicuously successful. Like most migrants, they often came
from the rural South to work in Pittsburgh industries. Sharing
southern blacks' onerous work and poor living conditions in
Pittsburgh, they knew very well the difficulties incoming blacks
faced at their jobs and in their crowded lodgings. James S., who
came to Pittsburgh from the Albany, Georgia, area, both made a
living at industrial jobs and preached at many churches. In
order to pursue his religious calling, he refused more than one
supervisor's orders to work on Sundays. The North Carolinian
John T. also balanced his employment at Westinghouse Electric
and Manufacturing Company with his efforts to become an
ordained Baptist minister. Both he and James S. belonged to a
ministers' union, which supported lay preachers' efforts to promote themselves and obtain pastorships. Members of the union
preached as guests of black churches whenever there were
opportunities and in places as far from Pittsburgh as Ohio and
West Virginia.[56] Some migrants probably saw in these preachers'
attempts to become ordained and win their own pulpits reflec-
tions of their own struggles to overcome the barriers of poverty,
low social status, and lack of education.

The migrant preachers who managed to get Pittsburgh pastorships drew some of the members of their southern churches to
the congregations over which they presided in the city.[57] Their
sermons were more likely to appeal to the migrants, many of
whom preferred the rousing, emotional deliveries of the southern rural churches. This "down home" oratory was not the
exclusive possession of southern-born preachers, but it flourished
especially in the storefront Baptist and Pentecostal churches,
most of whose members were recent arrivals in Pittsburgh.[58]

The clear differences in the social composition of Pittsburgh's
black churches meant that the congregation could be as important as the preacher in attracting migrant settlers. Seeking
more than a place to worship, migrants wanted to find fellowship and a sense of belonging in the churches they joined.
Southern blacks were unlikely to feel accepted in the elite black
Episcopal or Congregational churches, or in the less exclusive
but larger congregations at long-established Baptist and Methodist churches. Olive W. attended services at an African Methodist Episcopal church in the lower Hill District just after she and

her husband reached Pittsburgh in 1919. This church seated light-skinned members apart from darker worshippers. She "wanted none of that" and joined the Wesley African Methodist Episcopal Zion Church instead.[59] The relationship between migrants' perception of a congregation and how much "at home" they felt in a church came through clearly in one woman's experiences in Homestead. Julia D. lived in the Hilltop neighborhood, and visited Clark Memorial Church the first Sunday she spent in the North. Then she was invited to go to Second Baptist Church: "The women, especially the older women—they were so friendly . . . they put their arms around me and made me feel so welcome!" The next Sunday she met Clark Memorial's pastor on his way to services. "Don't be late!" he told her. She replied, "I'm going to *my* church." He said, "*Your* church? What do you mean, 'your' church?" "Second Baptist," she said. "Those people down there were the most friendly and lovingest people I ever met."[60]

The networks of kin and friends from southern homes drew the migrants into churches simply by contributing to the sense of familiarity that was essential for southern blacks' affiliation. It was not uncommon for devout southern men and women to go to church in Pittsburgh on the first Sunday after they arrived in the company of parents, siblings, aunts and uncles, in-laws, boarding families, or friends.[61] Though the relatives or friends might be nearly as new to the churches as the migrants, nonetheless they could act as hosts and hostesses, sometimes introducing their guests to other church members, officers, or the pastor. Charner C. went to Homestead's Second Baptist Church for the first time with a buddy from his steel mill work gang. A migrant from Mississippi, this friend asked C. if he went to church and then told him about Second Baptist. C. liked what he found at the church, "The way they do, talk, and everything— so I joined."[62]

Proximity, migrant preachers, welcoming congregations, and migrant networks all contributed to the "southernizing" of some black churches in Pittsburgh. The new churches that were founded between World War I and the Depression in lower-class neighborhoods often took in predominantly recent migrants to the Pittsburgh area. Certainly this was the case for Union

Baptist near Rankin, White Lily Baptist in the West End, the Church of God in Christ in the Hill District, and Second Baptist in McKees Rocks.[63] In these churches and in older congregations that absorbed large numbers of migrants, kin and friendship networks continuously added more southern blacks.[64] These networks also established groups of blacks from certain southern regions and states. Some of Clark Memorial's Petersburg, Virginia, migrants came to the church through the auspices of Lillyan P. and her husband. These former Petersburg residents boarded men from the same part of Virginia and often invited them to services at Clark Memorial. Caleb B. likewise urged the friends he had invited north from his Marion, South Carolina, home to attend Second Baptist Church, where he was a member and strong admirer of the Reverend Morton.[65]

The way in which migrant networks brought southern blacks into Pittsburgh churches did not result in a neat correlation of southern localities or states with separate congregations. Instead, those black churches that gained large numbers of migrant members included many different, regionally based groups within their congregations. In Homestead, however, the Baptist churches diverged in the composition of their congregations between migrants from the Upper and Deep South areas. Of sixteen Homestead migrants interviewed for this study, half belonged to Second Baptist and half to Clark Memorial. Of the members of Second Baptist, six came from South Carolina, one from North Carolina, and one from Virginia.[66] Of the eight who belonged to Clark Memorial, six came from Virginia, one from South Carolina, and one from Alabama.[67] Corroboration of this geographic difference between the congregations came from a former secretary of Second Baptist's missionary circle, who had also been a member of Clark Memorial. She recollected many states of origin among the migrants at Second Baptist, but a preponderance of men and women from North Carolina, South Carolina, and Georgia. Clark Memorial migrants, in her memory, came from the Upper South.[68]

The networks of relatives and friends that undergirded southern blacks' chain migration to the North and their residential clusters in the Pittsburgh area were also partly responsible for the Upper South–Deep South difference between these two churches. But the histories of Clark Memorial and Second Baptist and their identification with separate black social groups in Homestead may also have keys to understanding which migrants were attracted to which congregation. Blacks from the more affluent and more urbanized Upper South may have found more to like in the atmosphere at Clark Memorial, while their counterparts from the poorer plantation areas of the Deep South might have felt more comfortable with Second Baptist's members. The way in which migrants' backgrounds meshed with existing differences between black churches in the Pittsburgh area thus could have resulted in making such differences ones of geographic origins as well as those of social status, culture, and education. In any case, the migrants' native regions in some instances were used as a basis for grouping church members into teams for church rallies and fund-raising events. "States" rallies were held as friendly competitions to see which state group could bring in the greatest financial contributions for the church. When men and women from the same southern state or locality cooperated in these functions, they maintained their identity not just as migrants, but as South Carolina, Georgia, or Virginia migrants.[69]

If the migrant settlers maintained kin and friend groups in Pittsburgh, they also in many cases returned to the South to nurture ties with those relatives and neighbors who remained in their places of origin. Some went back on brief visits to the places where their journeys had begun, but others stayed for months or even years before returning north. It was not for love of the South that migrants returned, but for love of family, friends, and childhood homes. Their settlement in Pittsburgh did not come about by the severing of these bonds, but by their strengthening under new forms and meanings.

Pittsburgh migrants more often went home because they wanted to, not because they had to. The line dividing choice from necessity often blurred, since obligations to family or to friends played a part in many migrants' decisions to return south. Walter H. left Homestead to run his family's Virginia farm during his brother's illness. His brother recovered after several months and resumed management of the farm, and Walter H. moved north to the Pittsburgh area again. Laura L.

also returned to Virginia from the Pittsburgh area. Her stepchildren needed care after their grandparents died, so she looked after them until other guardians could be found. More common obligations for the migrants were funerals, weddings, graduations, and family reunions. Though few migrants would have dreamed of missing one of these occasions, few attended them solely to discharge family responsibilities.[70]

There were also times when Pittsburgh migrants were forced to move back to their native region. Unemployment, injury, illness, a strike, trouble with the law, or some other unforeseen change in their fortunes could send individuals or families fleeing from the city. Sadie M.'s parents moved back to Alabama with all of their children in fear of falling prey to the influenza epidemic that ravaged Pittsburgh in 1918. Gilbert M. returned to South Carolina from Buffalo, New York, to avoid conscription during World War I. On a much larger scale, thousands of southern blacks who lost jobs in the 1920–21 depression left Pittsburgh. Many apparently took refuge in the South to await the revival of northern industry.[71]

It was the time of year migrants chose to go south more than the length of time they spent there that enabled them to maintain ties with the communities where they had grown up. The alternating periods of fieldwork and rural festivities in cotton-growing regions afforded Pittsburgh migrants at least two different ways to refresh their acquaintance with their places of origin. By choosing a season of heavy farm work to return south, migrants could keep their hand in their families' rural labors. Or, if they visited their native communities during one of the rural festival periods, Pittsburgh migrants could participate in the country social events and holiday celebrations. Though southern blacks' movement between north and south was influenced by other factors as well, the rural timetable of work and leisure is an important clue in revealing the nature of migrants' ties to their places of origin.

The transient southern black workers at the A. M. Byers Company moved to and from Pittsburgh on the same schedule most migrants used—traveling in both directions in the months of fair, warm weather and staying put during the cold months (figure 1). This meant that they did not for the most part

Figure 1
Byers Company Migrants' Arrivals and Departures, Pittsburgh, 1916-30

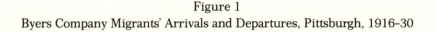

—————— Arrivals (N = 344)

— — — — Departures (N = 121)

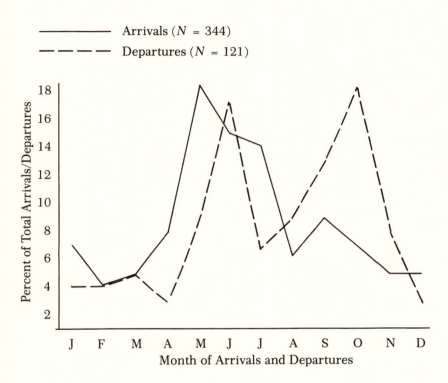

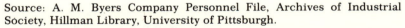

Month of Arrivals and Departures

Source: A. M. Byers Company Personnel File, Archives of Industrial Society, Hillman Library, University of Pittsburgh.

Note: "Arrivals" are months when migrants reached Pittsburgh; "departures" are months when migrant employees voluntarily left A. M. Byers Company after their first job assignment.

coordinate their migration with the annual cycle of cotton cultivation. There were, however, two points in these migrants' seasonal movements that suggested efforts to respond to the swings in demand for field labor in the South. During August, just as the cotton harvest began in the Deep South, departures from the Byers mill went up sharply. Men who had headed north during the spring groundbreaking now seemed to return South to help pick what their kinsmen and neighbors had grown. Then, too, as the cotton harvest drew to a close, more black men began arriving in Pittsburgh. Though this change might have signaled a reaction to the annual growth in demand for steel labor in Pennsylvania, it also fit the seasonal drop in demand for field labor in the South.[72]

The black men at the Byers Company may have been trying to balance their need for northern wages with their commitment to southern farms and families, but migrants who were gradually settling in Pittsburgh necessarily had to decrease their involvement with their former communities and develop a different relationship with them. Some settlers went home more frequently in the first months of their Pittsburgh residence than they did later. As the deaths of parents, siblings, and close friends gradually removed the primary bonds between Pittsburgh and the scenes of their earlier lives, visits to the South decreased. In fact, the passing of all loved ones in their places of origin may have been a decisive factor in convincing some southern blacks to remain permanently in the North.[73] For other Pittsburgh migrants, marriage marked a similar shift in their involvement with their birthplaces. Harrison G. and Charner C. both went back to the South for the last time to get married and to bring their new wives to the homes that they had prepared in Pittsburgh.[74]

A gradual slackening of bonds with former homes did not always end in a total lapse of connections between Pittsburgh migrants and their birthplaces. The migrants kept visiting southern communities after they had established permanent residences in the city. Unlike the transient black workers at Byers, these settlers most often went south either in mid-summer or at Christmas, timing their visits "back home" to coincide with periods when black farmers were holding their seasonal festivals. In December 1919 a Pittsburgh social worker discovered that "quite a few of the women of new families returned South for the Holidays and we find that frequently they remain until Spring leaving the husband to get along as best he can."[75] Those who visited the South in August, when black communities turned their energies from fieldwork to church revivals, barbecues, and picnics, mingled with the celebrants. When large numbers of migrants returned to a locality at this time of year, a homecoming celebration was added to other forms of socializing. In such a setting as this, Pittsburgh migrants could enter into old associations or renew friendships in the larger community, beyond the boundaries of their own kinship group. Return migration during the Christmas holiday could also affirm the sense of belonging to institutions and a way of life with which the migrants still felt some affinity.

The migrants' return trips to the South thus answered several needs, from sheltering laid-off, injured, or sick mill laborers, to bringing extra hands to the fields for harvest, to maintaining participation in communal and family networks. This last need became the most important one for those southerners who eventually settled in Pittsburgh. Annual visits to Union Springs, Alabama, New Kent County, Virginia, or Orangeburg, South Carolina, revived that part of the migrants' identity that remained bound up with their communities of origin. Here was a source of affinal and communal feelings to complement those surrounding Pittsburgh homes, a source of pride in being a *southern* black man or woman that could counter northerners' scorn for rural migrants.

Many years after they crossed the threshold between southern rural and northern urban worlds, the black migrants reflected on the immense changes encompassed by their lives. Harrison G., the Georgia migrant, explained that the implication of his northward movement came to him all at once. After finding steady work, marrying, and establishing a household, he thought to himself one day: "My daddy was a farmer and I thought I was going to be a farmer. But it looks like I'm going to be a city man now."[76]

However appropriate this statement seemed to Harrison G. at a particular point in his life, it simplified two problems of southern blacks' settlement in the North. One concerned dating of the end of the settlement process. Few migrants awoke one morning with the realization that they had become permanent urban workers in Pittsburgh. The growth of commitment to a new home necessarily came about in small degrees. John B. could look back on his migration, work, and Pittsburgh residence and say: "I kind of got stuck here, I think. After I got to working in the church and made quite a few friends around . . . I was just stuck, that was all. I never accumulated any property." Exactly when he knew he was "stuck," though, he could not say. Repeated periods of joblessness, unremitting restrictions on blacks' opportunities to prosper, and strong ties to southern homes all made migrants' status in Pittsburgh uncertain for many years. Perhaps not until the war-spawned economic boom of the 1940s, when blacks in Pittsburgh worked steadily for several years at relatively high wages, could some of them cap their settlement efforts by buying a small home.[77]

In another sense, which is hidden by the phrase, "I'm going to be a city man now," southern blacks who came to Pittsburgh never completely transformed themselves to northern wage workers. Queen W.'s feelings remained suspended between her adopted home in the city and her native Appomattox, Virginia. She nearly gave up on Pittsburgh soon after she came north to live with her husband, and even after she reconciled herself to the city, she went back to Virginia every summer. Yet she always bought a round-trip ticket for her journeys to the South. "I didn't want to go down there and get stranded," she admitted. "I'd keep my car fare home."[78] Matthew J. summarized his experience in Pittsburgh by enumerating the "houses" to which he had devoted his life. "I have spent most of my life at the firehouse, church house, school house, Westinghouse, and my house." But this migrant was one of the many southern blacks in Pittsburgh who also spent part of each year after moving north vacationing in the South Carolina rural district where he was born and grew up.

Matthew J. was like many black migrants in another respect: most of the blacks he knew in his new home were also southern-born men and women.[79] Pittsburgh migrants who succeeded in making northern homes in fact lived, worked, socialized, and worshipped primarily among other blacks from the South. Their geographic origins and social status in Pittsburgh remained the basis of their identity even after many years of residence in the North. The drawn-out series of changes that they had set in motion when they departed from the South bore fruit in a wholly northern, urban identity only in their children's and grandchildren's lives.

NOTES

1. "Negro Leadership of Negro Workers in Industrial Plants," speech by George E. Haynes, Oct. 22, 1920, typescript in U.S. Department of Labor, Division of Negro Economics, Record Group (RG) 174, File H, National Archives and Records Administration, Washington, D.C.; Robert C. Hanson and Ozzie G. Simmons, "The Role Path: A Concept and Procedure for Studying Migration to Urban Communities," *Human Organization* 27 (Summer 1968), 152, 154.

2. "From Slaves to Statesmen. A History of Blacks in Pittsburgh," Pittsburgh *Press,* "Roto Magazine" Oct. 17, 1982, 6-7, 10-11; Victor Ullman, *Martin R. Delany: The Beginnings of Black Nationalism* (Boston: Beacon Press, 1971), 11-34.

3. Helen Tucker, "The Negroes of Pittsburgh," in *Wage-Earning Pittsburgh,* The Pittsburgh Survey, ed. Paul U. Kellogg (New York: Survey Associates, 1914), 429-31; Richard R. Wright, Jr., *The Negro in Pennsylvania* (Philadelphia: AME Book Concern, 1912), 74-75.

4. Wright, *Negro in Pennsylvania,* 179; Works Progress Administration, Historical Survey, Pennsylvania Writers' Project, "The Negro in Pittsburgh," ch. 9, 3-4 (manuscript in Pennsylvania State Archives, Harrisburg); interview: William L., Nov. 3, 1975.

5. Richard R. Wright, Jr., "One Hundred Negro Steel Workers," in *Wage-Earning Pittsburgh,* 102.

6. Ibid., 102.

7. Margaret Byington, *Homestead: The Households of a Mill Town,* The Pittsburgh Survey, ed. Paul U. Kellogg (New York: Charities Publication Committee, 1910), 40-42; Tucker, "Negroes of Pittsburgh," 426-27.

8. Tucker, "Negroes of Pittsburgh," 427-28. For another description of a settlement of lower-class blacks in Pittsburgh, see Florence L. Lattimore, "Skunk Hollow," in *The Pittsburgh District: Civic Frontage,* The Pittsburgh Survey, ed. Paul U. Kellogg (New York: Survey Associates, 1914), 124-30.

9. Home Economics Worker's report, Aug. 1919, Administration File, "Miscellaneous," Urban League of Pittsburgh (ULP) Records, Archives of Industrial Society, Hillman Library, University of Pittsburgh.

10. Pennsylvania Department of Welfare, *Negro Survey of Pennsylvania* (Harrisburg, 1928), 10.

11. Pittsburgh *Courier,* June 16, 1923, 14.

12. Ibid., Feb. 16, 1924, 16.

13. Interviews: Harrison G., Aug. 23, 1974, John B., Mar. 10, 1976.

14. WPA, "Negro in Pittsburgh," ch. 14, 15-16.

15. Interviews: Harrison G., Aug. 23, 1974, Charner C., Feb. 21, 1976, Gilbert M., Apr. 9, 1976, Matthew J., May·28, 1976, Ed R., June 10, 1976.

16. Interviews: Ed R., June 10, 1976, John T., Nov. 1, 23, 1973.

17. For information on the social welfare programs conducted by black churches and charitable organizations in Pittsburgh, see Pittsburgh *Courier,* Nov. 24, 1923, 16; Ira De A. Reid, *Social Conditions of the Negro in the Hill District of Pittsburgh* (Pittsburgh: General Committee on the Hill Survey, 1930), 107–10; Tucker, "Negroes of Pittsburgh," 433–34; Wright, *Negro in Pennsylvania,* 180–81; *Survey* 43 (Jan. 17, 1920), 416; Arthur J. Edmunds, *Daybreakers: The Story of the Urban League of Pittsburgh* (Pittsburgh: Urban League of Pittsburgh, 1983), 10–16.

18. "The Urban League's Work in the Field of Industrial Relations" (typescript), 6–7; *Urban League of Pittsburgh* 1 (Mar. 1918); and "Annual Report of the Work of the Urban League of Pittsburgh for 1924," 3, all in ULP Records; John T. Clark to James Byrd, Jan. 30, 1923, Clark Papers, Carter G. Woodson Collection, Library of Congress, Washington, D.C.; Edmunds, *Daybreakers,* 17–28.

19. This analysis of the Urban League's work with black migrants in Pittsburgh does not cover several important League programs: Traveler's Aid, room registry, fellowships for black students at the University of Pittsburgh, baby health care, and health programs.

20. Home Economics Worker's report, Dec. 8, 1925, ULP Records; Edmunds, *Daybreakers,* 42.

21. Ruth Stevenson, "Pittsburgh Urban League" (M.A. thesis, University of Pittsburgh, 1936), 66–76; Home Economics Worker's report, Dec. 8, 1925, ULP Records.

22. Home Economics Worker's report, Dec. 8, 1925, ULP Records; John T. Clark, "The Migrant in Pittsburgh," *Opportunity* 1 (Oct. 1923), 304.

23. Home Economics Worker's report, Dec. 8, 1925, ULP Records.

24. Urban League of Pittsburgh, *Bulletin* 2 (May 1919), ULP Records.

25. Stevenson, "Pittsburgh Urban League," 77.

26. Ibid., 89–90; Clark, "Migrant in Pittsburgh," 305–6; Edmunds, *Daybreakers,* 36–40, 59–62.

27. Stevenson, "Pittsburgh Urban League," 55; Edmunds, *Daybreakers,* 33–34, 36.

28. Ira De A. Reid, "The Negro in the Major Industries and Building Trades of Pittsburgh" (M.A. thesis, University of Pittsburgh, 1925), 24; Reid, *Social Conditions,* 13; "Report on Visit to Pittsburgh, Pa., August 12 and 13, 1920," U.S. Department of Labor, Division of Negro Economics, RG 174, File "Miscellaneous."

29. Interviews: John B., Mar. 10, 1976, Charles B., July 16, 1976.

30. Minutes of Industrial Welfare Workers' meeting, Nov. 12, 1919, ULP Records.

31. Publicity File (no date), ULP Records.

32. Stevenson, "Pittsburgh Urban League," 90.

33. John T. Clark to James F. Malone, Mar. 8, 1924, ULP Records.

34. John T. Clark to James Byrd, Jan. 30, 1923, Clark Papers.

35. Nancy J. Weiss, *The National Urban League, 1910–1940* (New York: Oxford University Press, 1974), 117, 119.

36. J. T. Boris, ed., *Who's Who in Colored America* (New York: WWICA Publications, 1929), 78, 357-58.

37. Dennis C. Dickerson, "Black Steelworkers in Western Pennsylvania, 1915–1950" (Ph.D. thesis, Washington University, 1978), 83.

38. "Report on Visit to Pittsburgh . . . ," RG 174, File "Miscellaneous." Dennis C. Dickerson has found that Nelson also pastored churches in Ford City, Rankin, and Pittsburgh. See Dickerson, "The Black Church in Industrializing Western Pennsylvania," *Western Pennsylvania Historical Magazine* 64 (Oct. 1981), 335-36.

39. Edmunds, *Daybreakers*, 32-34, 36-40, 59-62.

40. Pittsburgh *Courier*, Nov. 17, 1923, 9.

41. Tucker, "Negroes of Pittsburgh," 432; "From Slaves to Statesmen," 36-37; interview: Olive W., July 23, 1976.

42. Pittsburgh *Courier*, June 6, 1925, 6; John Bodnar, Roger Simon, and Michael P. Weber, *Lives of Their Own: Blacks, Italians, and Poles in Pittsburgh, 1900–1960* (Urbana: University of Illinois Press, 1982), 74.

43. U.S. Census Bureau, *Religious Bodies: 1916,* Part 1 (Washington: Government Printing Office, 1919), 345, 422, 470; U.S. Census Bureau, *Religious Bodies: 1926,* 1 (Washington: Government Printing Office, 1930), 293, 510-11.

44. Reid, *Social Conditions,* 101-3; interviews: Sadie M., Apr. 9, 1976, Willie S., July 15, 1974; Carter G. Woodson, *History of the Negro Church,* 3d ed. (Washington: Associated Publishers, 1972), 297.

45. Pittsburgh *Courier*, Jan. 10, 1925, 3; interviews: Harvey C., Dec. 2, 1973, Lillyan P., Nov. 9, 10, 1973, Laura L., Nov. 21, 1973.

46. Pittsburgh *Courier*, Jan. 10, 1925, 3.

47. "History of the Second Baptist Church" (no date, no pages). I wish to thank the Reverend Donald Turner for providing me with this document. Interviews: Sadie M., Apr. 9, 1976, Alfred B., Apr. 21, 1976.

48. Interviews: Sadie M., Apr. 9, 1976, Alfred B., Apr. 21, 1976.

49. Interview: Alfred B., Apr. 21, 1976.

50. Pittsburgh *Courier*, Apr. 4, 1923, 13, Apr. 28, 1923, 15, June 9, 1923, 13, June 23, 1923, 13, June 30, 1923, 13, July 21, 1923, 13, Aug. 18, 1923, 13.

51. Interview: Alfred B., Apr. 21, 1976.

52. Reid, *Social Conditions,* 100; interviews: Elonzo H., Oct. 23, 1973, Laura L., Nov. 21, 1973, Joseph M., Nov. 16, 1973.

53. Interviews: Maria B., June 1, 1976, Alfred B., Apr. 21, 1976, Lee C., June 9, 1976, Jonathan W., June 28, 1974, Willie S., July 15, 1974, Ed R., June 10, 1976.

54. Interview: Ben E., July 31, 1974.

55. Pittsburgh *Courier,* Nov. 24, 1923, 16, Dec. 1, 1923, 12; Reid,

Social Conditions, 104-5; Dennis C. Dickerson, "Black Workers and Black Churches in Western Pennsylvania, 1915-1950," in *Blacks in Pennsylvania History,* ed. David McBride (Harrisburg: Pennsylvania Historical and Museum Commission, 1983), 57.

56. Interviews: James S., June 7, 14, 1974, John T., Nov. 1, 23, 1973.

57. Interview: Carrie J., July 23, 1976.

58. Interviews: Caleb B., Apr. 9, 1976, Alfred B., Apr. 21, 1976; Melvin D. Williams, *Community in a Black Pentecostal Church* (Pittsburgh: University of Pittsburgh Press, 1974), 103-8.

59. Interview: Olive W., July 23, 1976.

60. Interview: Julia D. (pseudonym), May 3, 1976.

61. Interviews: Laura L., Nov. 21, 1973, Walter H., Oct. 25, 30, 1973, Mrs. Abraham L., Mar. 11, 1976, Ed R., June 10, 1976.

62. Interview: Charner C., Feb. 21, 1976.

63. Interviews: Sadie M., May 19, 1976, Willie S., July 15, 1974, Jonathan W., June 28, 1974; Williams, *Community in a Black Pentecostal Church,* 17-26.

64. Interviews: Sadie M., Apr. 9, 1976, Ed R., June 10, 1976, Matthew J., May 28, 1976.

65. Interviews: Lillyan P., Nov. 9, 10, 1973, Caleb B., Apr. 9, 1976, Walter H., Oct. 25, 30, 1973.

66. Interviews: John B., Mar. 10, 1976, Wesley M., Apr. 2, 1976, Gilbert M., Apr. 9, 1976, Caleb B., Apr. 9, 1976, Julia D. (pseudonym), May 3, 1976, Charner C., Feb. 21, 1976, Mrs. Abraham L., Mar. 11, 1976, Joseph G., Nov. 26, 1973.

67. Interviews: Joseph M., Nov. 16, 1973, Lillyan P., Nov. 9, 10, 1973, Laura L., Nov. 21, 1973, Silas B., Oct. 29, 1973, John A., Oct. 29, 1973, Walter H., Oct. 25, 30, 1973, Benjamin B., Nov. 30, 1973, Harvey C., Dec 2, 1973.

68. Interview: Sadie M., Apr. 9, 1976.

69. Interview: Sadie M., Apr. 9, 1976.

70. Interviews: Walter H., Oct. 25, 30, 1973, Laura L., Nov. 21, 1973, Jean B., July 29, 1976.

71. Interviews: Sadie M., May 19, 1976, Gilbert M., Apr. 9, 1976; Reid, "Negro in the Major Industries," 9; R. W. Edmonds, "The Negro Exodus: Will It Be Permanent?" *Manufacturers Record* 85 (Apr. 17, 1924), 77. Another indication of the extent of return migration is in the migrants' letters in the Clark Papers. Several southern men who wrote to the Urban League of Pittsburgh in 1922-23 to inquire about job openings in industry explained that they had previously been in the city or elsewhere in Pennsylvania. See, e.g., Samuel Moore, Jan. 30, 1923, James Purdy, Feb. 7, 1923, Cicero Whitehead, Mar. 2, 1923, Horace Rollins, Mar. 5, 1923, J. W. Mitchell, Dec. 12, 1922.

72. A. M. Byers Company Personnel File, Archives of Industrial Society, Hillman Library, University of Pittsburgh.

73. Interviews: Jean B., July 29, 1976, Julia D. (pseudonym), May 3, 1976.

74. Interviews: Harrison G., Aug. 23, 1974, Charner C., Feb. 21, 1976.

75. Home Economics Worker's report, Dec. 1919, ULP Records.

76. Interview: Harrison G., Aug. 23, 1974.

77. Interview: John B., Mar. 10, 1976.

78. Interview: Queen W., Oct. 8, 1976.

79. Interview: Matthew J., May 28, 1976.

Epilogue

THE GREAT DEPRESSION radically altered the dynamics of southern blacks' movement to and from Pittsburgh. Mass unemployment, sharp reductions of working hours, and failures of companies that formerly sought black employees practically closed the migrants' approaches to the city. Unlike earlier periods of joblessness, however, blacks who lost jobs in Pittsburgh in the 1930s found themselves stranded. Their native communities in the South, gripped by a severe agricultural depression, could scarcely sustain them. There was little chance of finding jobs in other northern cities, either. The severity of the economic crisis during the early 1930s removed incentives for the far-flung searches to which job-seeking migrants had once resorted.

Pittsburgh blacks suffered from the economic hardship of the 1930s and from the loss of alternatives for supporting themselves and their families. They had to survive in the city against even greater odds than they had faced in the preceding era. Some were fortunate to have their spouses' incomes to maintain their households above a level of utter destitution. Others never were laid off by their employers, but worked only one or two days during each pay period. Black workers who lost their jobs had to enroll on local, state, or federal relief programs and works projects. In addition to the other means of survival, there was a great deal of foraging and scavenging. Collecting bottles and tin cans, culling bits of coal from slag heaps, fishing in the polluted rivers and streams around Pittsburgh, or hunting for small game were all ways to keep warm, keep fed, and keep

busy. Still, black migrants who in earlier years had scarcely
enough time to relax between their work shifts and their nights'
sleep now had countless hours of idle time to pass playing
cards with friends, chatting with neighbors, or simply sitting in
their rooms.[1]

A less direct but equally important consequence of the Depression for the black migrants was the unionization of Pittsburgh
mass production industries. The revitalization of the United
Mine Workers (UMW) began a chain of events that led to union
victories in the steel, electrical, rubber tire, cement, automobile,
and other basic industries. Blacks' attitudes toward the labor
movement changed gradually but perceptibly, especially with
the advent of the Committee for Industrial Organization (CIO).
This new federation of unions, led by men from unions that,
like the UMW, had long been more favorable to enrolling blacks
and giving them equal treatment, clearly set out to recruit
workers of all ranks, nationalities, and races, making special
appeals to blacks in Pittsburgh industry. Black workers themselves were more willing to listen to union organizers in the
1930s, having seen enough of open shop policies and the deterioration of living standards in the early 1930s. The change in
blacks' thinking about unions certainly did not occur overnight,
but there were signs of a shift even before the CIO achieved
breakthroughs in Pittsburgh. Black miners joined the UMW in
large numbers, and black steelworkers took an active part in the
abortive attempt to organize Pittsburgh area steel employees
into the Amalgamated Association of Iron and Steel Workers in
1933 and 1934. These activists and many other formerly indifferent black workers joined the new Steel Workers Organizing
Committee after 1936 and broke the long tradition of black
antiunionism in the steel industry.[2]

By the time World War II finally stimulated full levels of
industrial production in Pittsburgh, former southern migrants
had achieved a new status in the local labor market. They were
no longer newcomers just breaking into industrial jobs where
few blacks had previously worked. They were now veteran
employees who had become settled in the Pittsburgh area, survived the Depression, and enrolled in the labor movement.
Their actions during the 1930s also changed the way black

migrants of the 1940s would fit into the Pittsburgh economy and black community. Yet Pittsburgh after the 1930s was not an entirely new world for black workers. Stringent social and economic barriers to black advancement remained, even in the unionized work places where all employees supposedly worked under the same seniority and work transfer rules. Housing for blacks in the Pittsburgh area remained in a state of crisis, worsened by the expansion of mills and factories and by the redevelopment of downtown neighborhoods for which some black lower-class residential areas were razed. Black women's work opportunities did not change significantly up to the 1950s, either. Though some got better-paid factory jobs in World War II, these positions, like the few industrial jobs that women had filled in World War I, were mostly temporary. The majority of black women remained confined to domestic work beyond the 1930s, as they had been before.[3]

The continuities and changes for black migrants in Pittsburgh after 1930 bring the northward movement between World War I and the Depression into sharper focus. Though black migration to the city was continuous throughout the twentieth century, the dynamics of geographic movement changed from one period to another. Before World War I southern blacks came in relatively small numbers and only infrequently in response to demand for industrial laborers. After the late 1920s black migrants fled the collapse of the tenancy system in the cotton South, whether to share blacks' deprivation in the city during the 1930s or to work in war industries in the 1940s. But from World War I to the Depression the conjuncture of forces repelling blacks from the South and attracting them to the North, as well as blacks' responses to these forces, created a unique migration process. Except for brief interludes in particular southern regions, there was no upheaval in the cotton economy to send rural blacks fleeing northward.[4] The migrants were able to control the timing, organization, and direction of their movement to a greater degree than at other times. They could also coordinate the movements of family members and friends to maintain kinship and community networks. As long as there were sufficient work opportunities in Pittsburgh, therefore, strategies of movement in these years had greater chances for success than in years either earlier or later. Despite the forbidding long-term prospects for their northern urban lives, migrants had some reason to be optimistic at this time, to approach Pittsburgh with their own goals and high expectations.

Southern blacks moved to Pittsburgh in these years in ways that closely resemble the rural-urban migration of peoples at other times and places. While we are accustomed to thinking of the Great Migration as the foremost achievement of Afro-Americans in the early twentieth century, it is also a part of a worldwide pattern of urbanization. Under circumstances that vary from one instance to another, populations long bound to the land by a traditional agricultural economy and society gradually stretch their lives outward toward growing manufacturing or marketing centers. Like the post–Civil War changes in southern rural blacks' family organization, land tenure, and geographic mobility, the preparation for cityward migration takes place over a span of generations. The apparent suddenness of a "flight" from the countryside masks the lengthy seasoning that Afro-Americans and rural peoples in many places undergo before they attempt moves to urban areas.

For all the important differences between them and other groups of rural migrants to American cities, Pittsburgh's black migrants relied on many of the same resources and strategies for making good in their migration as those who arrived in the slums before them. Wherever possible, southern blacks relied on members of their nuclear and extended families for assistance in their northward trips. Such support was also given and received among friends, neighbors, workmates, and fellow church and lodge members from the home community in the South. The importance of such assistance within families and community groups may even have strengthened bonds among the newcomers to Pittsburgh and to other northern cities. They partially mitigated the difficulties of long-distance migration and home and job searches in Pittsburgh. They also cast some doubt on black novelist Richard Wright's assertion, "Perhaps never in history has a more utterly unprepared folk wanted to go to the city."[5] To a limited extent at least, Pittsburgh migrants readied themselves and tried to ready those who followed them for a different kind of work and home environment.

Despite the importance of blacks' sharing resources within family and communal groups, Pittsburgh migrants apparently cohered around social networks from their places of origin less than did black migrants to other cities. More research on patterns of movement and settlement will be needed to measure differences in this regard from one city to another, but in Pittsburgh we infrequently find the tightly knit groups of migrants from a particular southern locality belonging to the same northern church, living in close proximity, or gathering at social affairs in the city that are found among newcomers in other northern destinations.[6] There was no black church composed mainly of migrants from Marion, South Carolina, but instead a group of Marion residents congregated within the generally Deep South membership of Second Baptist in Homestead. Many Pittsburgh migrants settled in the city only after a period of transiency during which their family and friendship networks in the city became less vital to their social lives than they were when they arrived. By that time they were ready to affiliate with organizations and groups more on the basis of socioeconomic status and culture and less on the basis of kinship or common place of origin.

Thus, in Pittsburgh the migrants' orientation to their northern homes may have been influenced by a different mix of race, culture, social class, and kinship than that operating among southern blacks in other northern cities. Their race set them apart from other working-class newcomers to the city, targeting them for discrimination wherever they turned. In other ways, they snugly fit the historic mold of the city's common laborers — primarily young, male workers living in bunkhouses and boardinghouses, working hard, drinking hard, and often quitting their jobs to escape the city with cash earnings. Not surprisingly, both long-term black residents and white workers in Pittsburgh greeted the black migrants coolly. Similar receptions had been given each newly arriving supply of labor by those who had attained some standing or security in the city. But the local economy in the end most directly shaped southern blacks' experiences. Absorbing and then casting off southern blacks in time to the irregular cycles of industrial growth and decline, Pittsburgh industry made permanent space for relatively few of those who came to the mines, mills, and machine shops. The essential relationship between the city and these migrants during the years from World War I to the Depression was captured in the words of a 1914 study of black workers in Pittsburgh: "Pittsburgh is debtor to the South. . . . The steel district beckons, uses up, and beckons to more."[7]

NOTES

1. Dennis C. Dickerson, "Black Steelworkers in Western Pennsylvania, 1915-1950" (Ph.D. thesis, Washington University, 1978), 95-101; interviews: Richard C., Aug., 8, 1974 (on spouses supporting households), Lee T., May 26, 1976, Gilbert M., Apr. 9, 1976, Matthew J., May 28, 1976, Lee C., June 9, 1976 (on part-time work), Jerome G., Aug. 1, 1974, Richard C., Aug. 8, 1974, Queen W., Oct. 8, 1976 (on welfare and works projects), Gilbert M., Apr. 9, 1976 (on scavenging); Philip Klein, *A Social Study of Pittsburgh* (New York: Columbia University Press, 1938), 273, 279-80.

2. Robert R. R. Brooks, *As Steel Goes* (New Haven: Yale University Press, 1940), 18; George Powers, *Cradle of Steel Unionism: Monongahela Valley, Pa.* (East Chicago, Ind.: Figueroa Printers, 1972), 37, 42-43, 96; Horace R. Cayton and George S. Mitchell, *Black Workers and the New Unions* (Chapel Hill: University of North Carolina Press, 1939), 123-224.

3. Dickerson, "Black Steelworkers," 131-70; Roy Lubove, *Twentieth Century Pittsburgh: Government, Business, and Environmental Change* (New York: John Wiley & Sons, 1969), 83-86, 130-32.

4. James H. Street, *The New Revolution in the Cotton Economy* (Chapel Hill: University of North Carolina Press, 1957), 41-64, 107-91; Dwayne E. Walls, *The Chickenbone Special* (New York: Harcourt, Brace, Jovanovich, Inc., 1970), 3, and passim; Daniel M. Johnson and Rex R. Campbell, *Black Migration in America: A Social Demographic History* (Durham: Duke University Press, 1981), 120-51.

5. Richard Wright, *Twelve Million Black Voices* (New York: Viking Press, 1941), 93.

6. Clyde V. Kiser, *Sea Island to City* (New York: Columbia University Press, 1932), 210-12; Emmett J. Scott, *Negro Migration during the War* (New York: Oxford University Press, 1920), 96; Allen B. Ballard,

One More Day's Journey (New York: McGraw-Hill, 1984), 16, 174–76, 181–82.

7. Richard R. Wright, Jr., "One Hundred Negro Steel Workers," in *Wage-Earning Pittsburgh,* The Pittsburgh Survey, ed. Paul U. Kellogg (New York: Survey Associates, 1914), 110.

Appendix A

Oral History Interviews

The interviews used in this study were conducted from October 1973 to January 1977. Of the sixty-five interviews listed below, thirty-two were conducted under the auspices of the Ethnic Studies Program of the Pennsylvania Historical and Museum Commission. I contacted the subjects of my interviews through the institutions and organizations to which they belonged: churches, labor unions, community groups, and senior citizens' programs. I relied on ministers, church and union secretaries, and social workers to develop lists of potential interviewees, from which I selected my respondents.

The questions I asked each migrant were designed with two goals in mind: first, to develop a body of information on places of origin, migration patterns, Pittsburgh occupations, family relationships, and institutional affiliations; second, to elicit the migrants' memories of their attitudes, aspirations, and reactions to new experiences during their northward movement. The questions that I prepared for the interviews are found on pages 226–29.

I departed from this interview schedule whenever it was necessary to explore facets of the respondents' lives on which my questions did not touch. Thus the questionnaire includes only those questions that I asked most frequently.

The problems in collecting information through personal interviews hinged both on the kind of people I questioned and the reliability of their memories. The elderly black men and women whom I interviewed, most of them born between 1890 and 1910 and living in Pittsburgh in the mid-1970s, were survivors. That they were available to be interviewed also meant that they had persisted where thousands of other migrants had not. Those respondents I reached through churches also tended to hold deep religious convictions and to be prominent in their congregations: deacons, Sunday school teachers, members of missionary circles, for example. Fewer of the members of labor unions, community groups, and senior citizens' programs were devout church-goers or active supporters of congregations. Though interviewees selected in this manner were not a cross-section of Pittsburgh's migrants, they did include part of the migrant networks that were created by and through the process of northward movement. This was the advantage of working, for example, through the Homestead churches and community organizations and of being referred to friends and relatives of people whom I had already interviewed.

In answering my questions, the subjects of my interviews were recalling events and experiences long past. I found in most cases that their memories were very keen. Men and women could often tell me without much hesitation the exact day they arrived in Pittsburgh, how much they were paid in their first Pittsburgh jobs, and each different address they had in the city. Those who had more trouble remembering their activities did not dissemble. Their occasional confusion over a date or event was plain enough to allow me to move on to other topics or to probe a question from another angle. Distortions produced by viewing events far in the past undoubtedly crept into the interviews. I tried to phrase questions in such a way as to lessen the impact of these problems ("What were your goals when you *first* came north?"; "how did Pittsburgh look to you *in 1923?*").

The methodological difficulties of using oral interviews in historical research have been thoroughly discussed in recent years, and I have nothing to add here to the general points that have been made. Aside from what I have already said about selecting respondents for this study, I can only comment briefly on the problems of obtaining relatively unbiased information in my interviews. These problems can arise through both intentionally and unintentionally inaccurate answers. The men and women I interviewed may have wanted to evade, conceal, or withhold what they knew to be true because I was an outsider in their communities and because I was a member of the white race. As an outsider to their communities, however, I often felt I had an advantage in seeking information, since a stranger who does not live among the people who are being interviewed can be told about matters that friends and relatives do not want each other to know, or at least cannot tell each other comfortably.

As a white interviewer questioning black interviewees, I undoubtedly faced a curtain carefully drawn around some important matters of black social life, including the resentments and frustrations of black workers toward white authorities. I accepted this as a limit on my research and allowed my respondents to answer questions as they wanted to. In many instances, it was hard for me to judge where and how certain attitudes, perceptions, or factual information was being withheld, partly because the respondents were almost always friendly and unfailingly polite. In other instances, including those where I was denied interviews, refusals to answer questions were indignantly blunt. I was occasionally suspected of seeking financial information from black households, either to use in selling insurance or perhaps in evaluating bank or credit union loans. My interest in the 1919 steel strike also made some male interviewees wary of my real intentions. On these topics, the fact of my race added to the problems inherent in oral history research.

With these limitations and considerations in mind, I felt that I could largely rely on the information I gathered through my interviews. An important question, but one difficult to answer, was the *pattern* of bias resulting both from inaccuracies and from withheld information. Concerning this problem, I might conclude on a general observation. First, we will not be able to analyze and compensate for this bias until we have more sources of information about southern blacks' lives. Until then, we must work with the available sources — including oral history — with the best tools of our historical training. Second, and more obvious, this manner of adapting to flawed sources is no more necessary or important for oral interviews than for any other kind of primary material.

INTERVIEW QUESTIONNAIRE

Family and Education in the South

Where were your parents born? Your grandparents?
What kind of work did your father do? Your mother?
Where were you born? In what year?

How many children did your parents have?

What place were you in the birth order of your parents' children?

Did anyone besides your parents and siblings live in your home?

Did your aunts, uncles, cousins, grandparents, parents, or siblings migrate to the North? To what city? When? Why did they go?

For how many years did you go to school in the South?

What time of year was school held?

Why did you stop attending school?

Rural Work and Migration

What tasks were involved in your family's farm work?

What jobs did you and your brothers and sisters have to do?

How old were you when you started working on your parents' farm?

Did the boys and girls in your family perform different kinds of farm work?

At what times of year were different farm chores done?

What kind of work was done after the crops were harvested?

What were the most important social events in your home community? What times of year did they take place?

How old were you when you first worked off your family's farm? Where did you look for work? Why did you work off your family's farm?

What kinds of nonfarm jobs did you get? Were they seasonal?

What did you use your nonfarm wages for?

Did your parents encourage or discourage you to work away from home?

How old were you when you left home? Why did you leave? Where did you go first? Where did you go subsequently? Why did you choose particular destinations?

Why did you decide to go north? Why did you decide to go to Pittsburgh? What places did you stop on your way to Pittsburgh? What mode of transportation did you take?

What did you bring with you? How much money did you have? Did you know anyone in Pittsburgh when you arrived? Did they help you in any way? How?

Did you return home after leaving? How often? At what times of
  year?

Did you send money home? How much? How often?

How long would you stay at home when you returned?

Working in Pittsburgh

How did you find a job in Pittsburgh?

Where did you go to look for jobs?

Did anyone tell you where you could find a job?

Who actually hired you? A foreman? A personnel officer?

What kind of job did you get first? What department and what
  mill?

Did most new employees begin in the job you were first given?

How did the job suit you? Was it difficult for you to adjust to?

Did you get better positions in the mill as time passed?

Did you ever want a particular kind of job which you didn't get?

How many different jobs have you had in Pittsburgh? What
  kinds of jobs were they?

On your first job in Pittsburgh, did you work with other southern migrants? With friends from the South?

Did you ever socialize with the men you worked with? Did you
  visit their homes after work?

Do you remember any of the foremen under whom you worked?
  How did they treat you? How did they treat southern blacks?
  How did the company treat blacks in general?

Were blacks segregated from whites in the mill?

Residences and Community Relationships

Where did you stay when you first arrived in Pittsburgh?

Did you lodge with relatives or friends? With a private family?

Did you board with other men from the South? From your
  home state?

Who owned the boardinghouse where you stayed? How did the
  owner treat the boarders? How much did it cost to live there?

What other addresses have you lived at in Pittsburgh? Why did you move to each address?

Were the places you have lived in segregated neighborhoods? Did foreigners live there? White Americans?

Did you notice any difference in Pittsburgh between southern-born and northern-born blacks? Did northern blacks look down on southern migrants?

Marriage and Family in Pittsburgh

When did you get married? How did you meet your wife/husband? Had you known your spouse before you came north?

Did you go back to the South to get married? How long did you stay for the wedding?

Had you found a place for your wife to live before she came to Pittsburgh? How long was it between the time you came to Pittsburgh and the time your wife arrived in the city?

How many children did you and your wife have? When did you start to have children?

Did any of your relatives ever come to Pittsburgh? Did they come to visit or to live in the city?

Did you encourage them to come? Did you help them in any way? How?

Institutional Affiliations in Pittsburgh

Did you join a church in Pittsburgh? When? Why?

Why did you join that particular congregation? Was it very different from the church you had attended in the South?

Were many of the members of the church you joined in Pittsburgh from your home state or locality?

What church organizations have you been active in?

Did you belong to any social organizations, fraternal associations, or athletic clubs? When did you join? Why?

What activities did these organizations sponsor?

Did you ever become an officer of these organizations?

RESPONDENTS

In order to maintain the anonymity of the men and women whom I have interviewed, I have referred to them throughout this study by first names and the first initial of their last names. Three respondents requested that I not use their names in connection with this study, and their interviews are designated by pseudonyms.

All but four of the interviews listed below were tape-recorded. The recorded interviews have been deposited in two places. Those that I conducted for the Pennsylvania Historical and Museum Commission (marked *) can be found at the offices of the Division of History, Pennsylvania Historical and Museum Commission, Harrisburg. The remainder (marked +) have been stored at the Archives of Industrial Society, Hillman Library, University of Pittsburgh.

Jasper A.	July 12, 1976*
John A.	October 29, 1973 (notes)
Alfred B.	April 21, 1976+
Benjamin B.	November 30, 1973+
Caleb B.	April 9, 1976+
Charles B.	July 16, 1976+
George B.	July 30, 1974*
Henry B.	August 2, 1974*
Jean B.	July 29, 1976*
John B.	March 10, 1976+
Maria B.	June 1, 1976+
Silas B.	October 29, 1973 (notes)
Charner C.	February 21, 1976+
Harvey C.	December 2, 1973+
Lee C.	June 9, 1976+
Richard C.	August 8, 1974*
Anthony D.	June 18, 1974*
Gertrude D.	November 3, 1976*
Julia D. (pseudonym)	May 3, 1976+
Ben E.	July 31, 1974*
Ernest F.	April 19, 1976*
Jonnie F.	April 23, 1976+
Harrison G.	August 23, 1974*
Jerome G.	August 1, 1974*
Joseph G.	November 26, 1973+

Elonzo H.	October 23, 1973+
Walter H.	October 25, 30, 1973+
William H.	June 17, 1976*
Carrie J.	July 23, 1976*
Matthew J.	May 28, 1976+
Mrs. Abraham L.	March 11, 1976 (notes)
Charles L.	January 28, 1977*
Laura L.	November 21, 1973+
Merril L.	August 22, 1974*
William L.	November 3, 1975
Betty M.	September 13, 1984
Clarence M.	August 5, 1974*
Francis M.	July 8, 1974*
Gilbert M.	April 9, 1976+
Hezekiah M.	October 8, 1976*
Joseph M.	November 16, 1973+
Leroy M.	July 9, 1974*
Sadie M.	April 9, 1976+
Sadie M.	May 19, 1976+
Sarah M. (pseudonym)	September 2, 1976*
Wesley M.	April 2, 1976+
Callie N.	June 23, 1976*
James N.	June 28, 1976*
Clarence P. (pseudonym)	December 16, 1974*
Freeman P.	July 11, 1974*
Lillyan P.	November 9, 10, 1973+
Ed R.	June 10, 1976+
James S.	June 7, 14, 1974*
Lucille S.	January 10, 1977*
Maria S.	May 13, 1976 (notes)
Sallie S.	June 18, 1976*
Victoria S.	May 25, 1976+
William S.	January 12, 1977*
Willie S.	July 15, 1974*
John T.	November 1, 23, 1973+
Lee T.	May 26, 1976+
Grant W.	July 12, 1976
Jonathan W.	June 28, 1974*
Olive W.	July 23, 1976*
Queen W.	October 8, 1976*
Walter W.	July 19, 1984 (notes)

Appendix B

Personnel Records of the A. M. Byers Company

The personnel records of the A. M. Byers Company permit analysis of individual southern black workers at one metal manufacturer in Pittsburgh. The Byers records identify employees not only by race and place of birth but also by the date they had arrived in Pittsburgh. This last information allows a researcher to isolate the men who had participated in the Great Migration from those black workers at Byers who had come to the city before that mass population movement. Further, the records focused mainly on the migrants' employment status at the company and on their work experience. Similar information about southern blacks in Pittsburgh generally or those employed at specific firms cannot be found in as detailed and systematic a form as that presented by the Byers records.

The A. M. Byers Company manufactured wrought iron tubing for industrial machinery and railroad locomotives. Its facilities included the mill in Pittsburgh's South Side neighborhood and furnaces in Ohio. Work processes at the Pittsburgh mill included the iron-making crafts of puddling, bending, and rolling as well as sequences of tasks in the intermediate and finishing stages of manufacture: inserting and withdrawing metal from furnaces, galvanizing, removing imperfections, testing water pressure of finished pipes, warehousing, and shipping. The Byers Company developed a mechanized puddling process and built a new mill near Ambridge, Pennsylvania, in the 1930s designed for this new technology. All the black workers analyzed in this study, however, worked at the Pittsburgh mill.

Byers Company's personnel records represented the application of scientific management to the firm's handling of its labor force. A card for each employee had spaces where employment office staff filled in information about physical characteristics, race, family status, residence, age, dates of beginning and ending of each work assignment, department and position, and so on. Additional spaces for information about prior employment, membership in clubs and societies, or participation in Byers Company's group insurance were seldom filled in. Employment managers presumably recorded this information before migrants were sent to their assigned jobs, since even the most transient employees had as complete data on physical characteristics, family status, place of birth, arrival in Pittsburgh, and residence as the men who stayed at the company for many years.

I drew a sample of the southern black migrants at the Byers Company by first grouping all the southern blacks who had arrived in Pittsburgh between 1916 and 1930 and then making a random selection of 40 percent. This proportion was equal to 669 individuals, a figure both manageable for the measurements I had in mind and also sufficiently large to leave enough individuals in each cell of cross-tabulations. The sample was also large enough to avoid problems of representativeness for the black migrant workers at Byers who came to Pittsburgh between World War I and 1930. How representative the men in my sample were of all the male migrants in Pittsburgh cannot be determined. However, the Byers Company apparently did not recruit blacks in the South for transportation to Pittsburgh, so any bias in the sample would not be the result of the company hiring men from a single southern locality. Distributions of ages, states of birth, and marital status for my sample were comparable to those for the southern black men in Pittsburgh whom Abraham Epstein surveyed in 1917.

Data from the personnel records were coded and entered into a machine-readable file. I coded job-assignment information (position name, wage/tonnage rates, dates of beginning and ending assignment, and reasons for leaving) only through the fourth position at the mill. This limit on machine-coded data captured the entire Byers employment of 87 percent of the sample. Identical information for those sample members with five or more job assignments was recorded by hand and analyzed separately. In addition to the information taken directly from the records, I generated new data for each member of the sample by calculating length of time spent in each work assignment, length of time spent in all work assignments, strikebreaking/striking in the 1919 steel strike, and so on.

A Note on Sources

Students of black migration face more than the usual difficulties in documenting the experience of "anonymous" individuals who participated in a mass movement. That black migrants' own writings have seldom survived is only one aspect of the problem. There is a broad geographic field to cover in the course of researching the northward movement, from southern rural settlements and small work sites, to the towns and cities along the routes of transportation, to the northern destinations themselves. And since the migration touched on almost every facet of black life in one way or another, the sources for a migration study must cover almost as many topics as places. In the chapter notes I have cited the sources for the interrelated themes of labor and black migration that I used most frequently. Here I wish to draw attention to published and unpublished materials that were important to the larger conception and design of the study.

Bibliographies

A useful listing of contemporary writing about black migration, much of which is little known yet enlightening, is Louise V. Kennedy and Frank Ross's *A Bibliography of Negro Migration* (New York, 1934). Kennedy and Ross included periodical literature and published reports of investigators and observers. Their bibliography pulls together in one place titles that a researcher could compile only painstakingly, if at all. In a similar fashion, "The Negro in Industry: A Selected Bibliography," compiled by Helen L. Pier and Mary L. Spalding, *Monthly Labor Review* 22 (January 1926), 216–30, assembles titles of contemporary publications on a subject that overlaps broadly with black migration and provides brief annotations for each entry.

Other bibliographies should also be consulted. J. J. Mangalam's *Human Migration: A Guide to Migration Literature in English, 1855-1962* (Lexington, 1968) notes works on the theories and concepts of migration and has a significant outline of the study of migration in the introduction. Thomas R. Brooks's *Labor and Migration: An Annotated Bibliography* (New York, 1970) includes works on international as well as U.S. population flows. Jack T. Kirby's historiographical essay on black and white out-migration from the South is valuable for references to recent monographs: "The Southern Exodus, 1910-1960: A Primer for Historians," *Journal of Southern History* 49 (November 1983), 585-600.

Secondary Sources

Social and behavioral scientists have contributed more to the conceptualization of migration than historians have. Some studies in these general areas have the added strength of analyzing migration in other countries and not just the United States, providing information that the researcher can use for comparisons. Helpful works are Harry Jerome, *Migration and Business Cycles* (New York, 1926); Carter Goodrich et al., *Migration and Economic Opportunity* (Philadelphia, 1936); Brinley Thomas, *Migration and Urban Development* (London, 1972); James S. Slotkin, *From Field to Factory* (Glencoe, 1960); Everett S. Lee, "A Theory of Migration," *Demography* 3 (1966), 47-58; William Petersen, "A General Typology of Migration," *American Sociological Review* 23 (June 1958), 256-66; Henry S. Shryock, Jr., and Hope T. Eldridge, "Internal Migration in Peace and War," *American Sociological Review* 12 (February 1947), 27-39; Reynolds Farley, *The Growth of the Black Population* (Chicago, 1970); T. L. Smith, "The Redistribution of the Negro Population of the United States, 1910-1960," *Journal of Negro History* 51 (July 1966), 155-73; C. Horace Hamilton, "The Negro Leaves the South," *Demography* 1 (1964), 273-95. A useful overview of rural-urban migration in the United States is Dale Hathaway's "Migration from Agriculture: The Historical Record and Its Meaning," *American Economic Review* 50 (May 1960), 379-91.

Analyses of particular aspects of rural-urban migration that informed the analysis in this book include Charles Tilly and C. Harold Brown, "On Uprooting, Kinship, and the Auspices of Migration," *International Journal of Comparative Sociology* 8 (September 1967), 139–64; Harvey M. Choldin, "Kinship Networks in the Migration Process," *International Migration Review* 7 (Summer 1973), 163–75; J. S. MacDonald and L. D. MacDonald, "Chain Migration, Ethnic Neighborhood Formation and Social Networks," *Milbank Memorial Fund Quarterly* 42 (January 1964), 82–97; Eugene Litwack, "Geographical Mobility and Extended Family Cohesion," *American Sociological Review* 25 (1960), 385–94; Nancy B. Graves and Theodore D. Graves, "Adaptive Strategies in Urban Migration," *Annual Review of Anthropology* 3 (1974), 117–51; Joan M. Nelson, "Sojourners versus New Urbanites: Causes and Consequences of Temporary Versus Permanent Cityward Migration in Developing Countries," *Economic Development and Cultural Change* 24 (July, 1976), 721–57; Basil G. Zimmer, "Migration and Changes in Occupational Compositions," *International Migration Review* 7 (Winter 1973), 437–47; Curtis C. Roseman, "Channelization of Migration Flows from the Rural South to the Industrial Midwest," Association of American Geographers, *Proceedings* 3 (1971), 140–46; Philip Nelson, "Migration, Real Income, and Information," *Journal of Regional Science* (Spring 1959), 43–74.

There is a rapidly growing literature on land tenure, credit, share tenancy agriculture, and labor relations in the postbellum South. My chapter notes refer to some of the recently published studies on these topics. Still valuable are M. B. Hammond's *The Cotton Industry* (New York, 1897) and Robert P. Brooks's *The Agrarian Revolution in Georgia, 1865–1912* (Madison, 1914). Carl Kelsey's *The Negro Farmer* (Chicago, 1903) also offers firsthand observations of black tenants in the Deep South around the turn of the century. Women's field labor in cotton-growing receives excellent treatment in Ruth Allen's *The Labor of Women in the Production of Cotton* (Austin, 1933); in Allison Davis, Burleigh B. Gardner, and Mary R. Gardner's *Deep South* (Chicago, 1941); and in Hortense Powdermaker's *After Freedom* (New York, 1939). Charles Wesley's *Negro Labor in the United States, 1850–1925* (New York, 1927) is still an important source on black wage earners, but other helpful materials are the chapters on labor in Charles S. Johnson's *The Negro in American Civili-*

zation (New York, 1930); Sterling D. Spero and Abram L. Harris's *The Black Worker* (New York, 1931); and Lorenzo J. Greene and Carter G. Woodson's *The Negro Wage Earner* (Washington, 1930). Two model investigations of black employment, occupations, and unions in northern industries are Alma Herbst's *The Negro in the Slaughtering and Meat-Packing Industry in Chicago* (New York, 1932) and August Meier and Elliott Rudwick's *Black Detroit and the Rise of the UAW* (New York, 1979).

Recently published oral narratives provide sharp insights from personal vantages on blacks' culture, family, and community in the rural South, from Emancipation to the 1920s. The best is Theodore Rosengarten's *All God's Dangers: The Life of Nate Shaw* (New York, 1974), but two others should also be consulted: Jane Maguire's *On Shares: Ed Brown's Story* (New York, 1975) and Nell I. Painter's *The Narrative of Hosea Hudson* (Cambridge, Mass., 1979). The bulletins of the University of Georgia are also vital sources for portrayals of blacks' social and economic lives in specific localities, especially John W. Fanning's *Negro Migration,* Bulletin 30 (June 1930); Francis T. Long's *The Negroes of Clarke County, Georgia, during the Great War,* Bulletin 19 (1919); and Donald D. Scarborough's *An Economic Study of Negro Farmers as Owners, Tenants, and Croppers,* Bulletin 25 (September 1924).

Abraham Epstein's *The Negro Migrant in Pittsburgh* (Pittsburgh, 1918) is the sole monograph that describes black migrants in that city, but it refers only to conditions in 1916 and 1917. Articles by the staff of the Urban League of Pittsburgh are the next most important sources of published information on migration to Pittsburgh: John T. Clark, "The Migrant in Pittsburgh," *Opportunity* 1 (October 1923), 303–7; Clark, "The Negro in Steel," *Opportunity* 2 (October 1924), 299–301; Clark, "The Negro in Steel," *Opportunity* 4 (March 1926), 87–88; W. P. Young, "The First Hundred Negro Workers," *Opportunity* 2 (January 1924), 15–19. The paucity of published information on southern blacks in Pittsburgh is made worse by the lack of a history of black Pittsburgh. There is good background information in several works, however, including R. R. Wright, Jr.'s *The Negro in Pennsylvania: A Study in Economic History* (Philadelphia, 1912); E. R. Turner's *The Negro in Pennsylvania* (Washington, 1911); and Andrew Buni's *Robert Lee Vann of the Pittsburgh Courier: Politics and Black Journalism* (Pittsburgh, 1974). Helen Tucker's "The Negroes of Pittsburgh," in *Wage-*

Earning Pittsburgh, The Pittsburgh Survey, ed. Paul U. Kellogg (New York, 1914), 424–36, and Ira De A. Reid's *Social Conditions of the Negro in the Hill District of Pittsburgh* (Pittsburgh, 1930) also provide a wealth of detail for periods at the beginning and end of the years covered by this study. John Bodnar, Roger Simon, and Michael P. Weber, in *Lives of Their Own: Blacks, Italians, and Poles in Pittsburgh, 1900–1960* (Urbana, 1982), compare southern black migrants with European immigrants in the city, emphasizing different trends in social mobility for each group and contrasting blacks' individualism with the Europeans' family and community cohesion.

Manuscript Sources

The letters of black migrants who wrote to the Urban League of Pittsburgh in 1922–23 are one of the richest lodes of material for southern blacks' self-expressed attitudes, perceptions, and values. These are in the John T. Clark Letters, a portion of the Carter G. Woodson Collection at the Library of Congress, Washington, D.C. Though seldom offering the migrants' own views, the records of the Urban League of Pittsburgh and the National Urban League are also extremely important for documentation on the migration to Pittsburgh. Unfortunately, the Pittsburgh League's records were partially destroyed by fire at 300 Fourth Avenue, Pittsburgh, after I had consulted them. What was saved from destruction is now at the Archives of Industrial Society, Hillman Library, University of Pittsburgh. This material is strongly complemented by several files in the National Urban League Papers at the Library of Congress.

The records of the Division of Negro Economics in the U.S. Department of Labor records have scant but important information on black migration to Pittsburgh during World War I and the immediate postwar period (Record Group 174, National Archives and Records Administration, Washington, D.C.). Less important but still helpful are the letters and reports of Karl Phillips in the files of the Bureau of Employment Security (Record Group 183, National Archives and Records Administration).

The manuscript prepared by the Federal Writers' Project, "The Negro in Pittsburgh," offers many interesting but uncited facts about Pittsburgh's black community. The manuscript is in the Pennsylvania State Archives, Harrisburg.

Newspapers

Generally speaking, newspapers had little information about black migrants in Pittsburgh or in towns nearby. The absence of copies of the Pittsburgh *Courier* from 1913 to 1922 further lessened the value of available newspapers for a study of black migration to the city. Both the black and white press usually took note of the migrants only when they ran afoul of the police or were perceived as a menace to community welfare. The *Courier,* however, is helpful for information on the black elite's attitudes toward the migrants and for information about the black community and its most important institutions. The daily and weekly newspapers published in Pittsburgh and the surrounding industrial towns had a few reports on black migration during World War I. The *National Labor Journal* and the *National Labor Tribune,* both published in Pittsburgh, are useful for occasional reports on black migration to western Pennsylvania and for expressions of the antipathy white craft unionists had for black workers and black strikebreakers.

Theses and Dissertations

A series of Master of Arts theses by University of Pittsburgh students contribute greatly to the knowledge of conditions among black migrants in Pittsburgh. The best are Abram L. Harris, "The New Negro Worker in Pittsburgh" (1924), and Ira De A. Reid, "The Negro in the Major Industries and Building Trades of Pittsburgh" (1925). The following theses in this series were also of great value: Wiley A. Hall, "Negro Housing and Rents in the Hill District of Pittsburgh" (1929); Gerald E. Allen, "The Negro Coal Miner in the Pittsburgh District" (1927); Floyd C. Covington, "Occupational Choices in Relation to Economic Opportunities of Negro Youth in Pittsburgh" (1928); Alonzo G. Moron, "Distribution of the Negro Population in Pittsburgh, 1910–1930" (1933); John N. Rathmell, "Status of Pittsburgh Negroes in Regard to Origin, Length of Residence, and Economic Aspects of Their Life" (1935); Ruth Stevenson, "The Pittsburgh Urban League" (1936). Less helpful is Lewis J. Carter, "Negro Migrant Labor in Pennsylvania, 1916–1936" (M.A. thesis, Pennsylvania State University, 1936), since it is based mainly on unsubstantiated evidence and readily available published sources. Two doctoral dissertations also should be consulted: Dennis C. Dickerson, "Black Steelworkers in Western Pennsylvania, 1915–1950" (Washington University, 1978), and Ralph L. Hill, "A View of the Hill — A Study of Experiences and Attitudes in the Hill District of Pittsburgh, Pennsylvania from 1900 to 1973" (University of Pittsburgh, 1974).

Government Documents and Publications

Aside from the decennial census figures and the important census monographs on blacks in the United States, there are significant data for a study of black migration in E. A. Boeger and E. A. Goldenweiser, *A Study of the Tenant System of Farming in the Yazoo-Mississippi Delta,* U.S. Department of Agriculture, Bulletin 337 (1916), and in U.S. Bureau of the Census, *Plantation Farming in the United States* (1916). Of the two publications of the U.S. Department of Labor, Division of Negro Economics, *Negro Migration in 1916–17* (1919) is by far the more important, offering much detail on conditions in each of the states from which the largest percentages of Pittsburgh migrants came. *The Negro at Work during the War and during Reconstruction* (1921) is more a review of the activities of the Division of Negro Economics than a treatment of the subject described by the title.

The Labor Department's *Monthly Labor Review* should be consulted for its articles on the movement of southern blacks to northern cities and for information on wages and hours in the industries that employed large numbers of black migrants. The Labor Department's Women's Bureau published two important studies on female black workers: Women's Bureau, Bulletin 20, *Negro Women in Industry* (1922) and Bulletin 39, *Domestic Workers and Their Employment Relations,* by M. V. Robinson (1924).

Hearings before committees of the U.S. Senate are excellent sources for information on the 1919 steel strike, the 1925–28 coal strike, and the black workers' roles in these conflicts. See U.S. Senate, Committee on Education and Labor, *Investigation of Strike in Steel Industries, Hearings,* September--October 1919 (Washington, 1919), 66th Congress, S-145-11A, and U.S. Senate, Committee on Interstate Commerce, *Conditions in the Coal Fields of Pennsylvania, West Virginia, and Ohio, Hearings,* February–March 1928 (Washington, 1928), 70th Congress, S475.

Index

Note: People interviewed for this book have been indexed by first name only.

Employment practices: of Pittsburgh manufacturers, 80–84

Epstein, Abraham, 69, 71, 75, 76, 98, 128, 233

European immigrants: and housing, 66–67, 73; job strategies of, 79–80; kinds of work performed by, 90, 95, 96, 102, 110; and unions, 154–55, 161–63; numbers of, 159, 194

"Exodusters," 1

Farm tenancy, 13–22

Farnham, Dwight, 137, 141

Festivities: seasonal, in rural South, 20–21, 206–9

First Baptist Church (Braddock), 201

Ford City (Pa.), 72, 130

Ford Motor Company, 169

Foster, William Z., 155, 156, 172

Frick, Henry Clay, 165

Frick Coal Company, 165

Frogs (elite black club), 185

Garfield Lodge (Amalgamated Association), 153

Gary, Elbert H. (Judge), 93

Gatekeepers, 32, 184, 190–97. *See also* Churches; Industrial welfare workers; Urban League of Pittsburgh

Gilbert M., 79, 137, 206

Girls: and farm work, 18–19

"Give Them a Chance" (editorial, Pittsburgh *Courier*), 187–88

Gompers, Samuel, 156

Grant, Robert, 3

Great Depression: effects on migrants, 217–18

Great Migration: significance of, 1–6, 219–22

Green, Cyrus, 195

Green, Will, 169

Group migration, 53–55, 72

Gutman, Herbert G., 5, 139

Harbison-Walker Refractory Brick Company, 72–73

Harris, Abram, 70, 162

Harrison G., 74, 77, 84, 188, 189, 208, 209

Harvey C., 72, 79, 158

Haynes, George E., 134, 184

Henri, Florette, 3, 4, 7

Henry B., 49, 79

Hezekiah M., 50

Hill, J. R., 54–55

Hill District (Pittsburgh): housing, 66–67, 69–71, 76; unemployment in, 104; miners in, 171; Leondi Club in, 185

Hillman Coal Company, 165

"Hilltop" (Homestead neighborhood), 73, 199

"Hiring boss," 80. *See also* Employment practices

Hod Carriers, Building, and Common Laborers Union, 150

Hoisting Engineers Union, 150

"Homecomings," 20–21, 219

"Home employment," 24

Homestead (Pa.): Carnegie Steel mill in, 40; black population in, 64; housing in, 70–73; black neighborhoods in, 73–74; skilled workers in, 90–91; churches in, 198–204; 1892 strike in, 153

Housing (in Pittsburgh): search for, 47, 63, 69–77, 219; lack of segregation in, 66–67, 69; condition of migrants', 69–71; employers' role in providing, 70–71; migrants' preferences in, 71–72; migrants' reactions to, 74–77, 123, 136; strikebreakers', 163. *See also* Boardinghouses; Bunkhouses; Rent

Immigrants. *See* European immigrants

Industrial welfare workers: roles of, 130–34, 192–93; limitations on, 133, 193; explanations of job turnover by, 136–37; attitudes toward unions, 173; backgrounds of, 195–96; mentioned, 72, 103, 123, 174, 175

Industrialization, 5–6, 8, 30–32, 139–41. *See also* Proletarianization

Industrial work: in South, 12, 22-24, 118-19. *See also* Wage employment
Industrial work sites (in Pittsburgh): migrants' reactions to, 121-23

Jacksonville Agreement (1924), 165-66
Jake's Run (Pittsburgh), 186
James S., 51-52, 72, 202
Jasper A., 45
Jean B., 54, 55, 72
Job turnover rates, 97, 123-27, 129, 133-34, 136, 140-41
Jobs: information about, 25-26, 40, 42-43, 45, 46, 51, 53, 79-81; "black," 32, 98-99, 120, 188; searches for, 63, 77-85; migrants' goals in, 117, 123-26; selectivity in, 140-41; migrants' pride in, 188. *See also* Job turnover rates; Occupational advancement; Occupational differentiation; Proletarianization; Unemployment; Wage employment; Wages
Joe G., 28, 126
John B., 28, 44-45, 58, 135, 188, 209
John T., 49, 53-54, 75, 81, 83, 97, 137-38, 189, 202
Johnson, Albert, 54
Johnson, C. H., 56
Johnson, Charles S., 140
Johnson, Robert E., 195
Jones and Laughlin Steel Company: its labor agent, 58; unskilled workers at, 94; employment practices of, 136; mentioned, 40, 82, 84, 157, 162, 188
Jonnie F., 27, 48
Joseph G., 45, 55
Joseph M., 97, 158
Julia D., 47, 50, 203

Kaufman Department Store, 152
Kelsey, Carl, 14
Kennedy, Louise V., 2
Kinship bonds: and migration, 4-5, 8, 49-51; and job placement,

79-80; and ties to South, 183, 205-10. *See also* Chain migration
Kiser, Clyde V., 2, 29
Knapp, J. W., 132
Knights of Labor, 164
"Ku Klux" coal mines, 174

L., Mrs., 47, 48
Labor: casual, 110-11
Labor agents, 43-45, 55-59, 128
Labor demand: fluctuations in, in cotton production, 19, in Pittsburgh industry, 63-66, 80-81, 93, 103, 177, 206
Labor gangs, 97, 119-23
Labor unions. *See* Unions
Landlord-tenant relations: under tenant farming, 13-22; in Pittsburgh, 70-71
Landownership: among southern blacks, 15-16
Lathers Union, 150
Laura L., 75, 205-6
Lawrenceville (Pittsburgh), 66, 191
Lawrenceville Community Uplift Club, 191
Lee C., 50, 73
Lee T., 54
Leisure: seasonal nature of, in South, 12, 19-22. *See also* Festivities
Leisure activities. *See* Recreation opportunities
Lennon, Macon, 195
Lewis, Edward E., 2
Life cycle: significance of, in migration, 12, 24, 26-29
Lillyan P., 48-49, 75, 204
Locke, Alain, 140
Lockhart Iron and Steel Company, 40, 92, 107, 130-31, 133, 195, 201
Loendi Club, 185
Lucille S., 50
Lynch, Hollis, 3

McKees Rocks (Pa.), 70, 131
Maria B., 48, 49, 201
Maria S., 72
Marriage: and women's migration, 47-48; and settling into

Marriage (*continued*)
  Pittsburgh, 183, 207; male
  migrants' preferences in, 189
Marx, Karl, 30
Massey, E. A., 55
Maxwell, John D., 54
Migrants: pre–World War I, 1, 32,
  66–67, 80, 89, 90, 94–95, 98,
  183–210; significance of life cycle
  of, 12, 24, 26–29; recreation
  opportunities for, 128–34, 136,
  192–94; and northern women,
  188–89; their self-image, 189;
  church attendance among, 201; as
  preachers, 201–2; Byers records
  as source of information about,
  232–34. *See also* Churches;
  Discrimination; Great Migration;
  Housing; Jobs; Kinship bonds;
  Migration; Unions; Work
Migration: causes of, 2–3, 29–30,
  104; patterns of, 4–5, 22–24,
  44–45; worldwide patterns of,
  30–31; of unmarried men, 43–46;
  of women, 46–49; of married men,
  51–53; seasonal, 12, 22–33;
  strategies of, 40–59. *See also*
  Great Migration; Labor agents;
  Return migration; Rural-urban
  migration
Ministers, 20, 199–202
Mitchell, J. W., 52
Monessen (Pa.), 157, 160, 173
Montgomery, David, 5
Morality: employers' involvement
  with, 132
Morals Court (Pittsburgh), 191–92
Morton, J. D. (Rev.), 199–200, 204
Murray, Philip, 167

National Association of Afro-
  American Steam and Gas Engi-
  neers and Skilled Laborers of
  America, 150
National Committee for Organizing
  Iron and Steel Workers, 155–56,
  159, 161
National Labor Tribune, 174
National Shirt Factory, 107
National Tube Company, 94

National Urban League, 196. *See
  also* Urban League of Pittsburgh
"Negro jobs," 32, 98–99, 120, 188
Negro Migration in 1916–17 (U.S.
  Dept. of Labor), 57
Negro Survey of Pennsylvania, 187
Nelson, Grover, 195
New Hope Baptist Church
  (Braddock), 77
New Negro, The (Locke), 140

Occupational advancement: blacks'
  prospects for, 95–96, 99–101,
  111–12, 138–39, 141; during
  strikes, 159, 164. *See also* Jobs;
  Work
Occupational differentiation:
  between black and white workers,
  104, 115n42
Off-farm employment. *See* Wage
  employment: as supplement to
  agriculture
Olive W., 48, 202
Oliver Iron and Steel Company, 40,
  92, 94
Open shop drive, 154, 167–70, 176,
  218
Operative Plasterers' Association,
  148
Oral history interviews, 224–31

Pennsylvania Chocolate Factory, 149
Pennsylvania Department of
  Internal Affairs, 64
Pennsylvania Department of
  Welfare, 76
Pennsylvania Federation of Labor,
  150
Pennsylvania Historical and Museum
  Commission, 224
Pennsylvania Railroad, 56
Pennsylvania State Employment
  Department, 52
Pennsylvania State Police, 157
Peonage, 13–15
Piece rates, 137
Pittsburgh: as site of study, 9;
  growth of black population in, 32,
  63–66; its physical geography,
  39–40; its attraction for male

A Note on the Author

Peter Gottlieb is head of the Historical Collections and Labor Archives and assistant professor in the Labor Studies Department at Pennsylvania State University, University Park. He received a B.A. with honors from the University of Wisconsin, Madison, and a M.A. and Ph.D. from the University of Pittsburgh. He was formerly associate curator of the West Virginia and Regional History Collection and a lecturer in the Department of History at West Virginia University. His previous publications include articles in the *Western Pennsylvania Historical Magazine* and *Appalachian Journal.*

BOOKS IN THE SERIES BLACKS IN THE NEW WORLD

Before the Ghetto: Black Detroit in the Nineteenth Century
David M. Katzman

Black Business in the New South: A Social History of the North Carolina
Mutual Life Insurance Company *Walter B. Weare*

The Search for a Black Nationality: Black Colonization and Emigration,
1787-1863 *Floyd J. Miller*

Black Americans and the White Man's Burden, 1898-1903
Willard B. Gatewood, Jr.

Slavery and the Numbers Game: A Critique of *Time on the Cross*
Herbert G. Gutman

A Ghetto Takes Shape: Black Cleveland, 1870-1930
Kenneth L. Kusmer

Freedmen, Philanthropy, and Fraud: A History of the Freedman's
Savings Bank *Carl R. Osthaus*

The Democratic Party and the Negro: Northern and National Politics,
1868-92 *Lawrence Grossman*

Black Ohio and the Color Line, 1860-1915
David A. Gerber

Along the Color Line: Explorations in the Black Experience
August Meier and Elliott Rudwick

Black over White: Negro Political Leadership in South Carolina
during Reconstruction *Thomas Holt*

Keeping the Faith: A. Philip Randolph, Milton P. Webster, and the
Brotherhood of Sleeping Car Porters, 1925-37 *William H. Harris*

Abolitionism: The Brazilian Antislavery Struggle
Joaquim Nabuco, translated and edited by Robert Conrad

Black Georgia in the Progressive Era, 1900-1920
John Dittmer

Medicine and Slavery: Health Care of Blacks in Antebellum
Virginia *Todd L. Savitt*

Alley Life in Washington: Family, Community, Religion, and Folklife in
the City, 1850-1970 *James Borchert*

Human Cargoes: The British Slave Trade to Spanish America,
1700-1739 *Colin A. Palmer*

Southern Black Leaders of the Reconstruction Era
Edited by Howard N. Rabinowitz

Black Leaders of the Twentieth Century
Edited by John Hope Franklin and August Meier

Slaves and Missionaries: The Disintegration of Jamaican Slave Society, 1787-1834 *Mary Turner*

Father Divine and the Struggle for Racial Equality
Robert Weisbrot

Communists in Harlem during the Depression
Mark Naison

Down from Equality: Black Chicagoans and the Public Schools, 1920-41 *Michael W. Homel*

Race and Kinship in a Midwestern Town: The Black Experience in Monroe, Michigan, 1900-1915 *James E. DeVries*

Down by the Riverside: A South Carolina Slave Community
Charles Joyner

Black Milwaukee: The Making of an Industrial Proletariat, 1915-45
Joe William Trotter, Jr.

Religious Philanthropy and Colonial Slavery: The American Correspondence of the Associates of Dr. Bray, 1717-1777
John C. Van Horne

Black History and the Historical Profession, 1915-80
August Meier and Elliott Rudwick

Rise to Be a People: A Biography of Paul Cuffe
Lamont D. Thomas

Making Their Own Way: Southern Blacks' Migration to Pittsburgh, 1916-30 *Peter Gottlieb*

Reprint Editions

King: A Biography
David Levering Lewis Second Edition

The Death and Life of Malcolm X
Peter Goldman Second Edition

Race Relations in the Urban South, 1865-1890
Howard N. Rabinowitz, with a Foreword by C. Vann Woodward

Race Riot at East St. Louis, July 2, 1917
Elliott Rudwick

W. E. B. Du Bois: Voice of the Black Protest Movement
Elliott Rudwick

The Negro's Civil War: How American Negroes Felt and Acted during the War for the Union *James M. McPherson*

Lincoln and Black Freedom: A Study in Presidential Leadership
LaWanda Cox

Slavery and Freedom in the Age of the American Revolution
Edited by Ira Berlin and Ronald Hoffman